FREE MONEY®
When You're Unemployed
Second Edition

Other Free Money® Books by Laurie Blum

Business

Free Money® for Small Businesses and Entrepreneurs, Fourth Edition
Free Money® from the Federal Government for Small Businesses and Entrepreneurs

Child Care/Education

Free Money® for Athletic Scholarships
Free Money® for College
Free Money® for College from the Government
Free Money® from Colleges and Universities
Free Money® for Day Care
Free Money® for Graduate School
Free Money® for Private Schools
Free Money® for Foreign Study

Health Care

Free Money® for Seniors and Their Families
Free Money® for Childhood Behavioral and Genetic Disorders
Free Money® for Children's Medical/Dental Expenses
Free Money® for Diseases of Aging
Free Money® for Heart Disease and Cancer Care
Free Money® for Infertility Treatments
Free Money® for Mental/Emotional Disorders

FREE MONEY®
When You're Unemployed
Second Edition

Laurie Blum

John Wiley & Sons, Inc.
New York · Chichester · Brisbane · Toronto · Singapore

Contents

Introduction

Maybe you are one of the unfortunate victims of a corporate restructuring. Or perhaps you are a middle- or even upper-management executive unemployed for the first time, losing your job as well as your pension and retirement benefits. Maybe you have been a wife and homemaker, and, because of a divorce or the death of your spouse, you just don't know how you are going to be able to manage financially.

Over and over, I am asked the same question on the radio and television broadcasts I do or in the thousands of letters I receive about my other *Free Money®* books: Are there really monies to help me if I lose my job or run into tough financial circumstances? Happily, the answer is yes.

Free Money® When You're Unemployed identifies private, corporate, and government sources that have millions of dollars to give to those who find themselves unemployed or in tough financial circumstances. These monies can be used to pay everything from the grocery bill to a mortgage payment. This is *free money*, money that is given simply because an individual needs financial help—money that never needs to be paid back.

Remember, however, that funding sources are not without restrictions. Do you just walk up, hold out your hand, and expect someone to put money in it? Of course not. It takes time, effort, and thought on your part. You are going to have to fill out applications. You may experience frustration or rejection at some point; but the odds are in your favor that you will qualify for some sort of funding.

The hardest part has always been finding the sources of money. That is why I wrote this book. Though I have written books on grant monies available for almost every conceivable need—from monies to pay for college to start-up capital for small businesses—over and over in my research I'd come across grants available for individuals in tough financial circumstances. Much of the information in this book has never been made available to the general public.

The book is divided into three sections:

1. Private Foundation Funding. This section covers the easiest and most accessible funding sources for the average individual seeking a grant.
2. Flow-Through Funding. This section provides information about foundation monies that are given to individuals through nonprofit organizations.
3. Federal Grants. This section identifies agencies that offer direct funding and/or essential referral information.

When possible, listings within each chapter are arranged state by state to make this book easy to use. Check your state's listings in all chapters to see which grants apply to you. You'll find funding parameters and an address and phone number to contact for further information (and for application forms).

By the time this book is published, some of the information it contains will have changed. No reference book can be as up-to-date as the reader or the author would like. Names, addresses, dollar amounts, telephone numbers, and other data are always in flux; however, most of the information will not have changed.

On the next few pages is a concise guide to applying for a grant and writing a proposal. Follow my instructions, and you should be successful in obtaining some sort of assistance.

Good luck.

How to Apply for a Grant

Thousands of resources are available from private foundations, corporations, and government sources throughout the country. Applying for this aid is the challenging part; it requires diligence, thought, and organization.

First is the sorting-out or research-gathering phase. Look through each chapter of this book and make a list of the potential assistance sources that meet your needs. When compiling your list, pay close attention to the restrictions and qualifications.

Then, politely contact each of your listed sources by mail or phone to verify all current information, such as address, telephone number, name of the proper contact (in cases where the contact's name is not listed, begin your letter, "To Whom It May Concern"), and his or her title. At this time, you can also arrange to get a copy of the source's most current assistance guidelines and an application form (if one is required). Use this opportunity to find out about any application deadlines and where you are in the funding cycle (i.e., if there is no deadline, when the best time to apply is). Also be sure to ask when awards will be announced and funds distributed. However, do not grill, or cross-examine, the person you reach on the phone. Always be prepared to explain why you are applying and what you are applying for—in case you ring through to the key decision maker, who decides to interview you on the spot!

Second is the application phase. Most often you will be asked to submit a formal application rather than a proposal. Always be sure to read (and follow!) the instructions for completing the application. Usually the material you use for one application can be applied with a little restructuring to most, if not all, of the other applications you fill out.

Make sure you answer each question as asked, in a manner appropriate to the application you are completing.

Grant applications take time (and thought) to fill out; so make sure you give yourself enough time to thoroughly complete the application before the deadline. Filling out the application can be a lengthy process because you may be required to write one or more essays. Often what is required is a "statement of purpose" that explains what you will use the money for and why you need the assistance for which you are applying. You may also need to assemble required attachments, such as tax returns and other financial records, and to include personal references. Be sure to get strong references. Call all the people you plan to list, and ask them if they feel comfortable giving you references. Remember, you have to convince the grantors to give money to you rather than to someone else.

Be clear, concise, and neat! You may very well prepare a top-notch application, but it won't look good if it's sloppy. Application and proposals should always be typed double-spaced. Make sure you keep a copy after you send the original. I have learned the hard way that there is nothing worse than having to reconstruct your application if problems arise simply because you didn't keep a copy.

Because no one application is guaranteed to win you a grant or an award, you should apply to a number of funding sources. Although none of the sources listed in this book requires an application fee, the effort you will have to put into the endeavor will probably limit you to a maximum of eight applications. (If you are ambitious and want to apply to more than eight sources, go right ahead.) Remember, the more sources you apply to, the greater your chances for success.

Components of a Successful Proposal

One of the largest categories of grants that are given to individuals is grants for general welfare, that is, *free money* for emergency or long-term personal, medical, or living expenses. Applying for these grants is generally a much simpler process than applying for other kinds of grants. Most, if not all, of the foundations to which you apply will require the following in order to consider your request for funding:

1. A brief but concise letter outlining the circumstances that caused your financial difficulty. In the final paragraph of your letter, you should specify a dollar amount that you feel confident would ease your financial burden (e.g., "I request a grant in the amount of $2,500 to help me through this difficult period"). Remember to carefully look at the money given in the foundation listing to which you are applying. If you need $20,000 but the foundation only gives grants ranging from $5,000 to $15,000, the most you can request is $15,000.

2. An application form. Don't panic! If an application form is required, it is usually self-explanatory.

3. A copy of your tax return. Don't worry! You won't be penalized for showing excellent earnings or having savings. The issue is how the costs associated with your present medical problems or care needs have altered your financial stability. If you are in financial need, you will certainly be given every consideration.

4. A personal interview. This may take place by phone or in person. Foundations are run by people committed to their mission of help-

ing those in need or in trouble. Simply state the facts of your case and needs, and all should go well.

Remember, the information in your application should be clear and concise. Your letter should not exceed two pages. Be sure to include any attachments the foundation might require. Follow my instructions, and you should qualify for some sort of *free money*.

Private Foundation Funding

The listings in this chapter are probably the most accessible funding sources for the average individual seeking a grant. Until now, this information has not been made readily available to the general public. And yet thousands of foundations give away millions of dollars to individuals to help them through tough financial times.

The information is organized by state. Wherever possible, each listing includes a description of what cases the foundation will fund, any restrictions (i.e., residency in a particular town or city), the total amount of money awarded annually, the range of money given, the average size of the award, information on how to apply, deadline date(s), and name(s) of contact person(s).

ALABAMA

Kate Kinloch
Middleton Fund
P.O. Drawer 2527
Mobile, AL 36622
(205) 438-9597

Application Address:
409 First Alabama Bank Building
Mobile, AL 36602

Description: Grants or 4 percent loans to middle-class residents of
Mobile County, to help pay the expenses of unexpected serious
illness involving hospitalization and medical services.
$ Given: $131,569 for 80 grants; average range: $39–$4,604
Application Information: Initial approach by interview to disclose
medical problem and related financial burden.
Deadline: Not available
Contact: Joan Sapp, Trustee

ARIZONA

Lorraine Mulberger Foundation, Inc.
c/o Burch & Cracciolo
702 East Osborn
Phoenix, AZ 85014
(602) 274-7611

Description: Welfare assistance to needy individuals in Arizona.
$ Given: $44,857 for 13 grants; average range: $100–$11,573
Application Information: Completion of formal application re-
quired.
Deadline: None
Contacts: Andrew Abraham, Lorraine J. Mulberger

Precious Thoughts Tape Ministry
P.O. Box 4560
Apache Junction, AZ 85278
(602) 982-6035

Description: Gifts to prison inmates and their families, including tapes, tape players, headphones, books, Bibles, postage stamps, newsletters, paper and envelopes, and adapters.
$ Given: $269 for 6 cash gifts; average range: $20–$68; in-kind gifts for 1,976 people, valued at $28,570.
Application Information: Initial approach by letter, indicating tapes or materials desired.
Deadline: None
Contact: Betty B. Stidam, President

ARKANSAS

Charlotte Hill Charitable Trust
P.O. Box 754
Winfield, KS 67156
(316) 221-4600

Description: Financial assistance to single women over 60 with limited income and assets in the Arkansas City and Winfield areas of Kansas.
$ Given: $24,275 for 27 grants; average range: $70–$2,589
Application Information: Completion of formal application required.
Deadline: None
Contact: Kay Roberts, Trustee

CALIFORNIA

Avery-Fuller Children's Center
251 Kearny Street, #301
San Francisco, CA 94108
(415) 986-1687

Description: Financial assistance to handicapped and disabled children in the California counties of San Francisco, Alameda, Contra Costa, San Mateo, and Marin, for the purpose of increasing their self-sufficiency.
$ Given: $156,289

Application Information: Initial approach by letter or phone; completion of formal application required; final notification by mail, within four weeks after deadline. Rejected applicants will be reconsidered at the next review date, providing applicants request review in writing.
Deadlines: February 15, May 15, August 15, November 15
Contact: Eve Nikkila, Executive Director

William Babcock Memorial Endowment
305 San Anselmo Avenue
Suite 219
San Anselmo, CA 94960
(415) 453-0901

Description: Assistance to residents of Marin County for medical costs.
$ Given: $405,978 for 491 grants; average range: $100–$10,000
Application Information: Call; completion of formal application required.
Deadline: None
Contact: Alelia Gillin, Executive Director

Albert B. Cutter Memorial Fund
Bank of America
P.O. Box 712
Riverside, CA 92506
(909) 781-1464

Description: Limited emergency grants only to persons who have been permanent residents of Riverside for a minimum of one year and have been referred by local agencies.
$ Given: $34,406 for grants to individuals
Application Information: Completion of formal application required; interview or presentation recommended. Individuals are referred by local agencies.
Deadline: None
Contact: Trust Department

Danish Cheer Committee
1557 Lakewood Way
Upland, CA 91786

Description: Grants to needy or destitute elderly persons living in Upland.
$ Given: $13,942 for grants to individuals
Application Information: Initial approach by detailed letter.
Deadline: Not available
Contact: Not available

German Ladies Benevolent Society
(also known as Allgemeiner Deutscher Frauen Verein)
P.O. Box 27101
San Francisco, CA 94127
(415) 391-9947

Description: Temporary assistance to needy women and children of German descent in the San Francisco Bay Area.
$ Given: $83,813 for grants to individuals
Application Information: Completion of formal application required.
Deadline: Not available
Contact: Inge Byrnes, Secretary

Giannini Foundation for Employees
c/o Bank of America
Trustee Department
P.O. Box 37121
San Francisco, CA 94137
(415) 662-4915

Description: Grants to employees of Bank of America and its subsidiaries for medical bills or other emergencies.
$ Given: $72,835 for 13 grants; average range: $520–$27,604
Application Information: Initial approach by letter, including reason for grant request, amount requested, and applicant's financial status.
Deadline: None
Contact: Susana Morales, Assistant Vice President, Bank of America

The Marguerite Home Association
555 Capitol Mall
Suite 200
Sacramento, CA 95814

Description: Support limited to financial assistance to needy, elderly, single women in the Sacramento area.
$ Given: $52,150 for 284 grants
Application Information: Contributes only to preselected individuals. Application not accepted.
Deadline: Not available
Contact: Not available

New Horizons Foundation
700 South Flower Street
Suite 1222
Los Angeles, CA 90017-4160
(213) 626-4481

Description: Grants to financially needy Christian Scientists who live in Los Angeles and are over 65.
$ Given: $16,127 for 8 grants; average range: $300–$6,000
Application Information: Call or write for guidelines; interview required.
Deadline: None
Contact: G. Grant Gifford, President

Peninsula Community Foundation
1700 South El Camino Real, # 300
San Mateo, CA 94402-3049
(415) 358-9369
Fax: (415) 358-9369

Description: Grants to artists, including painters, dancers, photographers, and poets, who are residents of San Mateo County or northern Santa Clara County.
$ Given: $125,020 for 202 grants; average range: $250–$5,000
Application Information: Initial approach by letter and phone.
Deadline: None
Contact: John D. Taylor, President

John Percival and Mary C. Jefferson Endowment Fund

114 East De La Guerra
Santa Barbara, CA 93101
(805) 963-8822

Description: Grants to residents of Santa Barbara, to help pay medical, dental, or living expenses.
$ Given: $80,919 for 38 grants; average range: $374–$7,100
Deadline: Not available
Contact: Patricia M. Brouard, Trustee

Pfaffinger Foundation

Times Mirror Square
Los Angeles, CA 90053
(213) 237-5743

Description: Grants to current and former employees of the Times Mirror Company.
$ Given: $2,093,625 in grants to individuals; average range: $500–$40,553
Application Information: Initial approach by letter.
Deadline: None
Contact: James C. Kelly, President

Rivendell Stewards' Trust

2661 Tallant Road, # 620
Santa Barbara, CA 93105
(805) 969-5856

Description: Grants to needy people who work within the Christian church in Santa Barbara.
$ Given: $192,100 for grants
Application Information: Not available
Deadline: Not available
Contact: K.N. Hansen Sr., Treasurer

Charles E. Saak Trust

c/o Wells Fargo Bank Trust Department
P.O. Box 63954
San Francisco, CA 93711

Application Address:
2222 West Shaw Avenue, # 11
Fresno, CA 93111
(209) 442-6206

Description: Dental and emergency medical assistance to children
under 21 years of age from low-income families residing in the
Porterville/Poplar area of Tulare County.
$ Given: $37,572 for 34 grants; average range: $417–$3,720
Application Information: Completion of formal application required; application must be submitted with purpose and estimate
statement, parents' financial statements, and copy of most recent
income tax return.
Deadline: March 31
Contact: Not available

Virginia Scatena Memorial Fund for San Francisco School Teachers

c/o Bank of America
P.O. Box 37121
San Francisco, CA 94137

Description: Grants to retired San Francisco public school teachers
who are needy, sick, or disabled.
$ Given: $9,000 for 4 grants; average range: $1,800–$2,700
Application Information: Formal application required.
Deadline: None
Contact: Susan Morlas

Sequoia Trust Fund

555 California Street
36th Floor
San Francisco, CA 94104
(415) 393-8552

Description: Financial assistance primarily in California to needy
people who, by their special talents, have given great pleasure to
others. This assistance is only for special and unusual medical
expenses.

$ **Given:** $33,000 for 3 grants; average range: $3,000–$22,000
Application Information: Initial approach by letter; completion of
formal application, with complete details, required.
Deadline: None
Contact: Walter M. Baird, Secretary

The Trustees of Ivan V. Koulaieff Educational Fund
c/o Stadler Rosenblum
2301 Market Street
Suite 200
San Francisco, CA 94118

Application Address:
651 11th Avenue
San Francisco, CA 94118

Description: Scholarships to Russian immigrants throughout the
world.
$ **Given:** $218,050 for 22 grants; average range: $400–$55,300
Application Information: Not available
Deadline: None
Contact: Stadler Rosenblum

Winnett Foundation
c/o Bullock's
Executive Offices
800 South Hope Street
Los Angeles, CA 90017-4684
(213) 612-5000

Description: Aid to needy employees and retirees of Bullock's
Department Store only.
$ **Given:** $46,584 for 15 grants; average range: $850–$6,404
Application Information: Not available
Deadline: Not available
Contact: Cara Green

COLORADO

Jane Nugent Cochems Trust

c/o Colorado National Bank of Denver
P.O. Box 5168
Denver, CO 80217

Application Address:
President
Colorado State Medical Society
6061 Willow Drive
Suite 250
Englewood, CO 80111

Description: Grants to indigent doctors in Colorado.
$ Given: $5,000 for 1 grant
Application Information: Write for guidelines.
Deadline: Write to Colorado State Medical Society.
Contact: President, Colorado State Medical Society

Colorado Masons Benevolent Fund Association

1770 Sherman Street
Denver, CO 80203
(303) 837-0367

Application Address:
1130 Panorama Drive
Colorado Springs, CO 80904
(719) 471-9589

Description: Grants to Colorado Masonic Lodge members and their
families who are in financial distress.
$ Given: $569,051 for grants awarded
Application Information: Write or call Lodge for which brother is
(was) a member in good standing.
Deadline: Not available
Contact: Local Lodge in Colorado

CONNECTICUT

Blue Horizon Health & Welfare Trust

c/o Reid & Reige
Lakeville, CT 06039
(203) 435-9251

Application Address:
17 Cobble Road
Salisbury, CT 06068

Description: Financial assistance for medical costs.
$ Given: $200,199 for 4 grants; range: $7,320–$96,876
Application Information: Write for guidelines.
Deadline: None
Contact: Frances M. Wagner, Trustee

Bridgeport Ladies Charitable Trust

c/o Citytrust
951 Main Street
Bridgeport, CT 06604

Description: Support available to the handicapped, the aged, and children for health and home care.
$ Given: $36,000 for 100 grants; average range: $100–$1,000
Application Information: Must be referred from Emily Woodside Service or other community agencies.
Deadline: None
Contact: Mrs. Jeffrey S. Lockhart, President

Charitable Society of Hartford

Connecticut National Bank
777 Main Street
Hartford, CT 06115

Application Address:
c/o Robinson & Cole
One Commercial Plaza
Hartford, CT 06103
(203) 725-8200

Description: Grants for Hartford residents, to help pay for food, shelter, clothing, heat, and so on.
$ Given: $75,592 to individuals
Application Information: Accepted only by recognized social service agencies.
Deadline: None
Contact: Raymond S. Andrews Jr., President

Marion Isabelle Coe Fund
c/o Bank of Boston
P.O. Box 2210
Waterbury, CT 06722

Description: Grants to worthy residents of Goshen, Litchfield, Morris, and Warren, for living and medical expenses.
$ Given: $15,594 for 107 grants; average range: $28–$885
Application Information: Write for guidelines.
Deadline: None
Contact: Mrs. Speers

James Crocker Testamentary Trust
c/o J. Fells & L. B. Plumbing
P.O. Box 1045
Canaan, CT 06018

Application Address:
117 Main Street
Canaan, CT 06018
(203) 824-5146

Description: Grants to residents of Winchester who can demonstrate financial need.
$ Given: $1,683 for 13 grants; average range: $65–$300
Application Information: Write letter describing needs.
Deadline: Not available
Contact: Kevin F. Nelligan, Manager

The de Kay Foundation
c/o Manufacturers Hanover Trust Company
270 Park Avenue
New York, NY 10017
(212) 270-6000

Description: Grants to elderly residents of New York, New Jersey, and Connecticut in financial need, particularly those who are sick or disabled or who lack proper care.
$ Given: $193,260 for 79 grants; average range: $20–$7,000
Application Information: Completion of formal application required.
Deadline: None
Contact: Peter McSparran

The Westport-Weston Foundation
c/o The Westport Bank & Trust Company
P.O. Box 5177
Westport, CT 06681
(203) 222-6988

Description: Grants for medical and basic living expenses.
$ Given: Range: $42–$350
Application Information: Write for guidelines.
Deadline: Not available
Contact: Susanne M. Allen, Trust Officer

Widows Society
c/o Connecticut National Bank
777 Main Street
Hartford, CT 06115

Application Address:
20 Bayberry Lane
Avon, CT 06001
(203) 467-3887

Description: Financial assistance to needy women.
$ Given: $128,554 for 182 grants; average range: $35–$4,800
Application Information: Application usually referred by social service agencies, but individuals may submit letters.
Deadline: Not available
Contact: Dorothy Johnson, President

Women's Seamen's Friend Society of Connecticut
74 Forbes Avenue
New Haven, CT 06512
(203) 467-3887

Description: Financial assistance to sick and disabled seamen and their families.
$ Given: $40,125 awarded to individuals
Application Information: Write for guidelines.
Deadline: Not available
Contact: M. Courtwright

DISTRICT OF COLUMBIA

Buchly Charity Fund of Federal Lodge No. 1
1212 Wisconsin Avenue, NW
Washington, DC 20007

Application Address:
7015 Leesville Road
Springfield, VA 22151
(703) 256-1253

Description: Grants to widows and orphans of deceased former members of Federal Masonic Lodge No. 1.
$ Given: $33,900 for 12 grants; average range: $500–$7,700
Application Information: Write letter to Trustees showing financial needs upon death of husband.
Deadline: None
Contact: Willard E. Griffing, Trustee

FLORIDA

Alfred I. du Pont Foundation
P.O. Box 1380
Jacksonville, FL 32201
(904) 396-6600

Description: Grants to older residents of the southeastern United States with financial, health, or educational needs.
$ Given: $403,092 for 322 grants; average range: $125–$18,872
Application Information: Formal application required; write initial letter.
Deadline: None
Contact: Rosemary C. Wills, Assistant Secretary

Hope Foundation
2335 Tamiami Trail, North
Suite 510
Naples, FL 33940

Description: Grants for cancer, mental health, and social services
$ Given: $50,000 awarded to individuals
Application Information: Initial approach by letter.
Deadline: None
Contact: Mr. Philip M. Francoerur, Trustee

The Ryan Foundation
1511 West Broadway
Oviedo, FL 32765
(407) 365-8390

Description: Emergency assistance for basic necessities, including essential medical care.
$ Given: $62,203 for 77 grants to individuals
Application Information: Initial approach by letter or telephone.
Deadline: None
Contact: Jean Beede

Roy M. Speer Foundation
1803 U.S. Highway 19
Holiday, FL 34691-5536

Description: Grants to individuals in financial difficulty as a result of medical problems.
$ Given: 2 grants awarded to individuals; average range: $250–$1,500
Application Information: Write for guidelines.
Deadline: None
Contact: Not available

Vero Beach Foundation for the Elderly
c/o First National Bank
255 South County Road
Palm Beach, FL 33480
(407) 770-0044

Application Address:
2800 Indian River Boulevard
Apartment U-2
Vero Beach, FL 32960

Description: Grants to residents of Vero Beach who are at least 65 and can demonstrate financial need.
$ Given: $86,774 for grants to individuals
Application Information: Application required through Indian River County Council on Aging.
Deadline: None
Contact: Not available

Winter Park Community Trust Fund
c/o Barnett Banks Trust Company, N.A.
P.O. Box 1000
Winter Park, FL 32790

Application Address:
2823 Amber Gate Road
Winter Park, FL 32789

Description: Grants to needy residents of Orange and Seminole Counties.
$ Given: $14,800 for 12 grants was awarded to individuals in FY 91; range: $400–$1,950.
Application Information: Not available
Deadline: None
Contact: Not available

GEORGIA

Clark and Ruby Baker Foundation
c/o Bank South N.A.
Personal Trust Department
P.O. Box 4956 (MC 45)
Atlanta, GA 30302-9824
(404) 529-4627

Description: Grants primarily to retired Methodist ministers for pensions and medical assistance.

$ **Given:** $23,028 for 13 grants to individuals
Application Information: Not available
Deadline: None
Contact: Richard L. Watton, Trust Officer

Savannah Widows' Society
P.O. Box 30156
Savannah, GA 31410
(912) 232-6312

Description: Grants to female residents of Chatham County who are single and 55 or older and who are seriously disabled or handicapped.
$ **Given:** $99,931 for 104 grants; average range: $10–$8,400
Application Information: Completion of formal application required.
Deadline: None
Contact: Becky Traxler, President

HAWAII

The Hawaii Community Foundation
222 Merchant Street
Honolulu, HI 96813
(808) 537-6333

Description: One-time assistance to adult residents of Oahu.
$ **Given:** $117,500 for 125 grants; average range: $250–$1,500
Application Information: Call for guidelines; application form required.
Deadline: None
Contact: Not available

The May Templeton Hopper Foundation
1412 Whitney Street
Honolulu, HI 96822
(808) 944-2807

Description: Assistance to cover costs of medication, rent, day care, and other services.

$ Given: $130,131 for 74 grants to individuals; average range: $240–$9,600
Application Information: Application required.
Deadline: Fifth working day of the month in which application is to be considered.
Contact: Diana H. Lord, President

ILLINOIS

Reade Industrial Fund
c/o Harris Trust & Savings Bank
P.O. Box 755
111 West Monroe Street
Chicago, IL 60690
(312) 461-2609

Description: Grants or emergency loans to individuals who have been or are employed in industries in Illinois.
$ Given: $147,772 for 35 grants; average range: $5–$369
Application Information: Write for guidelines; formal application required.
Deadline: None
Contact: Ronald F. Tuite Jr.

Swiss Benevolent Society of Chicago
P.O. Box 2137
Chicago, IL 60690

Description: Grants to needy or elderly individuals of Swiss descent or nationality in the Chicago area.
$ Given: $54,567 for 4 grants
Application Information: Formal application required; write for guidelines.
Deadline: None
Contact: Not available

INDIANA

Mary Jane Luick Trust

c/o American National Bank & Trust Co.
110 East Main Street
Muncie, IN 47305
(317) 747-7550

Description: Grants to indigent elderly women of Delaware County.
$ Given: $4,170 for 5 grants
Application Information: Not available
Deadline: None
Contact: July Polson

Frank L. and Laura L. Smock Foundation

c/o Lincoln National Bank & Trust Co.
P.O. Box 2363
Fort Wayne, IN 46801-0960
(219) 461-6451

Description: Medical and nursing-care assistance to ailing, needy,
crippled, blind, or elderly individuals of the Presbyterian faith
throughout Indiana.
$ Given: $130,820 for 28 grants; average range: $3–$30,189
Application Information: Write for guidelines.
Deadline: Not available
Contact: Alice Kopfer, Assistance Vice President

IOWA

Human Aid Society of Iowa

400 First Interstate Bank Building
Des Moines, IA 50309

Application Address:
550 39th Street
Des Moines, IA 50312
(515) 274-1450

Description: Welfare assistance to individuals who demonstrate immediate need of assistance in acquiring food, clothing, and other material goods.
$ Given: $7,603 for 200 grants
Application Information: Apply in writing; include information on applicant's need and situation.
Deadline: None
Contact: Joseph S. Brick, President

KANSAS

Charlotte Hill Charitable Trust
P.O. Box 754
Winfield, KS 67156
(316) 221-4600

Description: Grants to single women over 60 in Winfield or Arkansas City with financial needs and limited assets.
$ Given: $24,275 for 279 grants
Application Information: Formal completion of application required.
Deadline: None
Contact: Kay Roberts, Trustee

Walter S. and Evan C. Jones Foundation
527 Commercial Street
Room 515
Emporia, KS 66801
(316) 342-2714

Description: Assistance with medical expenses to persons who have been continuous residents of the counties of Lyon, Coffey, or Osage for at least one year and who are under the age of 21.
$ Given: $500,680 for 1,670 grants; average range: $20–$19,205
Application Information: Initial approach by letter; completion of formal application required; interview required.
Deadline: Prior to beginning of services
Contact: Sharon R. Brown, General Manager

LOUISIANA

Joe W. and Dorothy Dorsett Brown Foundation
1801 Pere Marquette Building
New Orleans, LA 70112
(504) 522-4233

Description: Scholarships primarily to Louisiana and Mississippi
residents.
$ Given: $30,955 for 5 grants; average range: $1,800–$14,200
Application Information: Initial approach by letter.
Deadline: None
Contact: D. P. Spencer, President

MAINE

Camden Home for Senior Citizens
66 Washington Street
Camden, ME 04843
(207) 236-2087

Application Address:
Belfast Road
Camden, ME 04843
(207) 236-2014

Description: Grants for medical care and medicine; limited to
residents of Camden, Rockport, Lincolnville, and Hope, Maine.
$ Given: $45,948 for 257 grants in FY 91; range: $50–$350
Application Information: Not available
Deadline: Not available
Contact: Charles Lowe, President

Anita Card Montgomery Foundation
20 Mechanic Street
Camden, ME 04843-1707

Description: Grants to needy individuals, including funding for
medical and dental expenses.
$ Given: $9,207 for 18 grants; average range: $50–$1,297

Application Information: Write for guidelines.
Deadline: None
Contact: Julia Libby, President

Lena P. Frederick Trust Fund
c/o Key Trust Company
P.O. Box 1054
Augusta, ME 04330
(207) 623-5625

Description: Grants for medical assistance; limited to residents of
Belfast, Maine.
$ Given: $13,783 awarded in FY 91
Application Information: Not available
Deadline: None
Contact: Not available

Portland Female Charitable Society
20 Noyes Street
Portland, ME 04103

Application Address:
142 Pleasant Street, # 761
Portland, ME 04101

Description: Grants to Portland residents for medical or dental
care, for health or food needs, or for care of the ill, elderly, or
children.
$ Given: $10,297 for 89 grants; average range: $15–$950
Application Information: Write for guidelines; social workers,
nurses, or counselors may apply on behalf of individuals; interview
required.
Deadline: None
Contact: Janet Matty

Portland Seamen's Friend Society
14 Lewis Street
Westbrook, ME 04092

Description: Grants to seamen with financial needs who live in
Maine.

$ Given: $39,700 for 61 grants; average range: $120–$720
Application Information: Write for guidelines; interview required.
Deadline: None
Contact: Lewis G. Emery

MARYLAND

The Baltimore Community Foundation
The Latrobe Building
Two East Read Street
Ninth Floor
Baltimore, MD 21202
(301) 332-4171

Description: Grants for widows and children of B & O Railroad employees.
$ Given: Not available
Application Information: Write for guidelines.
Deadline: None
Contact: Timothy D. Armbruster, Executive Director

The Eaton Fund, Inc.
c/o Mercantile-Safe Deposit & Trust Co.
Two Hopkins Plaza
Baltimore, MD 21201
(410) 237-5321

Application Address:
766 Old Hammods Ferry Road
Linthieom, MD 21090

Description: Relief assistance to women 60 years of age or older who are residents of Baltimore or its vicinity.
$ Given: $18,325 for 9 grants; average range: $525–$3,000
Application Information: Initial approach by letter.
Deadline: None
Contact: Scott Murphy

Steeplechase Fund
400 Fair Hill Drive
Elkton, MD 21921

Description: Grants to injured jockeys or their widows who can
demonstrate financial need.
$ Given: $9,369 for grants to individuals; average range: $167–
$4,200
Application Information: Write letter describing disability and
medical needs.
Deadline: None
Contact: Charles Colgan

Anna Emory Warfield Memorial Fund, Inc.
c/o Mercantile Bank & Trust
Two Hopkins Plaza
Baltimore, MD 21201
(410) 547-0612

Description: Relief assistance to elderly women in Baltimore area.
$ Given: $162,500 for 45 grants; average range: $325–$4,225
Application Information: Write to request application guidelines;
formal application required.
Deadline: None
Contact: Thelma K. O'Neal, Secretary

MASSACHUSETTS

Association for the Relief of Aged Women of New Bedford
27 South Sixth Street
New Bedford, MA 02740

Description: Relief aid to needy, aged women; limited to residents
of New Bedford.
$ Given: $328,004 for 19 grants in FY 91; range: $693–$34,677
Application Information: Not available
Deadline: None
Contact: Not available

German Ladies Aid Society of Boston, Inc.
2222 Centre Street
West Roxbury, MA 02132

Description: Grants to aid needy local individuals.
$ Given: $1,690 in grants awarded
Application Information: Not available
Deadline: None
Contact: Not available

Howland Benevolent Fund for Aged Women
c/o Child and Family Service
1061 Pleasant Street
New Bedford, MA 02740
(508) 993-4232

Description: Relief assistance to poor, aged women.
$ Given: $12,900 for 13 grants; average range: $300–$1,200
Application Information: Formal application required.
Deadline: None
Contact: Sally Ainsworth, President of the Trustees

Charlotte M. Robbins Trust
c/o State Street Bank & Trust Co.
P.O. Box 351, M-11
Boston, MA 02101
(617) 654-3360

Application Address:
c/o State Street Bank & Trust Co.
225 Franklin Street
Boston, MA 02110

Description: Financial assistance to aged couples and aged women.
$ Given: $24,764 to individuals
Application Information: Write letter to application address stating income, expenses, assets, and reason money is needed.
Deadline: Not available
Contact: Cheryl D. Curtin, Vice President

Salem Female Charitable Society

c/o Fiduciary Trust Company
175 Federal Street
Boston, MA 02110

Application Address:
30 Warren Street
Salem, MA 01970

Description: Financial aid to needy women of the Salem area.
$ Given: $21,050 for 17 grants; average range: $50–$1,800
Application Information: Write for guidelines.
Deadline: None
Contact: Mrs. Roseanne Dennis, Treasurer

MINNESOTA

Duluth-Superior Area Community Foundation

618 Missabe Building
227 West First Street
Duluth, MN 55802-1913
(218) 726-0257

Description: Grants to residents of the Wisconsin counties of
Douglas and Bayfield and the Minnesota counties of Koochiching,
Itasca, St. Louis, Lake, Cook, Carlton, and Aitkin.
$ Given: $13,230 for 12 grants; range: $400–$3,000
Application Information: Application form required; write or call
for guidelines.
Deadlines: February 1, May 1, October 1
Contact: Marna Banks

Charles D. Gilfillan

West 555 First National Bank Building
St. Paul, MN 55101

Application Address:
3537 Edward Street, NE
Minneapolis, MN 55418
(612) 788-9010

Description: Financial assistance for medical, surgical, and dental costs to the financially distressed, limited to Minnesota residents with preference given to those living in small rural communities.
$ Given: $39,771 for 79 grants in 1991
Application Information: Not available
Deadline: None
Contact: Ms. Leah Slye, Secretary

Fanny S. Gilfillan Memorial, Inc.
c/o Lawrence Harder
Route 4
Redwood Falls, MN 56283

Application Address:
Redwood County Welfare Department
Box 27
Redwood Falls, MN 56283
(507) 637-5741

Description: Financial aid to needy individuals of Redwood County, including hospitalization bills.
$ Given: $51,063 for 29 grants in FY 90
Application Information: Not available
Deadline: None
Contact: Lawrence Harder

Hanna R. Kristianson Trust
P.O. Box 1011
Albert Lea, MN 56007

Application Address:
Clarks Grove, MN 56016
(507) 256-4415

Description: Financial aid to needy individuals over 50 years of age; limited to residents of Freeborn County.
$ Given: $8,333 awarded in 1989
Application Information: Not available
Deadline: None
Contact: Richard S. Haug

Saint Paul Foundation
1120 Norwest Center
St. Paul, MN 55101
(612) 224-5463

Description: Relief assistance grants limited to residents of St. Paul and Minneapolis.
$ Given: $243,980 awarded in 1991
Application Information: Not available
Deadline: None
Contact: Paul A. Verret, President

MISSISSIPPI

Joe W. and Dorothy Dorsett Brown Foundation
1801 Pere Marquette Building
New Orleans, LA 70112
(504) 522-4233

See complete entry under Louisiana, this chapter.

MISSOURI

The Leader Foundation
7711 Carondelet Avenue
10th Floor
St. Louis, MO 63105
(314) 725-7300

Description: Funding for pensions, family services, and health organizations.
$ Given: $76,308 for 23 grants; range: $600–$6,000
Application Information: Write for guidelines.
Deadline: None
Contact: Edwin G. Shifrin, Vice President

NEW HAMPSHIRE

Abbie M. Griffin Hospital Fund
111 Concord Street
Nashua, NH 03060

Description: Support for payment of hospital bills. Limited to
residents of Merrimack and Hillsborough Counties.
$ Given: $10,001 for 7 grants
Application Information: Not available
Deadline: None
Contact: S. Robert Winer, Trustee

NEW JERSEY

The de Kay Foundation
c/o Manufacturers Hanover Trust Company
270 Park Avenue
New York, NY 10017
(212) 270-6000

See complete entry under New York, this chapter.

Otto Sussman Trust
P.O. Box 1374
Trainsmeadow Station
Flushing, NY 11370-9998

See complete entry under New York, this chapter.

NEW YORK

Emma J. Adams Memorial Fund, Inc.
603 Third Avenue
25th Floor
New York, NY 10036

Description: Welfare assistance primarily through institutions to the elderly and to indigent gentlemen and gentlewomen in the New York City metropolitan area.
$ Given: $77,695 for 61 grants; range: $100–$6,000
Application Information: Write letter detailing need; formal application and interview required.
Deadline: Not available
Contact: Edward R. Finch Jr., President

Benedict Family Charitable Foundation, Inc.
82 Wall Street
New York, NY 10005

Description: Grants to needy individuals.
$ Given: $16,349 for individual grants
Application Information: Write letter.
Deadline: None
Contact: Alfred Benedict, President

The James Gordon Bennett Memorial Corporation
c/o *New York Daily News*
220 East 42nd Street
New York, NY 10017

Description: Grants to journalists who have been employees for ten or more years on *New York Daily News* and who can demonstrate financial need. Funds to be used for "the physical needs of persons . . . who, by reason of old age, accident, or bodily infirmity or through lack of means, are unable to care for themselves."
$ Given: Range: $150–$6,000
Application Information: Write for guidelines; formal application required.
Deadline: None
Contact: Denise Houseman

The Clark Foundation
30 Wall Street
New York, NY 10005
(212) 269-1833

Description: Financial aid of medical and hospital care to needy individuals in upstate New York and New York City.

$ **Given:** $65,166 for 11 grants in FY 92
Application Information: Not available
Deadline: None
Contact: Joseph H. Cruikshank, Secretary

Josiah H. Danforth Memorial Fund

8 Fremont Street
Gloversville, NY 12078

Description: Financial aid for medical care; limited to residents of Fulton County.
$ **Given:** $25,309 for 112 grants in FY 91
Application Information: Application form required.
Deadline: None
Contact: Not available

The de Kay Foundation

c/o Manufacturers Hanover Trust Company
270 Park Avenue
New York, NY 10017
(212) 270-6000

Description: Grants to needy elderly residents of New York, New Jersey, and Connecticut, particularly those who are sick or disabled or who lack proper care.
$ **Given:** $193,260 for 79 grants; average range: $20–$7,000
Application Information: Completion of formal application required.
Deadline: None
Contact: Peter McSparran

Dubose and Dorothy Heyward Memorial Fund

c/o Bank of New York
48 Wall Street, 4M
New York, NY 10015
(212) 495-1177

Description: Support for cancer treatment and research, as well as for arts organizations.
$ **Given:** $2 million in total giving
Application Information: Not available
Deadline: None
Contact: Katherine W. Floyd

Mary W. MacKinnon Fund
c/o Wilber National Bank
Trust Department
245 Main Street
Oneonta, NY 13820

Description: Grants to older residents of Sidney, New York, who can demonstrate financial need; grants are in the form of medical, nursing home, and rehabilitative care.
$ Given: $85,884 awarded to individuals
Application Information: Submit application through a doctor or hospital.
Deadline: None
Contact: Trust Department

Otto Sussman Trust
P.O. Box 1374
Trainsmeadow Station
Flushing, NY 11370-9998

Description: Financial assistance for medical bills and care-giving expenses to individuals with serious or terminal illness; limited to residents of New York, New Jersey, Oklahoma, and Pennsylvania.
$ Given: $183,387 for 112 awards in FY 90
Application Information: Write letter requesting application form and guidelines; explain circumstances of need; formal application form required.
Deadline: None
Contact: Edward S. Miller, Trustee

VonderLinden Charitable Trust
c/o Leonard Rachmilowitz
26 Mill Street
Rhinebeck, NY 12572
(914) 876-3021

Description: Grants to residents of upstate New York who have financial needs; funds may be used to meet a variety of needs, including medical bills.
$ Given: $23,260 for 101 grants; average range: $4-$540
Application Information: Initial approach by letter or telephone.
Deadline: None
Contact: Not available

OHIO

Christian Business Cares Foundation
P.O. Box 1862
Akron, OH 44309
(216) 762-8825

Description: One-time-only support in times of life-threatening emergencies.
$ Given: $40,320 for 99 grants; range: $37–$5,711
Application Information: Application required.
Deadline: None
Contact: Don Wetzel, Treasurer

Virginia Gay Fund
751 Grandon Avenue
Columbus, OH 43209

Description: Relief assistance for women over age 55 who have been school teachers for a minimum of 20 years.
$ Given: $61,570 for 25 grants; average range: $400–$6,000
Application Information: Write for guidelines.
Deadline: Not available
Contact: Board of Trustees

Grace A. Gossens Testamentary Trust
One Seagate
24th Floor
P.O. Box 10032
Toledo, OH 10032

Application Address:
416 West Wayne
Maumee, OH 43537
(419) 893-8603

Description: Relief assistance to elderly women who reside in rest homes.
$ Given: $5,500 for 1 grant
Application Information: Written application stating applicant's financial needs.
Deadline: None
Contact: Alice J. Servais, Trustee

Paul Motry Memorial Fund
c/o Dean S. Lucal
P.O. Box 357
Sandusky, OH 44870-0357

Description: Funding to individuals for health services; limited to residents of Erie and western Ottawa counties.
$ Given: $57,800 for 132 grants
Application Information: Application for assistance must include doctor's letter.
Deadline: Not available
Contact: Dean S. Lucal

Virginia Wright Mothers Guild, Inc.
426 Clinton Street
Columbus, OH 43202-2741

Description: Grants to aged women in need.
$ Given: $7,485 for 9 grants; range: $540–$915
Application Information: Write for guidelines.
Deadline: None
Contact: M. Courtwright

OKLAHOMA

Otto Sussman Trust
P.O. Box 1374
Trainsmeadow Station
Flushing, NY 11370-9998

See complete entry under New York, this chapter.

OREGON

Elizabeth Church Clarke Testamentary Trust/Fund Foundation
U.S. National Bank of Oregon
P.O. Box 3168
Portland, OR 97208

Application Address:
Scottish Rite Temple
709 SW 15th Avenue
Portland, OR 97205
(503) 228-9405

Description: Grants for medical aid.
$ Given: $68,441 in 1990
Application Information: Not available
Deadline: None
Contact: Walter L. Peters, Executive Secretary

Louis G. & Elizabeth L. Clarke Endowment Fund

Scottish Rite Temple
709 SW 15th Avenue
Portland, OR 97205
(503) 228-9405

Description: Grants to needy Masons or their immediate families who require hospitalization in the Portland metropolitan area.
$ Given: $72,099 awarded in FY 91
Application Information: Not available
Deadline: None
Contact: G. L. Selmyhr, Executive Secretary

Blanche Fischer Foundation

1550 Security Pacific Building
1001 SW Fifth Avenue
Suite 1550
Portland, OR 97204
(503) 323-9111

Description: Financial aid to physically handicapped individuals.
$ Given: $42,724 for 132 grants; range: $20–$2,500
Application Information: Write for application guidelines.
Deadline: None
Contact: William K. Shepard, President

Sophia Byers McComas Foundation
c/o U.S. National Bank of Oregon
P.O. Box 3168
Portland, OR 97208
(503) 275-6564

Description: Grants to elderly and indigent residents of Oregon recommended to the trustees by various church groups, service agencies, and so on.
$ Given: $69,525 awarded in FY 91
Application Information: Applicants are recommended to the trustees. Individuals may not apply directly.
Deadline: Not available
Contact: Not available

Scottish Rite Oregon Consistory Almoner Fund, Inc.
709 SW 15th Avenue
Portland, OR 97205
(503) 228-9405

Description: Assistance to financially distressed Masons and their families for medical expenses.
$ Given: $14,526 awarded in FY 91
Application Information: Not available
Deadline: None
Contact: Walter Peters, Executive Director

PENNSYLVANIA

Margaret Baker Memorial Trust Fund
c/o Mellon Bank (East) N.A.
P.O. Box 7236
Philadelphia, PA 19101-7236

Application Address:
P.O. Box 663
Phoenixville, PA 19460

Description: Financial aid to widows and single women over age 30.

$ Given: $15,546 for 6 grants
Application Information: Include applicant's age, income, infirmity (if any), and other supportive material, plus name of person who can verify the request.
Deadlines: July, November
Contact: L. Darlington Lessig, Treasurer

Female Association of Philadelphia
c/o Provident National Bank
1632 Chestnut Street
Philadelphia, PA 19103
(215) 525-6234

Description: Relief assistance to women who earn an annual income of less than $10,000 and who are over age 60.
$ Given: $98,550 for 298 grants
Application Information: Write for guidelines.
Deadline: None
Contact: Not available

French Benevolent Society of Philadelphia
1301 Medical Arts Building
1601 Walnut Street
Philadelphia, PA 19102
(215) 563-3276

Description: Aid to persons born to French parents living in Philadelphia who are in need due to age, illness, or misfortune.
$ Given: $38,924 awarded in 1991
Application Information: Formal application required.
Deadline: None
Contact: Not available

William B. Lake Foundation
c/o Fidelity Bank, N.A.
Broad and Walnut Streets
Philadelphia, PA 19109
(215) 985-8712

Application Address:
Fox Craft Square, Apt. 185
Jenkintown, PA 19046

Description: Grants to residents of the Philadelphia area who have diseases of the respiratory tract.
$ Given: $30,000 for grants to individuals
Application Information: Write letter describing in detail the applicant's needs.
Deadlines: May 1, November 1
Contact: Sophia O'Lessker, Social Worker

Lottie Sleeper Hill and Josiah Sleeper Fund
c/o Fidelity Bank
Broad and Walnut Streets
Philadelphia, PA 19109
(215) 985-8712

Description: Support to individuals for health care.
$ Given: $35,000 to individuals
Application Information: Not available
Deadline: None
Contact: Sister Mary Margaret, Secretary/Treasurer

Otto Sussman Trust
P.O. Box 1374
Trainsmeadow Station
Flushing, NY 11370-9998

See complete entry under New York, this chapter.

RHODE ISLAND

Bristol Home for Aged Women
20 Harborview Avenue
Bristol, RI 02809-1710
(401) 253-7260

Description: Financial aid to elderly, needy women.
$ Given: $60,700 to individuals
Application Information: Include cost and description of service needed.
Deadline: None
Contact: Ms. Alfred E. Newton, Treasurer

Robert B. Cranston/Theophilus T. Pitman Fund
18 Market Square
Newport, RI 02840
(401) 847-4260

Description: Grants to the aged and to temporarily indigent and
indigent people of Newport County for medical assistance, food,
utilities, clothing, and housing.
$ Given: $67,454 awarded in FY 90
Application Information: Interview or reference from a local
welfare agency required.
Deadline: None
Contact: Reverend D. C. Hambly Jr.

Inez Sprague Trust
c/o Rhode Island Hospital Trust
One Hospital Trust Plaza
Providence, RI 02903
(401) 278-8880

Description: Financial assistance and medical expenses for needy
individuals.
$ Given: $28,317 awarded in FY 90
Application Information: Not available
Deadline: None
Contact: Trustee

Townsend Aid for the Aged
c/o Fleet National Bank
100 Westminster Street
Providence, RI 02903

Description: Financial assistance for needy, elderly individuals in
Newport.
$ Given: $76,575 awarded in FY 90
Application Information: Applications not accepted.
Deadline: None
Contact: Not available

SOUTH CAROLINA

Graham Memorial Fund
P.O. Box 533
Bennettsville, SC 29512

Application Address:
308 West Main Street
Bennettsville, SC 29512
(803) 479-6804

Description: Grants for medical assistance and general welfare.
$ Given: $9,367 for 36 grants
Application Information: Initial approach by letter.
Deadline: June 1
Contact: Chairperson

TEXAS

H. C. Davis Fund
P. O. Box 2239
San Antonio, TX 78298

Description: Grants to assist Masons living in the 39th District of Texas.
$ Given: $25,924 for 9 grants; range: $750–$6,000
Application Information: Write for guidelines.
Deadline: None
Contact: Not available

Pardee Cancer Treatment Association of Greater Brazosport
127-C Circle Way
Lake Jackson, TX 77566

Description: Support for treatment of cancer.
$ Given: $206,930 for 137 grants
Application Information: Initial approach by letter.
Deadline: None
Contact: Ms. Shirley Funk

VIRGINIA

A. C. Needles Trust Fund Hospital Care
c/o Dominion Trust Company
P. O. Box 13327
Roanoke, VA 24040

Description: Grants for hospital care to financially distressed individuals.
$ Given: $48,518 for 14 grants; range: $598–$7,000
Application Information: Write for guidelines.
Deadline: None
Contact: Not available

WASHINGTON

G. M. L. Foundation, Inc.
c/o Gordon Cook
P.O. Box 916
Port Angeles, WA 98362

Description: Grants to individuals who need medical help.
$ Given: $14,966 for grants to individuals
Application Information: Write for guidelines.
Deadline: None
Contact: Graham Ralston, Secretary

Carrie Welch Trust
P.O. Box 244
Walla Walla, WA 99362

Description: Financial assistance to needy and/or worthy senior citizens in Washington State, with preference to residents of Walla Walla.
$ Given: $13,270 for 12 grants in FY 91
Application Information: Application form required.
Deadline: None
Contact: Not available

George T. Welch Testamentary Fund
c/o Baker-Boyd National Bank
P.O. Box 1796
Walla Walla, WA 99362
(509) 525-2000

Description: Medical assistance to financially distressed individuals
in Walla Walla.
$ Given: $142,401 for 111 grants in FY 91
Application Information: Application form required.
Deadlines: February 20, May 20, August 20, November 20
Contact: Dennis D. Gisi, Trust Officer

Whatcom Foundation, Inc.
Bellingham National Bank Building
Room 423
Bellingham, WA 98225
(206) 733-9511

Description: Grants to needy individuals for basic life needs and
medical care; limited to residents of Whatcom County.
$ Given: $10,307 total grants awarded in FY 91
Application Information: Formal application form required.
Deadline: Applications are due by noon each Wednesday and are
reviewed each following Monday throughout the year.
Contact: Linda Lopez

WEST VIRGINIA

Good Shepard Foundation, Inc.
Route 4
Box 349
Kinston, NC 28501-9317
(919) 569-3241

Description: Financial assistance to residents of Trent Township for
medical care.
$ Given: $17,000 for 6 grants in FY 91
Application Information: Application form required.
Deadline: None
Contact: Sue White, Secretary-Treasurer

WISCONSIN

Duluth-Superior Area Community Foundation
618 Missabe Building
227 West First Street
Duluth, MN 55802-1913
(218) 726-0257

See complete entry under Minnesota, this chapter.

Margaret Wiegand Trust
c/o Bank One
Wisconsin Trust Co., N.A.
P.O. Box 1308
Milwaukee, WI 53201

Description: Grants to blind individuals for uses including medical care, education, and other support services.
$ Given: $7,230 for 11 grants; range: $155–$1,500
Application Information: Write for guidelines.
Deadline: None
Contact: Judith Holland, Trust Officer

Private Foundation Funding, No Geographical Restrictions

Charles and Elsa Bendheim Foundation
1 Parker Plaza
Fort Lee, NJ 07024

Description: Grants to individuals for charitable purposes, including aid to the sick and destitute. Applicants must be Jewish and in need of financial assistance.
$ Given: $171,880 awarded in 1989
Application Information: Not available
Deadline: None
Contact: Not available

Broadcasters Foundation, Inc.
320 West 57th Street
New York, NY 10019
(212) 586-2000

Description: Grants to needy members of the broadcast industry
and their families.
$ Given: $14,400 for 7 grants in 1990; range: $1,800–$2,400
Application Information: Not available
Deadline: None
Contact: Not available

Hugel Foundation
824 Gravier Street
New Orleans, LA 70112

Description: Grants for health care and Catholic giving.
$ Given: $3,500 for 1 grant
Application Information: Not available
Deadline: Not available
Contact: Not available

Island Memorial Medical Fund, Inc.
c/o Richard Purinon
Main Road
Washington Island, WI 54246

Description: Financial assistance to needy individuals for help
covering medical expenses. Funds paid directly to physicians or
treatment facilities.
$ Given: Grants range from $630–$8,760
Application Information: Not available
Deadline: Varies
Contact: Richard Purinon

Max Mainzer Memorial Foundation, Inc.
570 Seventh Avenue
Third Floor
New York, NY 10018
(212) 921-3865

Description: Grants to financially distressed members of the American Jewish KC Fraternity or their widows.
$ Given: $34,287 for 15 grants in FY 91; range: $52–$3,750
Application Information: Not available
Deadline: None
Contact: Not available

NFL Alumni Foundation Fund
c/o Sigmund M. Hyman
P.O. Box 248
Stevenson, MD 21153-0248

Description: Financial assistance to disabled former National Football League alumni (prior to 1959), including grants for death benefits and medical expenses.
$ Given: $49,335 for 10 grants; eligible persons receive grants that will supplement their total annual income up to $12,000 with a $250/month maximum.
Application Information: Not available
Deadline: None
Contact: Sigmund M. Hyman

Katherine C. Pierce Trust
c/o State Street Bank and Trust Company
P.O. Box 351
Boston, MA 02101
(617) 654-3357

Description: Financial assistance to needy women.
$ Given: $44,200 for 13 grants in 1991
Application Information: Not available
Deadline: None
Contact: Robert W. Seymour, Trust Officer

Corporate Employee Grants Arranged by State, According to Corporate Location

ALABAMA

William H. and Kate F. Stockham Foundation, Inc.
c/o Stockham Valves & Fittings, Inc.
4000 North Tenth Avenue
P.O. Box 10326
Birmingham, AL 35202

Application Address:
c/o Kathryn W. Miree
AmSouth Bank
Trust Department
P.O. Box 11426
Birmingham, AL 35202
(205) 326-5387

Description: Need-based grants.
$ Given: $57,293 for 29 grants in 1990
Application Information: Not available
Deadline: Not available
Contact: Herbert Stockham, Chairman

CALIFORNIA

George S. Ladd Memorial Fund
c/o V. M. Edwards
633 Folsom Street
Room 420
San Francisco, CA 94107
(800) 248-6130

Description: Financial assistance grants, including funding for medical treatment, to elderly and retired employees of Pacific Bell, Nevada Bell, and Pacific Northwest Bell.
$ Given: $54,251 for 21 grants in 1991

Application Information: Not available
Deadline: Not available
Contact: Not available

Mate Foundation
c/o I. Magnin Administration Center
P.O. Box 7651
San Francisco, CA 94120-7651
(415) 362-2100

Description: Support for medical and personal emergencies; limited
to present or former employees of I. Magnin Company.
$ Given: $37,805 awarded in 1991
Application Information: Not available
Deadline: Not available
Contact: Not available

Pfaffinger Foundation
Times Mirror Square
Los Angeles, CA 90053
(213) 237-5743

Description: Need-based grants; limited to employees and former
employees of the Times Mirror Company.
$ Given: $2.1 million awarded in 1991
Application Information: Application form required.
Deadline: Not available
Contact: James C. Kelly

Winnett Foundation
c/o Bullock's Executive Offices
800 South Hope Street
Los Angeles, CA 90017-4468
(213) 612-5000

Description: Need-based grants; limited to employees and former
employees of Bullock's Department Store.
$ Given: $46,584 awarded in FY 91
Application Information:
Deadline: Not available
Contact: Cara Green

ILLINOIS

Clara Abbott Foundation
One Abbott Road
Abbott Park, IL 60064-3500
(312) 937-1091

Description: Relief grants, loans, and aid to the aged who are
employees, retirees, and families of employees of Abbott Laborato-
ries.
$ Given: $3,653,000 for 1,600 grants in 1991
Application Information: Not available
Deadline: None
Contact: David C. Jeffries, Executive Director

MASSACHUSETTS

Charles F. Bacon Trust
c/o Bank of New England, N.A.
28 State Street
Boston, MA 02109
(617) 573-6416

Description: Assistance grants given to former employees of Conrad
and Chandler Company who have retired or resigned due to illness.
$ Given: $17,000 for 4 grants in 1990
Application Information: Formal application required.
Deadline: December 31
Contact: Kerry Herlihy, Senior Trust Officer

Henry Hornblower Fund, Inc.
Box 2365
Boston, MA 02107
(617) 589-3286

Description: Need-based grants given to current and former em-
ployees of Hornblower and Weeks.
$ Given: $4,000 for 2 grants in 1990
Application Information: Not available
Deadline: None
Contact: Nathan N. Withington, President

Sexton Can Company Employees Aid Fund
125 Cambridge Park Drive
Cambridge, MA 02149

Description: Support to individuals for medical expenses; limited to present or former employees of Sexton Can Company, or their dependents.
$ Given: $3,800 for 2 grants
Application Information: Not available
Deadline: None
Contact: Not available

MINNESOTA

CENEX Foundation
5500 Cenex Drive
Inver Grove Heights, MN 55075
(612) 451-5105

Description: Financial assistance grants; limited to former employees of Cenex and its affiliates.
$ Given: $80,745 for 34 grants in 1990
Application Information: Application form required.
Deadline: None
Contact: Mary Kaste, Manager

MISSOURI

Butler Manufacturing Company Foundation
Penn Valley Park
P.O. Box 419917
BMA Tower
Kansas City, MO 64141-0197
(816) 968-3208

Description: Hardship grants to aid individuals in emergency financial distress due to serious illness, fire, or natural disaster; limited to Butler Manufacturing Company employees, retirees, and their dependents.

$ **Given:** $3,672 for 3 grants in 1991
Application Information: Write for application guidelines and
program information; interviews required.
Deadline: Not available
Contact: Barbara Lee Fay, Foundation Administrator

Hall Family Foundations
c/o Charitable and Crown Investment Department 323
P.O. Box 419580
Kansas City, MO 64141-6580
(816) 274-8516

Description: Grants for emergency relief assistance for employees of
Hallmark.
$ **Given:** $273,082 for 147 grants in 1990
Application Information: Not available
Deadline: Not available
Contact: Margaret H. Pence, Director/Program Officer

Kansas City Life Employees Welfare Fund
3520 Broadway
Kansas City, MO 64111-2565
(816) 753-7000

Description: Medical assistance to Kansas City Life employees and
their spouses and/or dependents.
$ **Given:** $1,600 for 2 grants in 1990
Application Information: Not available
Deadline: None
Contact: Dennis M. Gaffney

David May Employees Trust Fund
c/o May Department Stores Company
Attn: Tax Department
Sixth and Olive Streets
St. Louis, MO 63101

Description: Need-based grants to employees and former employees
of the May Department Store Company.
$ **Given:** $11,000 for 4 grants in 1990

Application Information: Not available
Deadline: Not available
Contact: Tax Department

NEVADA

George S. Ladd Memorial Fund
c/o V. M. Edwards
633 Folsom Street
Room 420
San Francisco, CA 94107
(800) 248-0130

Description: Financial assistance grants, including funding for medical treatment; limited to elderly and retired employees of Pacific Bell, Nevada Bell, and Pacific Northwest Bell.
$ Given: $54,251 for 21 grants in 1991
Application Information: Not available
Deadline: Not available
Contact: V. M. Edwards

NEW JERSEY

Ittleson Beaumont Fund
(Formerly Ittleson Beneficial Fund)
c/o The C.I.T. Group Holdings, Inc.
135 West 50th Street
New York, NY 10020
(212) 408-6000

Application Address:
650 C.I.T. Drive
Livingston, NJ 07039

Description: Need-based grants for providing supplemental income to individuals demonstrating continuing financial hardship. Intended primarily, but not exclusively, for current and former employees of C.I.T. Financial Corporation and its affiliates, as well as for the families of employees.

$ **Given:** $37,885 for 17 grants in 1990
Application Information: Submit application letter stating reason for request and providing details of applicant's financial status.
Deadline: None
Contact: William M. Hopf, Controller

NEW YORK

Ernst and Young Foundation
(formerly the Ernst and Whinney Foundation)
277 Park Avenue
New York, NY 10171

Description: Financial assistance grants to Ernst and Young employees and their families.
$ **Given:** $2,400 for 1 relief grant
Application Information: Not available
Deadline: Not available
Contact: Bruce J. Mantia, Administrator

Hegeman Memorial Trust Fund
One Madison Avenue
Area 23VW
New York, NY 10010
(212) 578-3493

Description: Grants to employees, active and retired, and their New York dependents, including dependents of deceased employees of Metropolitan Life Insurance Company, for health and welfare.
$ **Given:** $468,700 for 15 grants in 1990
Application Information: Initial approach by letter, including financial statement to demonstrate need.
Deadline: None
Contact: Evelyn D. Ilari, Employees Advisory Services

Ittleson Beaumont Fund
(Formerly Ittleson Beneficial Fund)
c/o The C.I.T. Group Holdings, Inc.
135 West 50th Street
New York, NY 10020
(212) 408-6000

Application Address:
650 C.I.T. Drive
Livingston, NJ 07039

Description: Need-based grants for providing supplemental income
to individuals demonstrating continuing financial hardship. Intended primarily, but not exclusively, for current and former
employees of C.I.T. Financial Corporation and its affiliates, as well
as for the families of employees.
$ Given: $37,885 for 17 grants in 1990
Application Information: Submit application letter stating reason
for request and providing details of applicant's financial status.
Deadline: None
Contact: William M. Hopf, Controller

OHIO

National Machinery Foundation, Inc.
Greenfield Street
P.O. Box 747
Tiffin, OH 44883
(419) 447-5211

Description: Need-based grants to former employees of National
Machinery and to other financially distressed individuals in Seneca
County, Ohio.
$ Given: $11,390 awarded in 1990
Application Information: Not available
Deadline: Not available
Contact: D. B. Bero, Administrator

Richman Brothers Foundation
Box 657
Chagrin Falls, OH 44022
(216) 247-5426

Description: Relief assistance grants to employees, pensioners,
widows, and children of employees of the Richman Brothers
Company.
$ Given: Grants range from $100 to $1,995

Application Information: Write for guidelines; application form required.
Deadline: November 15
Contact: Richard R. Moore, President

OREGON

George S. Ladd Memorial Fund
c/o V. M. Edwards
633 Folsom Street
Room 420
San Francisco, CA 94107
(800) 248-0130

Description: Financial assistance grants, including funding for medical treatment, to elderly and retired employees of Pacific Bell, Nevada Bell, and Pacific Northwest Bell.
$ Given: $54,251 for 21 grants in 1991
Application Information: Not available
Deadline: Not available
Contact: Not available

PENNSYLVANIA

Vang Memorial Foundation
P.O. Box 11727
Pittsburgh, PA 15228
(412) 563-0261

Description: Grants-in-aid assistance to past, present, and future employees of George Vang, Inc., and related companies, and their dependents.
$ Given: $40,589 for 17 grants in 1991
Application Information: Submit introductory letter, including name, address, and telephone number of applicant, and specify type of grant requested and basis of need.
Deadline: None
Contact: E. J. Hosko, Treasurer

WASHINGTON

George S. Ladd Memorial Fund
c/o V. M. Edwards
633 Folsom Street
Room 420
San Francisco, CA 94107
(800) 248-0130

Description: Financial assistance grants, including funding for
medical treatment, to elderly and retired employees of Pacific Bell,
Nevada Bell, and Pacific Northwest Bell.
$ Given: $54,251 for 21 grants in 1991
Application Information: Not available
Deadline: Not available
Contact: Not available

Companies with Employees Nationwide and Abroad

The Correspondents Fund
c/o Roseman & Cohen
575 Madison Avenue
New York, NY 10022-2511

Application Address:
c/o New York Times
229 West 43rd Street
New York, NY 10036

Description: Emergency grants to individuals who have worked in
the U.S. press, television, radio, news, film, and other U.S. organizations within or outside the U.S. and to individuals who have
worked in the foreign press or other foreign news organizations
and to their dependents.
$ Given: Grants range from $2,500 to $3,000
Application Information: Submit an introductory letter, including
details of the circumstances for which aid is requested.
Deadline: None
Contact: James L. Greenfield, President

Flow-Through Funding

Flow-through funding is different from the other kinds of grant funding that this book describes. Flow-through funding is indirect funding: The foundations listed in this chapter do not provide money directly to individuals, but instead give money to nonprofit organizations, which, in turn, pass funds along to people in need. These nonprofit organizations serve as sponsors for individuals who require financial assistance.

Individuals cannot apply directly to these foundations for funding. The foundations listed in this chapter accept applications only from nonprofit organizations. If you wish to receive funds from any of these foundations, you must work through a sponsoring nonprofit organization.

Why should you bother with a sponsor? The number of foundations included in this chapter should give you an idea of the vast amount of grant money made available as flow-through funding.

Many times, monies awarded to an organization are applied to the needs of more than one person; one grant award usually benefits a group of individuals. In asking your nonprofit sponsor to contact these foundations on your behalf, you are, in a sense, promoting the interests of other individuals served by the sponsor. However, don't let this discourage you from making use of the information in this chapter.

How do you go about finding a nonprofit sponsor? Check any local directory of nonprofit organizations (your local library will usually have such directories, perhaps in the community services section). Contact local citywide consortium-style associations operating in your area of interest, such as the United Way or federations. Speak to their directors or public information officers and elicit their suggestions for possible sponsors. Also check national organization reference books, such as the *Encyclopedia of Associations*, for other potential candidates.

How do you apply? Although you cannot apply directly to any of the foundations listed in this chapter, your background work here can be extremely helpful to your sponsor organization. Use the information provided in this chapter to identify foundations that seem to address your specific situation. Following your nonprofit sponsor's directions, write to the appropriate foundations to request information, including application guidelines. Share any information you have received from potential funding sources.

ALABAMA

The Comer Foundation
P.O. Box 302
Sylacauga, AL 35150
(205) 249-2962

Description: Grants to charitable organizations and residents of Alabama, to help pay for higher education and medical expenses.
$ Given: $561,690 for 41 grants; average range: $1,000–$50,000
Application Information: Write for guidelines (see the important information in the chapter introduction about the need for institutional affiliation).
Deadline: None
Contact: R. Larry Edmunds, Secretary-Treasurer

The Daniel Foundation of Alabama
820 Shades Creek Parkway
Suite 1200
Birmingham, AL 35209
(205) 879-0902

Description: Grants to charitable organizations and residents of the southeastern United States, to help pay for higher education and medical expenses; preference is given to residents of Alabama.
$ Given: $1.5 million for 67 grants; average range: $2,000–$50,000
Application Information: Write for guidelines.
Deadline: None
Contact: S. Garry Smith, Secretary-Treasurer

The Greater Birmingham Foundation
P.O. Box 131027
Birmingham, AL 35213
(205) 328-8641

Description: Grants to support the health, welfare, and cultural and educational needs of Birmingham residents.
$ Given: $2.9 million for 304 grants; average range: $1,000–$50,000
Application Information: Write for guidelines (see the important information in the chapter introduction about the need for institutional affiliation).
Deadlines: April 1, October 1
Contact: Sheila S. Blair, Executive Director

D.W. McMillan Foundation
329 Belleville Avenue
Brewton, AL 36426
(205) 867-4881

Application Address:
P.O. Box 867
Brewton, AL 36427

Description: Grants for organizations and residents of Escambia County, to help pay for medical and general living expenses.
$ Given: $215,152 for 62 grants
Application Information: Write for guidelines.
Deadline: December 1
Contact: Ed Leigh McMillan II, Managing Trustee

ARIZONA

Arizona Community Foundation
2122 East Highland Avenue
Suite 400
Phoenix, AZ 85016
(602) 381-1400
Fax: (602) 381-1575

Description: Grants to organizations in Arizona, to support community-based health and youth agencies and handicapped and social services.
$ Given: $2.4 million for 350 grants; average range: $1,000–$10,000
Application Information: Formal application required; write for guidelines (see the important information in the chapter introduction about the need for institutional affiliation).
Deadlines: February 1, June 1, October 1
Contact: Stephen D. Mittenthal, President

The Marshall Fund of Arizona
4000 North Scottsdale Road
Suite 203
Scottsdale, AZ 85251
(602) 941-5249

Description: Grants to organizations in Arizona, for human and social problems, social services, the homeless, and child welfare.
$ Given: $177,278 for 16 grants; average range: $2,500–$20,000
Application Information: Application form not required; write for guidelines (see the important information in the chapter introduction about the need for institutional affiliation).
Deadlines: March 1, August 1, November 1
Contact: Maxine Marshall, Vice President

Margaret T. Morris Foundation
P.O. Box 592
Prescott, AZ 86302
(602) 455-4010

Description: Grants to organizations in Arizona, for social programs, youth and child welfare, homeless, handicapped, disadvantaged, and mental health services.
$ Given: $1.2 million for 69 grants; average range: $1,000–$25,000
Application Information: Application form not required; write proposal or letter (see the important information in the chapter introduction about the need for institutional affiliation).
Deadline: Submit proposal May–November
Contact: Eugene P. Polk, Trustee

Steele Foundation, Inc.
702 East Osborn Road
Phoenix, AZ 85014-5215
(602) 230-2038

Application Address:
P.O. Box 1112
Phoenix, AZ 85001

Description: Grants to organizations and residents of Phoenix, for education, religious welfare, and medical expenses.
$ Given: $801,000 for 27 grants; average range: $5,000–$50,000
Application Information: Write for guidelines.
Deadline: None
Contact: Bea Baker, Controller

ARKANSAS

Arkansas Community Foundation, Inc.
700 South Rock
Little Rock, AR 72202
(501) 372-1116

Description: Grants to residents and charitable organizations of Arkansas, for social services, health services, and scholarships. Grants are also available for cultural programs, community development, and environmental programs.
$ Given: $1.85 million for grants
Application Information: Write or call; formal application required.
Deadlines: January 15, July 15
Contact: Martha Ann Jones, President

DeQueen General Hospital Foundation, Inc.
P.O. Box 674
DeQueen, AR 71832

Application Address:
Cassatot Technical College
P.O. Box 960
DeQueen, AR 71832
(501) 584-4471

Description: Grants to residents and organizations of Sevier County
to help pay for medical expenses.
$ Given: $139,000 for 7 grants
Application Information: Write for application form.
Deadline: None
Contact: Not available

Murphy Foundation
200 North Jefferson Avenue
Suite 400
El Dorado, AR 71730
(501) 862-6884

Description: Grants to residents and organizations of Arkansas for
higher education, social services, and the arts.
$ Given: $444,110 for 52 grants; average range: $500–$10,000
Application Information: Write or call for required application
form.
Deadline: Not available
Contact: Perry Silliman, Secretary-Treasurer

CALIFORNIA

The Abelard Foundation, Inc.
2530 San Pablo Avenue
Berkeley, CA 94702
(415) 644-1904

West Coast Application Address:
2530 San Pablo Avenue
Suite B
Berkeley, CA 94702

East Coast Application Address:
c/o Susan Collins
P.O. Box 148
Lincoln, MA 01773

Description: Grants to organizations in New York, the southern
and western states, and Appalachia that support social programs,
urban and rural economic equality, the disadvantaged, and those
individuals with financial needs.

$ Given: $245,000 for 35 grants; average range: $6,000–$7,000
Application Information: Write or call for guidelines or send proposal (see the important information in the chapter introduction about the need for institutional affiliation).
Deadline: None
Contacts: Susan Beaudry, Executive Director (West Coast); Susan Collins (East Coast)

The Ahmanson Foundation
9215 Wilshire Boulevard
Beverly Hills, CA 90210
(310) 278-0770

Description: Grants to residents and organizations of southern California to support a wide range of human service programs, including education, health, youth, and housing services.
$ Given: $19.6 million for 463 grants; average range: $10,000–$25,000
Application Information: Send letter of inquiry or proposal (see the important information in the chapter introduction about the need for institutional affiliation).
Deadlines: Quarterly
Contact: Lee W. Walcott, Vice President and Managing Director

Alliance Healthcare Foundation
5251 Viewridge Court
San Diego, CA 91213
(619) 278-2273

Description: Grants to residents and organizations of southern California to help pay for medical expenses, including those for people with AIDS.
$ Given: $1.1 million for grants
Application Information: Write for guidelines (see the important information in the chapter introduction about the need for institutional affiliation).
Deadline: Not available
Contact: Judy Montsatson, Program Associate

Argyros Foundation
950 South Coast Drive
Suite 200
Costa Mesa, CA 92626
(714) 241-5000

Description: Grants to residents and organizations of Orange
County, for culture, education, religious giving, social services,
recreation, and health services.
$ Given: $1.2 million for 54 grants
Application Information: Write for guidelines; formal application
required (see the important information in the chapter introduction
about the need for institutional affiliation).
Deadline: June 1
Contact: Charles E. Packard, Trustee

The Kathryne Benyon Foundation
199 South Los Robles Avenue
Suite 711
Pasadena, CA 91101-2460

Description: Grants to organizations and residents of southern
California, for health services, drug rehabilitation programs, child
welfare, Catholic Church support, and higher education.
$ Given: $231,000 for 18 grants
Application Information: Write letter; formal application form not
required.
Deadline: None
Contact: Robert D. Bannon, Trustee

George and Ruth Bradford Foundation
P.O. Box E
San Mateo, CA 94402-0017
(415) 345-5789

Description: Grants to education, health services, youth programs,
and the homeless in the San Francisco Bay Area.
$ Given: $199,000 for 47 grants
Application Information: Write for guidelines (see the important

information in the chapter introduction about the need for institutional affiliation).
Deadline: None
Contact: Robert Bradford, Director

Broderbund Foundation
500 Redwood Boulevard
P.O. Box 6121
Novato, CA 94948-6121

Description: Grants to residents and organizations of the San Francisco Bay Area, for social services, child welfare, and education.
$ Given: $202,612 for 49 grants
Application Information: Write for guidelines (see the important information in the chapter introduction about the need for institutional affiliation).
Deadline: None
Contact: Patsy Murphy, Secretary

Carbonel Foundation
c/o The Tides Foundation
1388 Sutter Street
10th Floor
San Francisco, CA 94109
(415) 771-4308

Application Address:
c/o Sheehan & Co., CPA
233 Broadway
New York, NY 10279
(212) 962-4470

Description: Grants to support organizations serving families in crisis, human needs, and the disadvantaged.
$ Given: $303,000 for grants
Application Information: Write for guidelines (see the important information in the chapter introduction about the need for institutional affiliation).
Deadline: None
Contact: Jacqueline Schad

Community Foundation of Santa Clara County
960 West Hedding
Suite 220
San Jose, CA 95126-1215
(408) 241-2666

Description: Grants to residents and organizations of Santa Clara County, for education, AIDS programs, child welfare, women and minorities, employment and housing, the arts, community development and urban affairs, and the environment.
$ Given: $2.7 million for 481 grants; average range: $1,500–$10,000
Application Information: Write letter or call; application form not required.
Deadlines: Generally quarterly
Contact: Winnie Chu, Associate Director

Elks of Los Angeles Foundation Fund
c/o Wells Fargo Bank, N.A.
333 South Grand
Los Angeles, CA 90071

Application Address:
5013 Dobkin Avenue
Tarzana, CA 91356

Description: Grants to residents of Los Angeles, for youth, child welfare, the homeless, and health services.
$ Given: $192,196 for 50 grants; average range: $1,000–$9,000
Application Information: Write letter; formal application required (see the important information in the chapter introduction about the need for institutional affiliation).
Deadline: None
Contact: Lee S. Linden

The Esprit de Corps Foundation
900 Minnesota Street
San Francisco, CA 94107

Description: Grants for housing and general charitable giving, primarily in San Francisco.

$ Given: $1.1 million for 146 grants; average range: $5,000–
$75,000
Application Information: Write for guidelines (see the important
information in the chapter introduction about the need for institu-
tional affiliation).
Deadline: None
Contact: Not available

Fireman's Fund Foundation
777 San Marin Drive
P.O. Box 777
Novato, CA 94998

Description: Grants to organizations in the counties of San Francisco, Marin, and Sonoma for human services, including programs
for the aged, homeless, disabled, disadvantaged, and youth.
$ Given: $986,004 for 844 grants; average range: $2,500–$5,000
Application Information: Write for guidelines (see the important
information in the chapter introduction about the need for institutional affiliation).
Deadline: None
Contact: Barbara B. Friede, Director

Audrey and Sydney Irmas Charitable Foundation
11835 West Olympic Boulevard
Suite 1160
Los Angeles, CA 90064
(310) 477-7979

Description: Grants to residents and organizations of Los Angeles,
to help pay housing expenses. Grants are also available for charitable foundations, the arts, education, drug rehabilitation, and
Jewish welfare.
$ Given: $1.0 million for 67 grants; average range: $1,000–$50,000
Application Information: Write letter; formal application not
required.
Deadline: None
Contact: Robert Irmas, Manager

General and Mrs. William Lyon Family Foundation
P.O. Box 8858
Newport Beach, CA 92658-8858
(714) 833-3600

Application Address:
4490 Von Karman
Newport Beach, CA 92660

Description: Grants to residents and organizations of California to support higher education and social service programs.
$ Given: $578,330 for 14 grants
Application Information: Send typed letter requesting the required application form (see the important information in the chapter introduction about the need for institutional affiliation).
Deadline: None
Contact: General or Mrs. William Lyon

MCA Foundation, Ltd.
100 Universal City Plaza
Universal City, CA 91608
(818) 777-1208

Description: Grants for health and welfare programs in the Los Angeles and New York City areas, including support for minorities, children, and women.
$ Given: $831,000 for 45 grants
Application Information: Write for guidelines or send proposal of not more than three pages (see the important information in the chapter introduction about the need for institutional affiliation).
Deadline: None
Contact: Helen D. Yatsko, Administrator

The Milken Family Foundation
c/o Foundations of the Milken Families
1250 Fourth Street
Sixth Floor
Santa Monica, CA 90401

Description: Grants to residents and organizations of the Los Angeles area, to help pay for general living expenses. Grants are also available for education, health and medical research, and community services.

$ Given: $3.7 million for 89 grants; average range: $1,000–$75,000
Application Information: Write letter or send proposal (see the important information in the chapter introduction about the need for institutional affiliation).
Deadline: None
Contact: Dr. Julius Lesner, Executive Director

Orange County Community Foundation
675 Town Center Drive
17th Floor
Costa Mesa, CA 92626
(714) 641-3874
Fax: (714) 979-1921

Description: Grants to support the disadvantaged, youth, women, and minorities of Orange County, including funds for scholarships and medical expenses.
$ Given: $161,332 for grants
Application Information: Write for guidelines.
Deadline: Spring
Contact: Judith Swayne, Executive Director

The Ralph M. Parsons Foundation
1055 Wilshire Boulevard
Suite 1701
Los Angeles, CA 90017
(213) 482-3185

Description: Grants to organizations in Los Angeles, to support health and social services for the disadvantaged, as well as women, families, and seniors.
$ Given: $8.3 million for 172 grants; average range: $10,000–$75,000
Application Information: Write for guidelines (see the important information in the chapter introduction about the need for institutional affiliation).
Deadline: None
Contact: Christine Sisley, Executive Director

The Riordan Foundation

300 South Grand Avenue
29th Floor
Los Angeles, CA 90071
(213) 229-8402

Description: Grants for job training, youth programs, and medical
expenses for young children, primarily in California.
$ Given: $2.0 million for 68 grants; average range: $1,000–$25,000
Application Information: Write for guidelines (see the important
information in the chapter introduction about the need for institutional affiliation).
Deadline: None
Contact: Mary Odell, President

Rivendell Stewards' Trust Dated February 23, 1985

2661 Tallant Road, #620
Santa Barbara, CA 93105
(805) 969-5856

Description: Grants to Christian residents and organizations of
California, for missionary efforts, education, and needy individuals
who work in the Christian church.
$ Given: $1.1 million for grants
Application Information: Write for guidelines.
Deadlines: January–April for education grants; September
1–October 15 for all others
Contact: K.N. Hansen Sr., Treasurer

Transamerica Foundation

600 Montgomery Street
San Francisco, CA 94111
(415) 983-4333

Description: Grants to organizations in the San Francisco Bay Area,
for housing, education, and AIDS and drug abuse programs.
$ Given: $568,125 for 60 grants; average range: $1,000–$25,000
Application Information: Write for required application form (see
the important information in the chapter introduction about the
need for institutional affiliation).
Deadline: None
Contact: Mary M. Sawai, Program Director

Lawrence Welk Foundation
1299 Ocean Avenue
Suite 800
Santa Monica, CA 90401
(213) 451-5727

Description: Grants to residents and organizations of southern California for social services, family services, and child welfare.
$ Given: $300,120 for 59 grants; average: $5,000
Application Information: Send letter of inquiry during the first half of the year (see the important information in the chapter introduction about the need for institutional affiliation).
Deadline: Not available
Contact: Shirley Fredricks, Executive Director

COLORADO

Community Foundation Serving Northern Colorado
c/o The Nicol Building
528 South College
Fort Collins, CO 80524
(303) 224-3462

Description: Support for health and social services in northern Colorado, with emphasis on Larimer and Weld counties.
$ Given: $162,700 for 60 grants; average range: $1,000–$5,000
Application Information: Write for guidelines; formal application not required (see the important information in the chapter introduction about the need for institutional affiliation).
Deadlines: February 1, May 1, August 1, November 1
Contact: Diane M. Hogerty, Executive Director

Adolph Coors Foundation
3773 Cherry Creek North Drive
Suite 955
Denver, CO 80209
(303) 388-1636

Description: Grants to organizations in Colorado, to support health, social, and youth services for the disadvantaged.

$ Given: $5.4 million for 138 grants; average range $10,000–$50,000
Application Information: Send letter; formal application not required (see the important information in the chapter introduction about the need for institutional affiliation).
Deadlines: February 1, May 1, August 1, November 1
Contact: Linda S. Tafoya, Executive Director

Henry W. Rabb Foundation
6242 South Elmira Circle
Englewood, CO 80111

Description: Grants to hospitals, Jewish welfare funds, and needy senior citizens of Denver.
$ Given: $112,600 for grants
Application Information: Write for guidelines (see the important information in the chapter introduction about the need for institutional affiliation).
Deadline: None
Contact: Richard A. Zarlengo, Secretary-Treasurer

Someone Cares Charitable Trust
P.O. Box 2062
Wheatridge, CO 80034

Description: Grants to support immigration services, Christian programs, and the needy of Colorado.
$ Given: $102,665 for 34 grants; average range: $500–$5,000
Application Information: Write for guidelines; application form not required.
Deadline: Not available
Contact: Philip Yancey, President

The Bal F. and Hilda N. Swan Foundation
c/o First Interstate Bank of Denver, N.A.
P.O. Box 5825
Terminal Annex
Denver, CO 80217
(303) 293-5275

Description: Grants to residents and organizations of Colorado, for handicapped services, medical research, child welfare, cultural programs, social services, and higher education.
$ Given: $375,692 for 53 grants; average range: $1,000–$30,000
Application Information: Write letter; formal application required.
Deadline: None
Contact: Julie Dines, Trust Officer, First Interstate Bank of Denver, N.A.

CONNECTICUT

The Community Foundation of Greater New Haven
70 Audubon Street
New Haven, CT 06510
(203) 777-2386

Description: Grants to residents and organizations of greater New Haven and lower Naugatuck River Valley, for health and social services, youth and education programs.
$ Given: $4.6 million for 526 grants; average range: $5,000–$30,000
Application Information: Call for guidelines and send letter of intent (see the important information in the chapter introduction about the need for institutional affiliation).
Deadline: Not available
Contact: Helmer N. Ekstrom, Executive Director

Fisher Foundation, Inc.
36 Brookside Boulevard
West Hartford, CT 06107
(203) 523-7247

Description: Grants to residents and organizations of the greater Hartford area, for health services, education, senior citizens, the disadvantaged, employment, and housing.
$ Given: $590,315 for 111 grants; average range $1,000–$50,000
Application Information: Write letter; formal application required.
Deadlines: January 15, April 15, September 15
Contact: Martha Newman, Executive Director

DELAWARE

Stephen and Mary Birch Foundation, Inc.
3650 Silverside Road, #1048
Wilmington, DE 19809

Description: Grants to residents and organizations of Delaware, for the blind, health services, youth services, cultural programs, social services, and civic services.
$ Given: $1.7 million for 35 grants; average range: $1,500–$100,000
Application Information: Write letter; formal application not required.
Deadline: None
Contact: Elfriede Looze

Crystal Trust
1088 du Pont Building
Wilmington, DE 19898
(302) 774-8421

Description: Grants to organizations in Delaware, especially Wilmington, to support social, family, and youth services for the disadvantaged.
$ Given: $2.6 million for 41 grants; average range: $10,000–$100,000
Application Information: Application form not required; write for guidelines (see the important information in the chapter introduction about the need for institutional affiliation).
Deadline: October 1
Contact: Stephen C. Doberstein, Director

DISTRICT OF COLUMBIA

Charles S. Abell Foundation, Inc.
8401 Connecticut Avenue
Chevy Chase, MD 20815
(301) 652-2224

See complete entry under Maryland, this chapter.

The Morris and Gwendolyn Cafritz Foundation
1825 K Street, NW
14th Floor
Washington, DC 20006
(202) 223-3100

Description: Grants for programs that offer direct assistance to the
disadvantaged, youth, homeless, minorities, and women in the
Washington, D.C., area.
$ Given: 8.6 million for 195 grants; average range: $10,000–
$50,000
Application Information: Write for guidelines or send proposal (see
the important information in the chapter introduction about the
need for institutional affiliation).
Deadlines: July 1, November 1, March 1
Contact: Calvin Cafritz, President

Aaron and Cecile Goldman Foundation
1725 K Street, NW
Suite 907
Washington, DC 20006
(202) 833-8714

Description: Grants to residents and organizations of the District of
Columbia and New York, for Jewish welfare, cultural activities,
social services, and education.
$ Given: $121,570 for 101 grants; average range $500–$5,000
Application Information: Write letter; formal application not
required.
Deadline: None
Contact: Aaron Goldman, Trustee

Walter G. Ross Foundation
c/o ASB Capital Management Inc.
1101 Pennsylvania Avenue, NW
Washington, DC 20004

Description: Grants to support family services and child welfare
and development for the disadvantaged in the Washington, D.C.,
area and Florida.
$ Given: $1.0 million for 12 grants; average range: $10,000–
$100,000

Application Information: Application form not required; send letter (see the important information in the chapter introduction about the need for institutional affiliation).
Deadline: September 15
Contact: Ian W. Jones, Secretary

FLORIDA

Broward Community Foundation
2601 East Oakland Park Boulevard
Suite 202
Fort Lauderdale, FL 33306
(305) 563-4483

Description: Grants for education, health and social services, and child welfare for organizations in Broward County.
$ Given: $990,823 for grants; average range: $1,000–$5,000
Application Information: Write for guidelines (see the important information in the chapter introduction about the need for institutional affiliation).
Deadline: September 1
Contact: Jan Crocker, Executive Director

Dade Community Foundation, Inc.
200 South Biscayne Boulevard
Suite 2780
Miami, FL 33131-2343
(305) 371-2711

Description: Grants for health and social programs that "promise to affect a broad segment of residents of Dade County," including the disadvantaged and homeless.
$ Given: $3.1 million for 484 grants
Application Information: Write for guidelines.
Deadline: November 30
Contact: Ruth Shack, President

Jacksonville Community Foundation
112 West Adams Street, #1414
Jacksonville, FL 32202
(904) 356-4483

Description: Grants for general charitable giving, including emergency funds, loans, and seed money, primarily in northeastern Florida.
$ Given: $2.2 million for 594 grants; average range: $1,000–$10,000
Application Information: Write or call for guidelines (see the important information in the chapter introduction about the need for institutional affiliation).
Deadline: None
Contact: L. Andrew Bell III, President

Walter G. Ross Foundation
c/o ASB Capital Management Inc.
1101 Pennsylvania Avenue, NW
Washington, DC 20004

See complete entry under District of Columbia, this chapter.

The Ryder System Charitable Foundation, Inc.
c/o Ryder System, Inc.
3600 NW 82nd Avenue
Miami, FL 33166
(305) 593-3642

Description: Grants given primarily in areas of company operations–southern Florida; Atlanta, Georgia; Detroit, Michigan; St. Louis, Missouri; Cincinnati, Ohio; and Dallas, Texas–to support health and human services for the disadvantaged.
$ Given: $2.0 million for 478 grants; average range: $1,000–$30,000
Application Information: Application form not required; send letter and one proposal (see the important information in the chapter introduction about the need for institutional affiliation).
Deadline: First half of calendar year
Contact: Office of Corporate Programs

Van Pelt Foundation
P.O. Box 88
Demerest, NJ 07627-9998

See complete entry under New Jersey, this chapter.

Hugh and Mary Wilson Foundation, Inc.
7188 Beneva Road
Sarasota, FL 34238
(813) 921-2856

Description: Grants for social and family services, women, and child welfare as well as general charitable giving, in the Manatee–Sarasota area.
$ Given: $249,335 for 23 grants; average range: $1,500–$35,000
Application Information: Write letter of inquiry (see the important information in the chapter introduction about the need for institutional affiliation).
Deadlines: Initial letter or inquiry must be received by June 1; proposal due September 1
Contact: John R. Wood II, Treasurer and Associate Director

GEORGIA

Francis L. Abreu Charitable Trust
c/o Trust Co. Bank
P.O. Box 4655
Atlanta, GA 30302-4655
(404) 588-7356

Description: Grants for social services, especially to women and youth, primarily in Atlanta.
$ Given: $91,544 for 35 grants; average range: $250–$5,000
Application Information: Write for guidelines (see the important information in the chapter introduction about the need for institutional affiliation).
Deadlines: March 31, September 30
Contact: Brenda Rambeau, Vice President, Trust Co. Bank

Colonial Foundation, Inc.
P.O. Box 576
Savannah, GA 31420-0576
(912) 236-1331

Description: Grants for various causes, including social services, primarily in Georgia.
$ Given: $132,155 for grants
Application Information: Write for guidelines (see the important information in the chapter introduction about the need for institutional affiliation).
Deadline: None
Contact: Frances A. Brown, Treasurer

John H. Harland Company Foundation
P.O. Box 105250
Atlanta, GA 30348
(404) 816-5205

Application Address:
c/o Piedmont Foundation
Seven Piedmont Center
Suite 100
Atlanta, GA 30305

Description: Grants for social services, youth, and general-purpose support.
$ Given: $106,238 for grants
Application Information: Write letter (see the important information in the chapter introduction about the need for institutional affiliation).
Deadline: None
Contact: J. William Robinson, President

The Stewart Huston Charitable Trust
76 South First Avenue
Coatesville, PA 19320
(610) 384-2666

See complete entry under Pennsylvania, this chapter.

J. C. Lewis Foundation, Inc.
P.O. Box 60759
Savannah, GA 31420
(912) 925-0234

Description: Grants for social services and general charitable causes, primarily in Savannah.
$ Given: $289,922 for grants
Application Information: Write letter (see the important information in the chapter introduction about the need for institutional affiliation).
Deadline: None
Contact: J. C. Lewis Jr., President

Harriet McDaniel Marshall Trust in Memory of Sanders McDaniel
c/o Trust Co. Bank
P.O. Box 4418, MC 041
Atlanta, GA 30302
(404) 588-8250

Description: Grants to organizations of metropolitan Atlanta for assisting the disadvantaged.
$ Given: $182,299 for grants; average range: $3,000–$5,000
Application Information: Formal application required; send letter (see the important information in the chapter introduction about the need for institutional affiliation).
Deadlines: March 1, June 1, September 1, December 1
Contact: Victor A. Gregory, First Vice President, Trust Co. Bank

The Nordsen Corporation Foundation
28601 Clemens Road
Westlake, OH 44145-1148
(216) 892-1580 or
(216) 988-9411

See complete entry under Ohio, this chapter.

HAWAII

Hawaiian Electric Industries Charitable Foundation
P.O. Box 730
Honolulu, HI 96808-0730
(808) 532-5867

Description: Grants and support services for the disadvantaged, family services, housing, and hunger programs, primarily in Hawaii.
$ Given: $615,328 for 89 grants; average: $1,000
Application Information: Application form not required; send letter with project data.
Deadlines: December 1, June 1
Contact: Scott Shirai, Director, Community Relations

IDAHO

Idaho Community Foundation
c/o Dr. Sally J. Thomas
205 North 10th Street
Suite 625
Boise, ID 83702
(208) 342-3535

Description: Grants for general charitable giving in Idaho.
$ Given: $563,033 for 59 grants
Application Information: Write for guidelines; formal application not required (see the important information in the chapter introduction about the need for institutional affiliation).
Deadlines: February 1, May 1, August 1, November 1
Contact: Bobette F. Youmans, Grants Coordinator

ILLINOIS

Alton Foundation
P.O. Box 1078
Alton, IL 62002
(618) 462-3953

Description: Grants for social services, women, youth, family services, and minorities, among others, in Madison County and adjoining counties.
$ Given: $229,364 for grants
Application Information: Write letter of inquiry; formal application required (see the important information in the chapter introduction about the need for institutional affiliation).
Deadline: None
Contact: R. S. Minsker, Secretary

AMCORE Bank Foundation
501 Seventh Street
P.O. Box 1537
Rockford, IL 60110-0037

Description: Grants to organizations in Rockford, Illinois, for health and social services, education, and youth activities.
$ Given: $157,725 for 42 grants
Application Information: Write for guidelines or send proposal (see the important information in the chapter introduction about the need for institutional affiliation).
Deadline: Not available
Contact: Charles E. Gagnier, President

AON Foundation
123 North Wacker Drive
Chicago, IL 60606
(312) 701-3000

Description: Grants for health and social services, higher education, and community development.
$ Given: $2.5 million for 225 grants; average range: $1,000–$10,000
Application Information: Write for guidelines (see the important information in the chapter introduction about the need for institutional affiliation).
Deadline: None
Contact: Arthur Quern, Vice President

The Bersted Foundation
c/o Continental Bank, N.A.
231 South LaSalle Street
Chicago, IL 60697
(312) 828-1785

Description: Grants for family and health services, including mental health, as well as handicapped and youth organizations serving Kane, DuPage, Dekalb, and McHenry counties.
$ Given: $475,834 for 25 grants
Application Information: Write for guidelines (see the important information in the chapter introduction about the need for institutional affiliation).
Deadline: Not available
Contact: M.C. Ryan

Doris and Victor Day Foundation, Inc.
1705 Second Avenue
Suite 424
Rock Island, IL 61201
(309) 788-2300

Description: Grants for social services, child welfare, housing, and general purposes in the quad-cities area of Rock County, Illinois, and Scott County, Iowa.
$ Given: $657,780 for 84 grants; average range: $1,000–$25,000
Application Information: Write or call for required application form (see the important information in the chapter introduction about the need for institutional affiliation).
Deadline: May 1
Contact: Alan Egly, Executive Director

Geifman Family Foundation, Inc.
2239 29th Street
Rock Island, IL 61201-5025
(309) 788-9531

Description: Grants for Jewish giving and welfare primarily in Illinois, with emphasis on Rock Island.
$ Given: $125,665 for 82 grants; average range: $50–$25,000
Application Information: Write letter.
Deadline: None
Contact: Morris M. Geifman, President

Hochberg Family Foundation

7233 West Dempster Street
Niles, IL 60648

Description: Grants for Jewish welfare services and giving primarily in Chicago.
$ Given: $235,386 for 101 grants
Application Information: Write letter (see the important information in the chapter introduction about the need for institutional affiliation).
Deadline: None
Contact: Larry Hochberg, Director

Katten, Muchin, & Zavis Foundation, Inc.

525 West Monroe Street
Suite 1600
Chicago, IL 60611-3693
(312) 902-5200

Description: Grants for Jewish welfare, primarily in the Chicago area.
$ Given: $375,010 for grants
Application Information: Write letter (see the important information in the chapter introduction about the need for institutional affiliation).
Deadline: None
Contact: Norman Steinberg

Albert and Anne Mansfield Foundation

400 North Michigan Avenue
Suite 409
Chicago, IL 60611
(312) 245-8000

Description: Grants for organizations in Illinois, Minnesota, and Massachusetts that support adult education, social and family services, and the disadvantaged.
$ Given: $106,830 for 16 grants
Application Information: Send letter of inquiry (see the important information in the chapter introduction about the need for institutional affiliation).

Deadline: None
Contact: Peter Van Cleave, Administrator

The Northern Trust Company Charitable Trust

c/o The Northern Trust Co.
Community Affairs Division
50 South LaSalle Street
Chicago, IL 60675
(312) 444-4059

Description: Grants to health and social services, including aid for the disadvantaged, homeless, and women's organizations in Cook County, with an emphasis on Chicago.
$ Given: $1.4 million for 190 grants; average range: $2,000–$5,000
Application Information: Write for guidelines (see the important information in the chapter introduction about the need for institutional affiliation).
Deadlines: February 1, October 1
Contact: Marjorie W. Lundy, Vice President, The Northern Trust Company

Polk Bros. Fifty-Five Plus

c/o Marian Egel
420 North Wabash Avenue
Suite 203
Chicago, IL 60611-3504

Description: Grants to organizations in Chicago serving the needs of residents over age 55.
$ Given: $212,060 for 637 grants
Application Information: Write for guidelines (see the important information in the chapter introduction about the need for institutional affiliation).
Deadline: Not available
Contact: Not available

The Rockford Community Trust

321 West State Street
13th Floor
Rockford, IL 61101
(815) 962-2110

Description: Grants for youth programs and health and social
services in the Rockford, Illinois, metropolitan area, including
Winnebago, Boone, Ogle, and Stephenson counties.
$ Given: $454,465 for 143 grants
Application Information: Write for required application form (see
the important information in the chapter introduction about the
need for institutional affiliation).
Deadlines: March 31, September 30
Contact: Gloria Lundin, Executive Director

Sara Lee Foundation
Three First National Plaza
Chicago, IL 60602-4260
(312) 558-8448

Description: Grants for social service organizations assisting
women, the homeless, and the disadvantaged of Chicago.
$ Given: $4.0 million for 343 grants; average range: $1,000–$5,000
Application Information: Write or call for application form and
guidelines (see the important information in the chapter introduction about the need for institutional affiliation).
Deadlines: First working day of March, September, December
Contact: Robin S. Tryloff, Executive Director

INDIANA

The Indianapolis Foundation
615 North Alabama Street
Room 119
Indianapolis, IN 46204
(317) 634-7497
Fax: (317) 684-0943

Description: Grants for family, social, and health services in Indianapolis and Marion counties.
$ Given: $4.2 million for 111 grants; average range: $10,000–
$50,000
Application Information: Write or call for required application form
(see the important information in the chapter introduction about
the need for institutional affiliation).

Deadlines: End of January, March, May, July, September
Contact: Kenneth L. Gladish, Executive Director

Frank L. & Laura L. Smock Foundation
c/o Norwest Bank Indiana, N.A.
P.O. Box 960
Fort Wayne, IN 46801-6632
(219) 461-6451

Description: Grants for the health and welfare of ailing, needy, crippled, blind, or elderly men and women.
$ Given: $367,537 for 26 grants
Application Information: Write letter; application form required.
Deadline: None
Contact: Alice Kopfer, Vice President, Norwest Bank Indiana, N.A.

IOWA

William C. Brown Company Charitable Foundation
2460 Kerper Boulevard
Dubuque, IA 52001-2293
(319) 588-1451

Description: Grants for health and social services in the Dubuque community.
$ Given: $131,296 for 74 grants
Application Information: Write letter (see the important information in the chapter introduction about the need for institutional affiliation).
Deadline: None
Contact: Marc Bigelow, Vice President, Human Resources

Doris and Victor Day Foundation, Inc.
1705 Second Avenue
Suite 424
Rock Island, IL 61201
(309) 788-2300

See complete entry under Illinois, this chapter.

Engman Foundation
P.O. Box 864
Des Moines, IA 50304

Description: Grants for welfare, social services, and Jewish organizations primarily in Iowa.
$ Given: $203,595 for 81 grants; average range: $1,000–$34,000
Application Information: Write letter (see the important information in the chapter introduction about the need for institutional affiliation).
Deadline: None
Contact: Lawrence B. Engman, Director

The John K. and Luise V. Hanson Foundation
P.O. Box 450
Forest City, IA 50436

Description: Grants for matching funds for community and general charitable causes serving individuals with financial needs primarily in northcentral Iowa.
$ Given: $240,395 for 39 grants; average range: $1,000–$2,000
Application Information: Write for guidelines (see the important information in the chapter introduction about the need for institutional affiliation).
Deadline: None
Contact: Linda Johnson

Peter H. and E. Lucille Gaass Kuyper Foundation
c/o Pella Corp.
Pella, IA 50219
(515) 628-1000

Description: Grants for general charitable causes serving individuals with financial needs in the Pella area.
$ Given: $658,089 for grants; average range: $5,000–$10,000
Application Information: Write for guidelines.
Deadline: None
Contact: William J. Anderson, Administrator

The Greater Cedar Rapids Foundation
101 Second Street, SE
Suite 306
Cedar Rapids, IA 52401
(319) 366-2862

Description: Grants for social services and community development in Linn County and surrounding area and in greater Cedar Rapids.
$ Given: $384,436 for grants; average range: $1,500–$5,000
Application Information: Write letter; encouraged to call (see the important information in the chapter introduction about the need for institutional affiliation).
Deadlines: May 21, October 20
Contact: Malcolm L. Peel, Executive Director

Mid-Iowa Health Foundation
550 39th Street
Suite 104
Des Moines, IA 50312
(515) 277-6411

Description: Grants for the disadvantaged, elderly, homeless, and general purposes in Polk County and seven surrounding counties.
$ Given: $517,050 for 41 grants
Application Information: Write or call; application required.
Deadlines: February 1, May 1, August 1, November 1
Contact: Kathryn Bradley

John Ruan Foundation Trust
P.O. Box 855
Des Moines, IA 50304
(515) 245-2552

Description: Grants in several areas, including child welfare, health services, and general charitable causes, primarily in Des Moines.
$ Given: $72,741 for 106 grants; average range: $100–$10,000
Application Information: Write letter.
Deadline: None
Contact: John Ruan, Trustee

W. A. Sheaffer Memorial Foundation, Inc.
817 Avenue G
Fort Madison, IA 52627-2912

Description: Grants for social services and community organizations primarily in Iowa.
$ Given: $64,500 for 7 grants; average range: $500–$28,000
Application Information: Write for guidelines (see the important information in the chapter introduction about the need for institutional affiliation).
Deadline: Not available
Contact: Walter A. Sheaffer, President

KANSAS

DeVore Foundation, Inc.
P.O. Box 118
Wichita, KS 67201

Application Address:
1199 East Central
Wichita, KS 67201
(316) 267-3211

Description: Grants for social services and community foundations primarily in Wichita.
$ Given: $124,133 for 77 grants
Application Information: Send letter or proposal (see the important information in the chapter introduction about the need for institutional affiliation).
Deadline: None
Contact: Richard A. DeVore, President

Ewing Marion Kauffman Foundation
4900 Oak Street
Kansas City, MO 64112-2776
(816) 932-1000
Fax: (816) 932-1100

See complete entry under Missouri, this chapter.

Ethel and Raymond F. Rice Foundation

700 Massachusetts Street
Lawrence, KS 66044
(913) 843-0420

Description: Grants for youth and social service agencies in Douglas County and Lawrence, Kansas, area.
$ Given: $333,225 for 93 grants; average $1,000–$20,000
Application Information: Write proposal (see the important information in the chapter introduction about the need for institutional affiliation).
Deadline: November 15
Contact: Robert B. Oyler, President, or George M. Clem, Treasurer

Topeka Community Foundation

5100 SW 10th Street
P.O. Box 4525
Topeka, KS 66604
(913) 272-4804

Description: Grants for social, health, and family services in Topeka and Shawnee counties.
$ Given: $242,862 for grants; average range: $500–$1,500
Application Information: Write for application form.
Deadline: February 15
Contact: Karen Welch, Executive Director

KENTUCKY

The Cralle Foundation

620 West Main Street
Suite 320
Louisville, KY 40202
(502) 581-1148

Description: Grants for general purpose support, including homeless, youth, and health services, primarily in Kentucky, with emphasis on Louisville.
$ Given: $388,000 for 22 grants; average range: $5,000–$25,000

Application Information: Write for application.
Deadline: None
Contact: James T. Crain Jr., Executive Director

Foundation for the Tri-State Community
P.O. Box 2096
Ashland, KY 41105
(606) 324-3888
Fax: (606) 324-5961

Description: Grants for general charitable purposes to residents of
Ashland, Kentucky; Ironton, Ohio; and Huntington, West Virginia.
$ Given: $175,714 for grants
Application Information: Write letter, call, or submit proposal.
Deadline: September 15 for grants from unrestricted funds
Contact: Theodore N. Burke Jr., CEO and President

Annie Gardner Foundation
South Sixth and College
Mayfield, KY 42066
(502) 247-5803

Description: Grants primarily to the disadvantaged in Graves
County, for rent, medical care, clothing, and other necessities.
$ Given: $407,426 for grants
Application Information: Write or call for application.
Deadline: July 1
Contact: Nancy H. Sparks, Education Director

Rudd Foundation, Inc.
3 River Front Plaza
Suite 320
Louisville, KY 40202
(502) 561-1609

Description: Grants for general charitable support primarily for
Jewish welfare funds.
$ Given: $241,510 for 6 grants
Application Information: Write for guidelines (see the important
information in the chapter introduction about the need for institutional affiliation).

Deadline: None
Contact: Mason C. Rudd, President

LOUISIANA

The Greater New Orleans Foundation
2515 Canal Street
Suite 401
New Orleans, LA 70119
(504) 822-4906

Description: Grants to residents and organizations in southeastern
Louisiana, including the greater New Orleans area, for health and
social service programs.
$ Given: $1.6 million for 236 grants; average range: $1,500–
$16,500
Application Information: Write for application or send proposal
(see the important information in the chapter introduction about
the need for institutional affiliation).
Deadline: Not available
Contact: Gregory Ben Johnson, Executive Director

Powers Foundation, Inc.
c/o Heard, McElroy and Vestal
P.O. Box 1607
Shreveport, LA 71165
(318) 221-0151

Description: Grants for social services, education, and music in
Shreveport and Bossier counties.
$ Given: $149,646 for 15 grants
Application Information: Send letter of inquiry or proposal (see the
important information in the chapter introduction about the need
for institutional affiliation).
Deadline: None
Contact: C. Cody White Jr., President

MAINE

The Maine Community Foundation, Inc.
210 Maine Street
P.O. Box 148
Ellsworth, ME 04605

Description: Grants to organizations in Maine for projects affecting the disadvantaged.
$ Given: $602,875 for 349 grants; average range: $500–$5,000
Application Information: Application form required; send letter and one copy of proposal (see the important information in the chapter introduction about the need for institutional affiliation).
Deadlines: January 15, April 1, July 15, October 1
Contact: Jay Davis, Program Director

MARYLAND

Charles S. Abell Foundation, Inc.
8401 Connecticut Avenue
Chevy Chase, MD 20815
(301) 652-2224

Description: Grants for church-related food and shelter centers, job training, abused women and children, the mentally handicapped, and especially homeless or disadvantaged individuals primarily in Washington, D.C., and five nearby Maryland counties.
$ Given: $408,950 for 26 grants; average range: $5,000–$60,000
Application Information: Write for guidelines (see the important information in the chapter introduction about the need for institutional affiliation).
Deadline: None
Contact: W. Shepherdson Abell, Secretary-Treasurer

Lockhart Vaughan Foundation, Inc.
250 West Pratt Street
13th Floor
Baltimore, MD 21201

Description: Grants to aid the disadvantaged in metropolitan
Baltimore, with special emphasis on children and family services.
$ Given: $471,390 for 45 grants; average range: $5,000–$20,000
Application Information: Send letter requesting required application
form (see the important information in the chapter introduction
about the need for institutional affiliation).
Deadlines: March 20, September 20
Contact: Not available

MASSACHUSETTS

Association for the Relief of Aged Women of New Bedford
27 South Sixth Street
New Bedford, MA 02740

Description: Grants to elderly female residents of New Bedford
who can demonstrate financial need.
$ Given: $296,182 for 23 grants; average range: $300–$40,000
Application Information: Write for guidelines.
Deadline: Not available
Contact: Mrs. Thorton Klaren, President

The Boston Foundation, Inc.
One Boston Place
24th Floor
Boston, MA 02108-4402
(617) 723-7415

Description: Grants to organizations serving the disadvantaged,
welfare, homeless, or women in the Boston metropolitan area.
$ Given: $18.6 million for grants; average range: $20,000–$40,000
Application Information: Send letter and one copy of proposal (see
the important information in the chapter introduction about the
need for institutional affiliation).
Deadlines: March, June, September, December
Contact: Anna Faith Jones, President

Greater Worcester Community Foundation, Inc.
44 Front Street
Suite 530
Worcester, MA 01608-1782
(508) 755-0980

Description: Grants to residents of greater Worcester or employees of Rotman's Furniture, "for the health, educational, social welfare, cultural, and civic needs of the residents of Greater Worcester," including grants for employment, homeless, and housing.
$ Given: $1.6 million for 354 grants; average range: $100–$100,000
Application Information: Write or call for application form.
Deadlines: January 1, April 1, September 1
Contact: Ann T. Lisi, Executive Director

The Hoche-Scofield Foundation
c/o Shawmut Bank, N.A.
446 Main Street
Worcester, MA 01608
(508) 793-4205

Description: Grants to organizations and social services serving women, youth, and the disadvantaged in the city and county of Worcester.
$ Given: $514,915 for 69 grants; average range: $1,000–$10,000
Application Information: Write or call for application form (see the important information in the chapter introduction about the need for institutional affiliation).
Deadlines: February 15, May 15, August 15, November 15
Contact: Stephen G. Fritch, Vice President, Shawmut Bank, N.A.

Albert and Anne Mansfield Foundation
400 North Michigan Avenue
Suite 409
Chicago, IL 60611
(312) 245-8000

See complete entry under Illinois, this chapter.

Amelia Peabody Charitable Fund
201 Devonshire Street
Boston, MA 02110-1401
(617) 451-6178

Description: Grants for health and social services to organizations serving families, youth, the aged, handicapped, and homeless of Massachusetts.
$ Given: $4.7 million for 107 grants; average range: $5,000–$25,000
Application Information: Write for guidelines (see the important information in the chapter introduction about the need for institutional affiliation).
Deadlines: April 1, July 1, October 1
Contact: Jo Anne Borek, Executive Director

MICHIGAN

The Barstow Foundation
c/o Chemical Bank
333 East Main Street
Midland, MI 48640
(517) 631-9200

Description: Grants to organizations in Michigan, primarily for the disadvantaged of the community.
$ Given: $181,500 for 12 grants; average range: $1,000–$50,000
Application Information: Write for guidelines or submit proposal (see the important information in the chapter introduction about the need for institutional affiliation).
Deadline: October 31
Contact: Bruce M. Groom, Senior Vice President, Chemical Bank

McGregor Fund
333 West Fort Street
Suite 2090
Detroit, MI 48226-3115
(313) 963-3495
Fax: (313) 963-3512

Description: Grants for health, education, and youth programs, with an emphasis on the homeless and hungry, for organizations primarily in Detroit.
$ Given: $5.0 million for 99 grants; average range: $5,000–$50,000
Application Information: Write for guidelines (see the important information in the chapter introduction about the need for institutional affiliation).
Deadline: None
Contact: Sylvia L. McNarney, Director of Programs

Steelcase Foundation
Location CH.5C
P.O. Box 1967
Grand Rapids, MI 49507-1967
(616) 246-4695

Description: Grants to organizations serving the disadvantaged, disabled, or elderly in areas of company operations, including Grand Rapids, Michigan; Orange County, California; Ashville, North Carolina; Athens, Alabama; and Toronto, Canada.
$ Given: $3.4 million for 93 grants; average range: $2,000–$25,000
Application Information: Write letter; application form required (see the important information in the chapter introduction about the need for institutional affiliation).
Deadline: None
Contact: Kate Pew Wolters, Executive Director

MINNESOTA

Hugh J. Anderson Foundation
287 Central Avenue
Bayport, MN 55003
(612) 439-1557
Fax: (612) 439-9480

Description: Grants for health and family services for the youth, disadvantaged, and homeless of Washington County, Minnesota, and Pierce, Polk, and St. Croix counties, Wisconsin.
$ Given: $1.1 million for 101 grants

Application Information: Write for guidelines (see the important information in the chapter introduction about the need for institutional affiliation).
Deadlines: March 15, June 15, September 15, November 15
Contact: Peggie Scott, Grants Consultant

The Emma B. Howe Foundation
A200 Foshay Tower
821 Marquette Avenue
Minneapolis, MN 55402
(612) 672-3831

Description: Grants to Minnesota organizations that serve "the poor, the disadvantaged, children, handicapped, and victims of discrimination."
$ Given: $1.5 million for 70 grants
Application Information: Send letter of inquiry (see the important information in the chapter introduction about the need for institutional affiliation).
Deadlines: June 1, December 1
Contact: Brian Malloy, Program Officer

Albert and Anne Mansfield Foundation
400 North Michigan Avenue
Suite 409
Chicago, IL 60611
(312) 245-8000

See complete entry under Ilinois, this chapter.

MISSOURI

Hallmark Corporate Foundation
P.O. Box 419580
Mail Drop 323
Kansas City, MO 64141-6580
(816) 274-8515

Description: Grants for employment, delinquent youth, social services, handicapped, housing, and hunger; limited to Kansas City and cities in which Hallmark corporate facilities and factories are located.
$ Given: $6.2 million for 1,000 grants; average range: $5,000–$50,000
Application Information: Send letter describing needs, purpose, and general activities of organization (see the important information in the chapter introduction about the need for institutional affiliation).
Deadline: None
Contact: Jeanne Bates, Vice President

Ewing Marion Kauffman Foundation
4900 Oak Street
Kansas City, MO 64112-2776
(816) 932-1000
Fax: (816) 932-1100

Description: Grants for the disadvantaged, at-risk youth, families in need, and general health services in Kansas and Missouri.
$ Given: $870,415 for 50 grants
Application Information: Application form not required; send brief concept paper (see the important information in the chapter introduction about the need for institutional affiliation).
Deadline: None
Contact: Lynn J. Spencer, Director of Communications

MONTANA

Sample Foundation, Inc.
14 North 24th Street
P.O. Box 279
Billings, MT 59103
(404) 256-5667

Description: Grants for social services for the disadvantaged in Montana and Collier County, Florida.
$ Given: $211,500 for 47 grants; average range: $500–$20,000

Application Information: Send letter of interest (see the important information in the chapter introduction about the need for institutional affiliation).
Deadline: Not available
Contact: Miriam T. Sample, Vice President

NEBRASKA

Woods Charitable Fund, Inc.
P.O. Box 81309
Lincoln, NE 68501
(402) 474-0707

Description: Grants to organizations serving children and families, for housing, education, and community development programs in Lincoln.
$ Given: $2.6 million for 137 grants; average range: $10,000–$20,000
Application Information: Write or call for guidelines (see the important information in the chapter introduction about the need for institutional affiliation).
Deadlines: April 15, July 15, October 15
Contact: Pam Baker, Executive Director

NEW HAMPSHIRE

Lou & Lutza Smith Charitable Foundation
c/o New Hampshire Charitable Foundation
37 Pleasant Street
P.O. Box 1335
Concord, NH 03302-1335
(603) 225-6641

Description: Grants for education, health, social services, and child welfare for residents and organizations of New Hampshire.
$ Given: $504,330 for 32 grants; average range: $5,000–$10,000

Application Information: Application form not required; write or call for guidelines (see the important information in the chapter introduction about the need for institutional affiliation).
Deadlines: February 1, May 1, August 1, November 1
Contact: Deborah Cowan, Program Director

NEW JERSEY

Mary Owen Borden Memorial Foundation
160 Hodge Road
Princeton, NJ 08540
(609) 924-3637

Description: Grants limited primarily to Monmouth and Mercer counties for programs focusing on the special needs of youth, including family planning, education, child care, and housing services, and for assistance to disadvantaged families.
$ Given: $436,635 for 56 grants; average: $7,500
Application Information: Application form not required; write for guidelines (see the important information in the chapter introduction about the need for institutional affiliation).
Deadlines: January 1, April 1, September 1
Contact: John C. Borden Jr., Executive Director

Innovating Worthy Projects Foundation
426 Shore Road
Suite E
Somers Point, NJ 08244
(609) 926-1111

Description: Grants for the education, service, or care of handicapped children, the aged, and the disadvantaged.
$ Given: $201,000 for 29 grants; average range: $500–$10,000
Application Information: Call for application guidelines (see the important information in the chapter introduction about the need for institutional affiliation).
Deadline: None

Contact: Dr. Irving W. Packer, Chair

L.P. Schenck Fund

c/o Midlantic National Bank, Trust Department
41 Oak Street
Ridgewood, NJ 07450
(201) 652-8499

Description: Grants to organizations in New Jersey, for youth,
social service, and mental health programs.
$ Given: $436,176 for 29 grants
Application Information: Write for guidelines or send proposal (see
the important information in the chapter introduction about the
need for institutional affiliation).
Deadline: August 1
Contact: Patricia H. Clarke, Vice President, Midlantic National
Bank

Van Pelt Foundation

P.O. Box 88
Demerest, NJ 07627-9998

Description: Grants to smaller organizations in New York State,
New Jersey, and Florida that have been hurt by federal and private
cutbacks; for support for child welfare, family services, and the
homeless.
$ Given: $198,300 for 67 grants
Application Information: Write and/or send proposal.
Deadlines: March 15, September 15
Contact: Lawrence Bass, President

NEW YORK

The Abelard Foundation, Inc.

2530 San Pablo Avenue
Berkeley, CA 94702
(415) 644-1904

East Coast Application Address:
c/o Susan Collins
P.O. Box 148
Lincoln, MA 01773

See complete entry under California, this chapter.

The Achelis Foundation
c/o Morris & McVeigh
767 Third Avenue
New York, NY 10017
(212) 418-0588

Description: Grants to organizations in New York City that serve children, the elderly, handicapped, and homeless.
$ Given: $914,852 for 63 grants; average range: $10,000–$25,000
Application Information: Send letter and proposal, or write for guidelines (see the important information in the chapter introduction about the need for institutional affiliation).
Deadline: None
Contact: Joe Dolan, Secretary and Executive Director

Altman Foundation
220 East 42nd Street
Suite 411
New York, NY 10017
(212) 682-0970

Description: Grants for social welfare programs providing long-term solutions to the needs of the disadvantaged in New York, with emphasis on the boroughs of New York City.
$ Given: $5.7 million for 168 grants; average range: $10,000–$100,000
Application Information: Application form not required; write for guidelines (see the important information in the chapter introduction about the need for institutional affiliation).
Deadline: None
Contact: John S. Burke, President

Louis Calder Foundation

230 Park Avenue
Room 1525
New York, NY 10169
(212) 687-1680

Description: Grants for programs designed to enhance the potential
and increase the self-sufficiency of disadvantaged children, youth,
and their families in New York City.
$ Given: $5.2 million for 154 grants; average range: $15,000–
$50,000
Application Information: Application form not required; send a
one- to three-page letter (see the important information in the
chapter introduction about the need for institutional affiliation).
Deadline: March 31
Contact: Barbara Sommer, Grants Program Manager

Aaron and Cecile Goldman Foundation

1725 K Street, NW
Suite 907
Washington, DC 20006
(202) 833-8714

See complete entry under District of Columbia, this chapter.

Stella and Charles Guttman Foundation, Inc.

445 Park Avenue
19th Floor
New York, NY 10022
(212) 371-7082

Description: Grants to organizations providing social and educational services for the disadvantaged in the New York City metropolitan area.
$ Given: $679,800 for 73 grants; average range: $5,000–$20,000
Application Information: Application form not required; write for
guidelines (see the important information in the chapter introduction about the need for institutional affiliation).
Deadline: None
Contact: Elizabeth Olofson, Executive Director

Daisy Marquis Jones Foundation
620 Granite Building
130 East Main Street
Rochester, NY 14604-1620
(716) 263-3331

Description: Grants to support improvement in the quality of
health care for residents of Monroe and Yates counties, with special
emphasis on the disadvantaged.
$ Given: $1.3 million for 105 grants; average range: $5,000–
$10,000
Application Information: Application form required; write for
guidelines (see the important information in the chapter introduction about the need for institutional affiliation).
Deadline: None
Contact: Pearl W. Rubin, President

MCA Foundation, Ltd.
100 Universal City Plaza
Universal City, CA 91608
(818) 777-1208

See complete entry under California, this chapter.

The Pinkerton Foundation
725 Park Avenue
New York, NY 10021-5008
(212) 772-6110
Fax: (212) 734-4982

Description: Grants for economically disadvantaged children, youth,
and families at risk in New York City.
$ Given: $1.9 million for 65 grants; average range: $20,000–
$50,000
Application Information: Application form not required; write for
guidelines (see the important information in the chapter introduction about the need for institutional affiliation).
Deadlines: February 1, September 1
Contact: Joan Colello, Executive Director

Rauch Foundation
401 Franklin Avenue
Suite 103
Garden City, NY 11530-5928
(516) 873-9808
Fax: (516) 873-0708

Description: Grants "to benefit young children and their families in Nassau County, New York, including prenatal care, family support, and early childhood education."
$ Given: $678,400 for 64 grants
Application Information: Send concept paper of one or two pages (see the important information in the chapter introduction about the need for institutional affiliation).
Deadline: None
Contact: Elisabeth Marx, Executive Director

Van Pelt Foundation
P.O. Box 88
Demerest, NJ 07627-9998

See complete entry under New Jersey, this chapter.

NORTH CAROLINA

Kate B. Reynolds Charitable Trust
128 Renolda Village
Winston-Salem, NC 27106-5123
(910) 723-1456

Description: Grants for health and social services in rural areas of North Carolina serving individuals with financial needs. Some grants limited to the city of Winston-Salem and Forsyth County, but healthcare giving is statewide.
$ Given: $14.2 million for 220 grants; average range $20,000–$200,000
Application Information: Call or write for guidelines and application form (see the important information in the chapter introduction about the need for institutional affiliation).

Deadlines: January 1, May 1, August 1 for general grants; March 15, September 15 for health services grants
Contact: Ray Cope, Deputy Executive Director; or W. Vance Frye, Director Health Care Division

NORTH DAKOTA

North Dakota Community Foundation
P.O. Box 387
Bismarck, ND 58502-0387
(701) 222-8349

Description: Grants largely for aid to the elderly and disadvantaged of North Dakota, especially in area of health services.
$ Given: $327,182 for 432 grants; average: $1,000
Application Information: Application form required; write for guidelines.
Deadline: August 31
Contact: Richard H. Timmins, President

OHIO

Borden Foundation, Inc.
180 East Broad Street
34th Floor
Columbus, OH 43215-3799
(614) 225-4340

Description: Grants for programs benefiting disadvantaged children and community services in areas of company operation.
$ Given: $2.3 million for 210 grants; average range: $2,000–$25,000
Application Information: Application form not required; write for guidelines (see the important information in the chapter introduction about the need for institutional affiliation).
Deadlines: March 1, July 1, October 1
Contact: Judy Barker, President

Foundation for the Tri-State Community
P.O. Box 2096
Ashland, KY 41105
(606) 324-3888
Fax: (606) 324-5961

See complete entry under Kentucky, this chapter.

The Nordsen Corporation Foundation
28601 Clemens Road
Westlake, OH 44145-1148
(216) 892-1580 or
(216) 988-9411

Description: Grants for community programs, projects, human services, community development, disadvantaged, health services, homeless, hunger, and social services in the areas of northern Ohio and Atlanta, Georgia.
$ Given: $1.0 million for 87 grants; average range $550–$25,000
Application Information: Application form not required; write letter or proposal (see the important information in the chapter introduction about the need for institutional affiliation).
Deadline: None
Contact: Constance T. Hagg, Executive Director

Albert G. & Olive H. Schlink Foundation
401 Citizens National Bank Building
Norwalk, OH 44857

Description: Grants to organizations providing aid to the disadvantaged and the aged in Ohio.
$ Given: $393,891 for 20 grants; average range: $2,500–$65,000
Application Information: Application form not required; write for guidelines (see the important information in the chapter introduction about the need for institutional affiliation).
Deadline: None
Contact: Robert A. Wiedemann, President

OKLAHOMA

Harris Foundation, Inc.
6403 NW Grand Boulevard
Suite 211
Oklahoma City, OK 73116
(405) 848-3371

Description: Grants for social and health services to organizations in Oklahoma, with emphasis on Oklahoma City, Lawton, and Enid.
$ Given: $333,416 for 50 grants; average range $5,000–$25,000
Application Information: Write for guidelines (see the important information in the chapter introduction about the need for institutional affiliation).
Deadlines: February 1, May 1, September 1
Contact: Ann B. Patterson, Vice President

OREGON

The Elizabeth Church Clarke Testamentary Trust/Fund Foundation
c/o U.S. National Bank of Oregon
P.O. Box 3168
Portland, OR 97208

Application Address:
709 SW 15th Avenue
Portland, OR 97205
(503) 228-9405

Description: Grants for medical expenses to residents of Oregon.
$ Given: $66,035 for grants
Application Information: Write for guidelines.
Deadline: None
Contact: Walter C. Peters

PENNSYLVANIA

Dolfinger-McMahon Foundation
c/o Duane, Morris & Heckscher
One Liberty Place
Philadelphia, PA 19103-7396
(215) 979-1768

Description: Grants for community development, health services, education, and the disadvantaged in the Philadelphia area.
$ Given: $471,000 for 111 grants; average range: $1,000–$15,000
Application Information: Write for guidelines; application form not required (see the important information in the chapter introduction about the need for institutional affiliation).
Deadlines: April 1, October 1
Contact: Marlene Valcich, Executive Secretary

The Stewart Huston Charitable Trust
76 South First Avenue
Coatesville, PA 19320
(610) 384-2666

Description: Grants for family services and the disadvantaged in the city of Coatesville and Chester County and in the Savannah, Georgia, area.
$ Given: $755,725 for 92 grants
Application Information: Call for application form (see the important information in the chapter introduction about the need for institutional affiliation).
Deadline: Not available
Contact: Louis J. Beccaria, Ph.D., Executive Director

RHODE ISLAND

Citizens Charitable Foundation
c/o Citizens Bank
One Citizens Plaza
Providence, RI 02903
(401) 456-7285
Fax: (401) 456-7366

Description: Grants for community development, disadvantaged, or other social services; limited to agencies in Rhode Island.
$ Given: $430,650 for 59 grants; average: $2,500
Application Information: Write for guidelines; application form not required (see the important information in the chapter introduction about the need for institutional affiliation).
Deadline: None, but preferably in June
Contact: D. Faye Sanders, Chair

The Rhode Island Foundation/The Rhode Island Community Foundation
70 Elm Street
Providence, RI 02903
(401) 274-4564

Description: Grants for improving the living conditions of residents of Rhode Island, including the elderly, and to health and social service agencies.
$ Given: Not available
Application Information: Write for guidelines; application form not required.
Deadline: None
Contact: Robert D. Rosendale, Vice President, Finance & Administration

TENNESSEE

H. W. Durham Foundation
5050 Poplar Avenue
Suite 1522
Memphis, TN 38157
(901) 683-3583

Description: Grants for programs for the elderly, disadvantaged, and health and social services, limited to organizations in Memphis and the mid-South region of the United States.
$ Given: $283,652 for 27 grants; average range: $1,500–$6,500

Application Information: Write for guidelines (see the important information in the chapter introduction about the need for institutional affiliation).
Deadlines: January 1, April 1, August 1
Contact: Jenks McCrory, Program Director

TEXAS

M. D. Anderson Foundation
P.O. Box 2558
Houston, TX 77252-8037
(713) 658-2316

Description: Grants to organizations in Texas for health and housing for the disadvantaged, including the aged.
$ Given: $2.4 million for 77 grants; average range: $5,000–$50,000
Application Information: Write for guidelines (see the important information in the chapter introduction about the need for institutional affiliation).
Deadline: None
Contact: John W. Lowrie, Secretary-Treasurer

The Effie and Wofford Cain Foundation
4131 Spicewood Springs Road
Suite A-1
Austin, TX 78759
(512) 346-7490

Description: Grants to organizations in Texas for health services, the handicapped, the disadvantaged, and community services.
$ Given: $2.1 million for 80 grants; average range: $2,000–$500,000
Application Information: Write or call for required application form (see the important information in the chapter introduction about the need for institutional affiliation).
Deadline: None
Contact: Harvey L. Walker, Executive Director

Communities Foundation of Texas, Inc.
4605 Live Oak Street
Dallas, TX 75204
(214) 826-5231

Description: Grants for education, health, and social services to organizations in Dallas, with an emphasis on youth.
$ Given: $25.1 million for grants
Application Information: Send letter requesting guidelines (see the important information in the chapter introduction about the need for institutional affiliation).
Deadlines: February 1, July 1, October 1
Contact: Jeverly R. Cook, Grants Administrator

VERMONT

The Ben and Jerry's Foundation
P.O. Box 299
Waterbury, VT 05676
(802) 244-7105

Description: Grants for programs serving disadvantaged groups, homelessness, and social change.
$ Given: $633,000 for 95 grants; average: $1,000–$5,000
Application Information: Write or call for guidelines and application form; three-page proposal required (see the important information in the chapter introduction about the need for institutional affiliation).
Deadlines: January 1, April 1, July 1, October 1
Contact: Rebecca Golden, Foundation Administrator

The Windham Foundation, Inc.
P.O. Box 70
Grafton, VT 05146
(802) 843-2211

Description: Grants for programs for the disadvantaged, youth, and handicapped, as well as for social services, in Vermont, especially Windham County.

$ Given: $382,331 for grants; average range: $100–$5,000
Application Information: Write for guidelines; formal application required.
Deadlines: January, April, June, September
Contact: Stephen A. Morse, President and CEO

VIRGINIA

Mustard Seed Foundation, Inc.
1001 North 19th Street
Suite 1900
Arlington, VA 22209
(703) 524-5620

Description: Grants and loans "to Christians to relieve human suffering," as well as for general charitable giving.
$ Given: $1.1 million for grants
Application Information: Write for guidelines; formal application and proposal required; a board member must recommend applicant.
Deadline: None
Contact: Craig E. Nauta, Executive Vice President

The Edgar A. Thurman Charitable Foundation for Children
c/o Crestar Bank, N.A.
P.O. Box 13888
Roanoke, VA 24038

Description: Grants for children and the disadvantaged with financial needs, youth agencies, and social services in Virginia, especially the Roanoke area.
$ Given: $267,700 for 43 grants; average range: $2,000–$10,000
Application Information: Write for guidelines; formal application required (see the important information in the chapter introduction about the need for institutional affiliation).
Deadline: July 15
Contact: Not available

WASHINGTON

Comstock Foundation
819 Washington Trust Financial Center
West 717 Sprague Avenue
Spokane, WA 99204
(509) 747-1527

Description: Grants to social service agencies, the disadvantaged, handicapped, and health organizations in Washington State, primarily the Spokane and Inland Empire areas.
$ Given: $887,159 for 50 grants; average range: $1,000–$35,000
Application Information: Write for guidelines; formal application and proposal required (see the important information in the chapter introduction about the need for institutional affiliation).
Deadline: None
Contact: Horton Herman, Trustee

Glaser Foundation, Inc.
P.O. Box 6548
Bellevue, WA 98008-0548

Description: Grants to health and social service agencies serving individuals with financial needs and children in Kings County and vicinity.
$ Given: $315,077 for 69 grants; average range: $3,000–$5,000
Application Information: Write for guidelines; application form and two copies of proposal required (see the important information in the chapter introduction about the need for institutional affiliation).
Deadline: None
Contact: Joann Van Sickle

WEST VIRGINIA

Clay Foundation, Inc.
1426 Kanawha Boulevard East
Charleston, WV 25301
(304) 344-8656

Description: Grants to programs serving the elderly, disadvantaged youth, and their families in West Virginia, especially the Kanawha Valley area.
$ Given: $1.2 million for 37 grants; average range: $10,000–$50,000
Application Information: Write letter in triplicate, or call for guidelines (see the important information in the chapter introduction about the need for institutional affiliation).
Deadline: None
Contact: Charles M. Avampato, President

Foundation for the Tri-State Community
P.O. Box 2096
Ashland, KY 41105
(606) 324-3888
Fax: (606) 324-5961

See complete entry under Kentucky, this chapter.

WISCONSIN

Hugh J. Anderson Foundation
287 Central Avenue
Bayport, MN 55003
(612) 439-1557
Fax: (612) 439-9480

See complete entry under Minnesota, this chapter.

Lindsay Foundation, Inc.
c/o The Milwaukee Foundation
1020 North Broadway
Milwaukee, WI 53202
(414) 272-5805

Description: Grants to organizations in Wisconsin for vocational education, social and health services, and services for the handicapped, disadvantaged, and elderly.
$ Given: $141,000 for grants

Application Information: Write or call for guidelines (see the important information in the chapter introduction about the need for institutional affiliation).
Deadline: August
Contact: Fred Gutierrez, Program Officer

WYOMING

Tom and Helen Tonkin Foundation
c/o Norwest Bank Wyoming, Casper, N.A.
P.O. Box 2799
Casper, WY 82606
(307) 266-1100

Description: Grants for Wyoming youth ages 6 to 21, particularly those handicapped by illness or injury or with financial needs; emphasis on the Casper area.
$ Given: $91,825 for 27 grants; average range: $1,000–$10,000
Application Information: Application form not required; write letter (see the important information in the chapter introduction about the need for institutional affiliation).
Deadline: None
Contact: Elona Anderson

Federal Grants

The federal government appropriates hundreds of millions of dollars each year for employment-related grants and job services, mostly through the Department of Labor. The bulk of this money is administered by the state Employment Security offices. There are also special programs and grants for women (through the Women's Bureau, Department of Labor), for farmers (through the Farmers Home Administration, Department of Agriculture), and for businesspersons (through the Small Business Administration).

ALABAMA

EMPLOYMENT SERVICE

United States Employment Service
Employment and Training Administration, Department of Labor
Washington, DC 20210
(202) 219-5257

Description: Provides placement services for job seekers and
employers. These include services to special applicant groups, such
as veterans, the handicapped, youth, minorities, and older workers;
a computerized interstate job listing; and other labor market
information.
$ Given: $847,220,000 est. FY 95
Application Information: Contact your state office.
Deadline: Established each year (contact federal agency for deadline
for application submission).
Contact: Leonora W. Pate, Director
            Department of Industrial Relations
            Industrial Relations Building
            649 Monroe Street
            Montgomery, AL 36130
            (205) 242-3960
            Fax: (205) 242-3960

UNEMPLOYMENT INSURANCE

Unemployment Insurance Service
Employment and Training Administration, Department of Labor
Washington, DC 20210
(202) 219-7831

Description: Provides unemployment insurance for workers whose
employers have contributed to state unemployment funds, federal
civilian employees, ex–service persons, those who have become
unemployed as a result of product imports, and those whose
unemployment comes under the purview of a presidentially declared
disaster.
$ Given: $23.7 billion est. FY 95
Application Information: Contact the Employment Security department for your state.
Deadline: Not available

Contact: Leonora W. Pate, Director
           Department of Industrial Relations
           Industrial Relations Building
           649 Monroe Street
           Montgomery, AL 36130
           (205) 242-3960
           Fax: (205) 242-3960

EMPLOYMENT AND TRAINING ASSISTANCE—DISLOCATED WORKERS

Employment and Training Administration, Department of Labor
200 Constitution Avenue, NW
Washington, DC 20210
(202) 219-5577

Description: Federal grants given to state and local programs to assist workers through training and employment services. These are workers who have been terminated or laid off or received notice of such and are not likely to return to their previous occupation or industry or who are long-term unemployed. Targeted individuals include those affected by mass layoffs and natural disasters.
$ Given: $571.1 million total nationwide for FY 93
Application Information: Inquire at Employment Security office listed below.
Deadline: None
Contact: Leonora W. Pate, Director
           Department of Industrial Relations
           Industrial Relations Building
           649 Monroe Street
           Montgomery, AL 36130
           (205) 242-3960
           Fax: (205) 242-3960

WOMEN'S SPECIAL EMPLOYMENT ASSISTANCE

Office of Administrative Management
Women's Bureau
Office of the Secretary
Department of Labor
Washington, DC 20210
(202) 219-6611

Description: Provides advisory services and counseling and also disseminates technical information to aid in the employment of women—especially in the realm of nontraditional women's jobs and jobs in new technologies.
$ Given: Not available
Application Information: Write to Women's Bureau in your region.
Deadline: None
Contact: Delores L. Crockett, Regional Administrator
            Region IV, Women's Bureau
            Department of Labor
            1371 Peachtree Street, NE
            Room 323
            Atlanta, GA 30367
            (404) 347-4461

EMERGENCY LOANS

Farmers Home Administration
Department of Agriculture
14th Street and Independence Avenue, SW
Washington, DC 20250
(202) 720-1632

Description: Provides loans to family farmers (either owner or tenant), ranchers, and aquaculture operators to cover losses resulting from natural or other major disasters. Recipients must be unable to obtain credit from other sources.
$ Given: $180 million est. FY 95; average range: $500–$500,000; average assistance: $66,200
Application Information: Consult local telephone directory under United States Government, Department of Agriculture, for Farmers Home Administration office.
Deadline: Not available
Contact: Farmers Home Administration
            Sterling Center
            Suite 601
            4121 Carmichael Road
            Montgomery, AL 36106-3683
            (205) 279-3400

ECONOMIC INJURY DISASTER LOANS

Office of Disaster Assistance
Small Business Administration (SBA)
409 Third Street, SW
Washington, DC 20416
(202) 205-6734

Description: Provides direct loans to small businesses suffering economic damage under Small Business Administration, Department of Agriculture, and/or presidentially declared disaster. Must be a small business or agricultural concern, located within declared disaster area and unable to obtain credit elsewhere.
$ Given: $78,209,000 est. FY 95; range: up to $1,500,000; average assistance: $50,725
Application Information: Applications are filed with nearest available SBA disaster area or special disaster office.
Deadline: Established for each declaration of disaster.
Contact: Small Business Administration, Region IV
1375 Peachtree Street, NE
Fifth Floor
Atlanta, GA 30367-8102
(404) 347-2797

ALASKA

EMPLOYMENT SERVICE

United States Employment Service
Employment and Training Administration, Department of Labor
Washington, DC 20210
(202) 219-5257

Description: Provides placement services for job seekers and employers. These include services to special applicant groups, such as veterans, the handicapped, youth, minorities, and older workers; a computerized interstate job listing; and other labor market information.
$ Given: $847,220,000 est. FY 95
Application Information: Contact your state office.
Deadline: Established each year (contact federal agency for deadline for application submission).

Contact: Judy Knight
          Employment Security Division
          Department of Labor
          111 West Eighth Street
          P.O. Box 25509
          Juneau, AK 99802-5509
          (907) 465-4537
          Fax: (907) 465-4537

UNEMPLOYMENT INSURANCE

Unemployment Insurance Service
Employment and Training Administration, Department of Labor
Washington, DC 20210
(202) 219-7831

Description: Provides unemployment insurance for workers whose
employers have contributed to state unemployment funds, federal
civilian employees, ex–service persons, those who have become
unemployed as a result of product imports, and those whose
unemployment comes under the purview of a presidentially declared
disaster.
$ Given: $23.7 billion est. FY 95
Application Information: Contact the Employment Security department for your state.
Deadline: Not available
Contact: Judy Knight
             Employment Security Division
             Department of Labor
             111 West Eighth Street
             P.O. Box 25509
             Juneau, AK 99802-5509
             (907) 465-4537
             Fax: (907) 465-4537

EMPLOYMENT AND TRAINING ASSISTANCE— DISLOCATED WORKERS

Employment and Training Administration, Department of Labor
200 Constitution Avenue, NW
Washington, DC 20210
(202) 219-5577

Description: Federal grants given to state and local programs to assist workers through training and employment services. These are workers who have been terminated or laid off or received notice of such and are not likely to return to their previous occupation or industry or who are long-term unemployed. Targeted individuals include those affected by mass layoffs and natural disasters.
$ Given: $571.1 million total nationwide for FY 93
Application Information: Inquire at Employment Security office listed below.
Deadline: Not available
Contact: Judy Knight
          Employment Security Division
          Department of Labor
          111 West Eighth Street
          P.O. Box 25509
          Juneau, AK 99802-5509
          (907) 465-4537
          Fax: (907) 465-4537

WOMEN'S SPECIAL EMPLOYMENT ASSISTANCE

Office of Administrative Management
Women's Bureau
Office of the Secretary
Department of Labor
Washington, DC 20210
(202) 219-6611

Description: Provides advisory services and counseling and also disseminates technical information to aid in the employment of women—especially in the realm of nontraditional women's jobs and jobs in new technologies.
$ Given: $8,054,000 est. FY 95
Application Information: Write to Women's Bureau in your region.
Deadline: None
Contact: Regional Administrator
          Region X, Women's Bureau
          Department of Labor
          1111 Third Avenue
          Room 885
          Seattle, WA 98101-3211
          (206) 553-1534

EMERGENCY LOANS

Farmers Home Administration
Department of Agriculture
14th Street and Independence Avenue, SW
Washington, DC 20250
(202) 720-1632

Description: Provides loans to family farmers (either owner or
tenant), ranchers, and aquaculture operators to cover losses resulting from natural or other major disasters. Recipients must be
unable to obtain credit from other sources.
$ Given: $180 million est. FY 95; average range: $500–$500,000;
average assistance: $66,200
Application Information: Consult local telephone directory under
United States Government, Department of Agriculture, for Farmers
Home Administration office.
Deadline: Not available
Contact: Farmers Home Administration
           634 South Bailey
           Suite 103
           Palmer, AK 99645
           (907) 745-2176

ECONOMIC INJURY DISASTER LOANS

Office of Disaster Assistance
Small Business Administration (SBA)
409 Third Street, SW
Washington, DC 20416
(202) 205-6734

Description: Provides direct loans to small businesses suffering
economic damage under Small Business Administration, Department of Agriculture, and/or presidentially declared disaster. Must be
a small business or agricultural concern, located within declared
disaster area and unable to obtain credit elsewhere.
$ Given: $78,209,000 est. FY 95; range: up to $1,500,000; average
assistance: $50,725
Application Information: Applications are filed with nearest
available SBA disaster area or special disaster office.
Deadline: Established for each declaration of disaster.

Contact: Small Business Administration, Region X
           2601 Fourth Avenue
           Room 440
           Seattle, WA 98121-1273
           (206) 553-1273

ARIZONA

EMPLOYMENT SERVICE

United States Employment Service
Employment and Training Administration, Department of Labor
Washington, DC 20210
(202) 219-5257

Description: Provides placement services for job seekers and
employers. These include services to special applicant groups, such
as veterans, the handicapped, youth, minorities, and older workers;
a computerized interstate job listing; and other labor market
information.
$ Given: $847,220,000 est. FY 95
Application Information: Contact your state office.
Deadline: Established each year (contact federal agency for deadline
for application submission).
Contact: Linda Blessing, Director
           Department of Economic Security
           1717 West Jefferson Street
           P.O. Box 6123
           Phoenix, AZ 85005
           (602) 542-5676
           Fax: (602)542-5432

UNEMPLOYMENT INSURANCE

Unemployment Insurance Service
Employment and Training Administration, Department of Labor
Washington, DC 20210
(202) 219-7831

Description: Provides unemployment insurance for workers whose
employers have contributed to state unemployment funds, federal
civilian employees, ex–service persons, those who have become

unemployed as a result of product imports, and those whose unemployment comes under the purview of a presidentially declared disaster.
$ Given: $23.7 billion est. FY 95
Application Information: Contact the Employment Security Department for your state.
Deadline: Not available
Contact: Linda Blessing, Director
Department of Economic Security
1717 West Jefferson Street
P.O. Box 6123
Phoenix, AZ 85005
(602) 542-5676
Fax: (602)542-5432

EMPLOYMENT AND TRAINING ASSISTANCE— DISLOCATED WORKERS

Employment and Training Administration, Department of Labor
200 Constitution Avenue, NW
Washington, DC 20210
(202) 219-5577

Description: Federal grants given to state and local programs to assist workers through training and employment services. These are workers who have been terminated or laid off or received notice of such and are not likely to return to their previous occupation or industry or who are long-term unemployed. Targeted individuals include those affected by mass layoffs and natural disasters.
$ Given: $571.1 million total nationwide for FY 93
Application Information: Inquire at Employment Security office listed below.
Deadline: Not available
Contact: Linda Blessing, Director
Department of Economic Security
1717 West Jefferson Street
P.O. Box 6123
Phoenix, AZ 85005
(602) 542-5676
Fax: (602) 542-5432

WOMEN'S SPECIAL EMPLOYMENT ASSISTANCE

Office of Administrative Management
Women's Bureau
Office of the Secretary
Department of Labor
Washington, DC 20210
(202) 219-6611

Description: Makes referrals as to sources for counseling and disseminates technical information to aid in the employment of women—especially in the realm of nontraditional women's jobs and jobs in new technologies.
$ Given: $8,054,000 est. FY 95
Application Information: Write to Women's Bureau in your region.
Deadline: None
Contact: Regional Administrator
           Region IX, Women's Bureau
           Department of Labor
           71 Stevenson Street
           Room 927
           San Francisco, CA 94105
           (415) 774-6679

EMERGENCY LOANS

Farmers Home Administration
Department of Agriculture
14th Street and Independence Avenue, SW
Washington, DC 20250
(202) 720-1632

Description: Provides loans to family farmers (either owner or tenant), ranchers, and aquaculture operators to cover losses resulting from natural or other major disasters. Recipients must be unable to obtain credit from other sources.
$ Given: $180 million est. FY 95; average range: $500–$500,000; average assistance: $66,200
Application Information: Consult local telephone directory under United States Government, Department of Agriculture, for Farmers Home Administration office.
Deadline: Not available

Contact: Farmers Home Administration
          3003 North Central Avenue
          Suite 900
          Phoenix, AZ 85012
          (602) 280-8700

ECONOMIC INJURY DISASTER LOANS

Office of Disaster Assistance
Small Business Administration (SBA)
409 Third Street, SW
Washington, DC 20416
(202) 205-6734

Description: Provides direct loans to small businesses suffering
economic damage under Small Business Administration, Department of Agriculture, and/or presidentially declared disaster. Must be
a small business or agricultural concern, located within declared
disaster area and unable to obtain credit elsewhere.
$ Given: $78,209,000 est. FY 95; range: up to $1,500,000; average
assistance: $50,725
Application Information: Applications are filed with nearest
available SBA disaster area or special disaster office.
Deadline: Established for each declaration of disaster.
Contact: Small Business Administration, Region IX
          71 Stevenson Street
          20th Floor
          San Francisco, CA 94105-2939
          (415) 744-6402

ARKANSAS

EMPLOYMENT SERVICE

United States Employment Service
Employment and Training Administration, Department of Labor
Washington, DC 20210
(202) 219-5257

Description: Provides placement services for job seekers and
employers. These include services to special applicant groups, such
as veterans, the handicapped, youth, minorities, and older workers;

a computerized interstate job listing; and other labor market information.

$ Given: $847,220,000 est. FY 95

Application Information: Contact your state office.

Deadline: Established each year (contact federal agency for deadline for application submission).

Contact: William D. Gaddy, Administrator
Arkansas Employment Security Division
P.O. Box 2981
Capitol Mall
Little Rock, AR 72203-2981
(501) 682-3713
Fax: (501) 682-3713

UNEMPLOYMENT INSURANCE

Unemployment Insurance Service
Employment and Training Administration, Department of Labor
Washington, DC 20210
(202) 219-7831

Description: Provides unemployment insurance for workers whose employers have contributed to state unemployment funds, federal civilian employees, ex–service persons, those who have become unemployed as a result of product imports, and those whose unemployment comes under the purview of a presidentially declared disaster.

$ Given: $23.7 billion est. FY 95

Application Information: Contact the Employment Security Department for your state.

Deadline: Not available

Contact: William D. Gaddy, Administrator
Arkansas Employment Security Division
P.O. Box 2981
Capitol Mall
Little Rock, AR 72203-2981
(501) 682-3713
Fax: (501) 682-3713

EMPLOYMENT AND TRAINING ASSISTANCE— DISLOCATED WORKERS

Employment and Training Administration, Department of Labor
200 Constitution Avenue, NW
Washington, DC 20210
(202) 219-5577

Description: Federal grants given to state and local programs to assist workers through training and employment services. These are workers who have been terminated or laid off or received notice of such and are not likely to return to their previous occupation or industry or who are long-term unemployed. Targeted individuals include those affected by mass layoffs and natural disasters.
$ Given: $571.1 million total nationwide for FY 93
Application Information: Inquire at Employment Security office listed below.
Deadline: Not available
Contact: William D. Gaddy, Administrator
Arkansas Employment Security Division
P.O. Box 2981
Capitol Mall
Little Rock, AR 72203-2981
(501) 682-3713
Fax: (501) 682-3713

WOMEN'S SPECIAL EMPLOYMENT ASSISTANCE

Office of Administrative Management
Women's Bureau
Office of the Secretary
Department of Labor
Washington, DC 20210
(202) 219-6611

Description: Makes referrals as to sources for counseling, and disseminates technical information to aid in the employment of women—especially in the realm of nontraditional women's jobs and jobs in new technologies.
$ Given: $8,054,000 est. FY 95
Application Information: Write to Women's Bureau in your region.
Deadline: None

Contact: Regional Administrator
            Region VI, Women's Bureau
            Department of Labor
            8625 King George Drive
            Building C
            Dallas, TX 75235-3391
            (214) 767-7633

EMERGENCY LOANS

Farmers Home Administration
Department of Agriculture
14th Street and Independence Avenue, SW
Washington, DC 20250
(202) 720-1632

Description: Provides loans to family farmers (either owner or tenant), ranchers, and aquaculture operators to cover losses resulting from natural or other major disasters. Recipients must be unable to obtain credit from other sources.
$ Given: $180 million est. FY 95; average range: $500–$500,000; average assistance: $66,200
Application Information: Consult local telephone directory under United States Government, Department of Agriculture, for Farmers Home Administration office.
Deadline: Not available
Contact: Farmers Home Administration
            700 West Capitol
            P.O. Box 2778
            Little Rock, AR 72203
            (501) 324-6281

ECONOMIC INJURY DISASTER LOANS

Office of Disaster Assistance
Small Business Administration (SBA)
409 Third Street, SW
Washington, DC 20416
(202) 205-6734

Description: Provides direct loans to small businesses suffering economic damage under Small Business Administration, Department of Agriculture, and/or presidentially declared disaster. Must be

a small business or agricultural concern, located within declared
disaster area and unable to obtain credit elsewhere.
$ Given: $78,209,000 est. FY 95; range: up to $1,500,000; average
assistance: $50,725
Application Information: Applications are filed with nearest
available SBA disaster area or special disaster office.
Deadline: Established for each declaration of disaster.
Contact: Small Business Administration, Region VI
            8625 King George Drive
            Building C
            Dallas, TX 75235-3391
            (214) 767-7633

CALIFORNIA

EMPLOYMENT SERVICE

United States Employment Service
Employment and Training Administration, Department of Labor
Washington, DC 20210
(202) 219-5257

Description: Provides placement services for job seekers and
employers. These include services to special applicant groups, such
as veterans, the handicapped, youth, minorities, and older workers;
a computerized interstate job listing; and other labor market
information.
$ Given: $847,220,000 est. FY 95
Application Information: Contact your state office.
Deadline: Established each year (contact federal agency for deadline
for application submission).
Contact: Thomas P. Nagle, Administrator
            Employment Development Department
            800 Capitol Mall
            P.O. Box 826880
            Sacramento, CA 94280-0001
            (916) 654-8210
            Fax: (916) 657-5294

UNEMPLOYMENT INSURANCE

Unemployment Insurance Service
Employment and Training Administration, Department of Labor
Washington, DC 20210
(202) 219-7831

Description: Provides unemployment insurance for workers whose
employers have contributed to state unemployment funds, federal
civilian employees, ex–service persons, those who have become
unemployed as a result of product imports, and those whose
unemployment comes under the purview of a presidentially declared
disaster.
$ Given: $23.7 billion est. FY 95
Application Information: Contact the Employment Security Department for your state.
Deadline: Not available
Contact: Thomas P. Nagle, Administrator
           Employment Development Department
           800 Capitol Mall
           P.O. Box 826880
           Sacramento, CA 94280-0001
           (916) 654-8210
           Fax: (916) 657-5294

EMPLOYMENT AND TRAINING ASSISTANCE—
DISLOCATED WORKERS

Employment and Training Administration, Department of Labor
200 Constitution Avenue, NW
Washington, DC 20210
(202) 219-5577

Description: Federal grants given to state and local programs to
assist workers through training and employment services. These are
workers who have been terminated or laid off or received notice of
such and are not likely to return to their previous occupation or
industry or who are long-term unemployed. Targeted individuals
include those affected by mass layoffs and natural disasters.
$ Given: $571.1 million total nationwide for FY 93
Application Information: Inquire at Employment Security office
listed below.
Deadline: Not available

Contact: Thomas P. Nagle, Administrator
           Employment Development Department
           800 Capitol Mall
           P.O. Box 826880
           Sacramento, CA 94280-0001
           (916) 654-8210
           Fax: (916) 657-5294

WOMEN'S SPECIAL EMPLOYMENT ASSISTANCE

Office of Administrative Management
Women's Bureau
Office of the Secretary
Department of Labor
Washington, DC 20210
(202) 219-6611

Description: Makes referrals as to sources for counseling and
disseminates technical information to aid in the employment of
women—especially in the realm of nontraditional women's jobs and
jobs in new technologies.
$ Given: $8,054,000 est. FY 95
Application Information: Write to Women's Bureau in your region.
Deadline: None
Contact: Regional Administrator
           Region IX, Women's Bureau
           Department of Labor
           71 Stevenson Street
           Room 927
           San Francisco, CA 94105
           (415) 774-6679

EMERGENCY LOANS

Farmers Home Administration
Department of Agriculture
14th Street and Independence Avenue, SW
Washington, DC 20250
(202) 720-1632

Description: Provides loans to family farmers (either owner or
tenant), ranchers, and aquaculture operators to cover losses result-

ing from natural or other major disasters. Recipients must be
unable to obtain credit from other sources.
$ Given: $180 million est. FY 95; average range: $500–$500,000;
average assistance: $66,200
Application Information: Consult local telephone directory under
United States Government, Department of Agriculture, for Farmers
Home Administration office.
Deadline: Not available
Contact: Farmers Home Administration
      194 West Maine Street
      Suite F
      Woodland, CA 95695-2915
      (916) 669-2000

ECONOMIC INJURY DISASTER LOANS

Office of Disaster Assistance
Small Business Administration (SBA)
409 Third Street, SW
Washington, DC 20416
(202) 205-6734

Description: Provides direct loans to small businesses suffering
economic damage under Small Business Administration, Department of Agriculture, and/or presidentially declared disaster. Must be
a small business or agricultural concern, located within declared
disaster area and unable to obtain credit elsewhere.
$ Given: $78,209,000 est. FY 95; range: up to $1,500,000; average
assistance: $50,725
Application Information: Applications are filed with nearest
available SBA disaster area or special disaster office.
Deadline: Established for each declaration of disaster.
Contact: Small Business Administration, Region IX
      71 Stevenson Street
      20th Floor
      San Francisco, CA 94105-2939
      (415) 744-6402

COLORADO

EMPLOYMENT SERVICE

United States Employment Service
Employment and Training Administration, Department of Labor
Washington, DC 20210
(202) 219-5257

Description: Provides placement services for job seekers and
employers. These include services to special applicant groups, such
as veterans, the handicapped, youth, minorities, and older workers;
a computerized interstate job listing; and other labor market
information.
$ Given: $847,220,000 est. FY 95
Application Information: Contact your state office.
Deadline: Established each year (contact federal agency for deadline
for application submission).
Contact: John J. Donlon, Executive Director
           Department of Labor and Employment Training
           600 Grant Street
           Ninth Floor
           Denver, CO 80203-3528
           (303) 837-3801
           Fax: (303) 837-3956

UNEMPLOYMENT INSURANCE

Unemployment Insurance Service
Employment and Training Administration, Department of Labor
Washington, DC 20210
(202) 219-7831

Description: Provides unemployment insurance for workers whose
employers have contributed to state unemployment funds, federal
civilian employees, ex–service persons, those who have become
unemployed as a result of product imports, and those whose
unemployment comes under the purview of a presidentially declared
disaster.
$ Given: $23.7 billion est. FY 95
Application Information: Contact the Employment Security Department for your state.
Deadline: Not available

Contact: John J. Donlon, Executive Director
Department of Labor and Employment Training
600 Grant Street
Ninth Floor
Denver, CO 80203-3528
(303) 837-3801
Fax: (303) 837-3956

EMPLOYMENT AND TRAINING ASSISTANCE— DISLOCATED WORKERS

Employment and Training Administration, Department of Labor
200 Constitution Avenue, NW
Washington, DC 20210
(202) 219-5577

Description: Federal grants given to state and local programs to assist workers through training and employment services. These are workers who have been terminated or laid off or received notice of such and are not likely to return to their previous occupation or industry or who are long-term unemployed. Targeted individuals include those affected by mass layoffs and natural disasters.
$ Given: $571.1 million total nationwide for FY 93
Application Information: Inquire at Employment Security office listed below.
Deadline: Not available
Contact: John J. Donlon, Executive Director
Department of Labor and Employment Training
600 Grant Street
Ninth Floor
Denver, CO 80203-3528
(303) 837-3801
Fax: (303) 837-3956

WOMEN'S SPECIAL EMPLOYMENT ASSISTANCE

Office of Administrative Management
Women's Bureau
Office of the Secretary
Department of Labor
Washington, DC 20210
(202) 219-6611

Description: Makes referrals as to sources for counseling and disseminates technical information to aid in the employment of women—especially in the realm of nontraditional women's jobs and jobs in new technologies.
$ Given: $8,054,000 est. FY 95
Application Information: Write to Women's Bureau in your region.
Deadline: None
Contact: Regional Administrator
          Region VII, Women's Bureau
          633 17th Street
          Seventh Floor
          Denver, CO 80202
          (303) 294-7186

EMERGENCY LOANS

Farmers Home Administration
Department of Agriculture
14th Street and Independence Avenue, SW
Washington, DC 20250
(202) 720-1632

Description: Provides loans to family farmers (either owner or tenant), ranchers, and aquaculture operators to cover losses resulting from natural or other major disasters. Recipients must be unable to obtain credit from other sources.
$ Given: $180 million est. FY 95; average range: $500–$500,000; average assistance: $66,200
Application Information: Consult local telephone directory under United States Government, Department of Agriculture, for Farmers Home Administration office.
Deadline: Not available
Contact: Farmers Home Administration
          655 Parket Street
          Room E-100
          Lakewood, CO 80215
          (303) 236-2801

ECONOMIC INJURY DISASTER LOANS

Office of Disaster Assistance
Small Business Administration (SBA)
409 Third Street, SW
Washington, DC 20416
(202) 205-6734

Description: Provides direct loans to small businesses suffering economic damage under Small Business Administration, Department of Agriculture, and/or presidentially declared disaster. Must be a small business or agricultural concern, located within declared disaster area and unable to obtain credit elsewhere.
$ Given: $78,209,000 est. FY 95; range: up to $1,500,000; average assistance: $50,725
Application Information: Applications are filed with nearest available SBA disaster area or special disaster office.
Deadline: Established for each declaration of disaster.
Contact: Small Business Administration, Region VIII
633 17th Street
7th Floor
Denver, CO 80202
(303) 294-7186

CONNECTICUT

EMPLOYMENT SERVICE

United States Employment Service
Employment and Training Administration, Department of Labor
Washington, DC 20210
(202) 219-5257

Description: Provides placement services for job seekers and employers. These include services to special applicant groups, such as veterans, the handicapped, youth, minorities, and older workers; a computerized interstate job listing; and other labor market information.
$ Given: $847,220,000 est. FY 95
Application Information: Contact your state office.
Deadline: Established each year (contact federal agency for deadline for application submission).

Contact: Bennett Pudlin, Executive Director
          Connecticut Labor Department
          State Office Building
          Employment Security Division
          200 Folly Brook Boulevard
          Wethersfield, CT 06109
          (203) 566-4280
          Fax: (203) 566-1520

UNEMPLOYMENT INSURANCE

Unemployment Insurance Service
Employment and Training Administration, Department of Labor
Washington, DC 20210
(202) 219-7831

Description: Provides unemployment insurance for workers whose employers have contributed to state unemployment funds, federal civilian employees, ex–service persons, those who have become unemployed as a result of product imports, and those whose unemployment comes under the purview of a presidentially declared disaster.
$ Given: $23.7 billion est. FY 95
Application Information: Contact the Employment Security Department for your state.
Deadline: Not available
Contact: Bennett Pudlin, Executive Director
          Connecticut Labor Department
          State Office Building
          Employment Security Division
          200 Folly Brook Boulevard
          Wethersfield, CT 06109
          (203) 566-4280
          Fax: (203) 566-1520

EMPLOYMENT AND TRAINING ASSISTANCE— DISLOCATED WORKERS

Employment and Training Administration, Department of Labor
200 Constitution Avenue, NW
Washington, DC 20210
(202) 219-5577

Description: Federal grants given to state and local programs to assist workers through training and employment services. These are workers who have been terminated or laid off or received notice of such and are not likely to return to their previous occupation or industry or who are long-term unemployed. Targeted individuals include those affected by mass layoffs and natural disasters.
$ Given: $571.1 million total nationwide for FY 93
Application Information: Inquire at Employment Security office listed below.
Deadline: Not available
Contact: Bennett Pudlin, Executive Director
           Connecticut Labor Department
           State Office Building
           Employment Security Division
           200 Folly Brook Boulevard
           Wethersfield, CT 06109
           (203) 566-4280
           Fax: (203) 566-1520

WOMEN'S SPECIAL EMPLOYMENT ASSISTANCE

Office of Administrative Management
Women's Bureau
Office of the Secretary
Department of Labor
Washington, DC 20210
(202) 219-6611

Description: Makes referrals as to sources for counseling and disseminates technical information to aid in the employment of women—especially in the realm of nontraditional women's jobs and jobs in new technologies.
$ Given: $8,054,000 est. FY 95
Application Information: Write to Women's Bureau in your region.
Deadline: None
Contact: Martha Izzi, Regional Administrator
           Region I, Women's Bureau
           Department of Labor
           One Congress Street, 11th Floor
           Boston, MA 02214
           (617) 565-1988

EMERGENCY LOANS

Farmers Home Administration
Department of Agriculture
14th Street and Independence Avenue, SW
Washington, DC 20250
(202) 720-1632

Description: Provides loans to family farmers (either owner or tenant), ranchers, and aquaculture operators to cover losses resulting from natural or other major disasters. Recipients must be unable to obtain credit from other sources.
$ Given: $180 million est. FY 95; average range: $500–$500,000; average assistance: $66,200
Application Information: Consult local telephone directory under United States Government, Department of Agriculture, for Farmers Home Administration office.
Deadline: Not available
Contact: Farmers Home Administration
451 West Street
Amherst, MA 01002
(413) 253-4300

ECONOMIC INJURY DISASTER LOANS

Office of Disaster Assistance
Small Business Administration (SBA)
409 Third Street, SW
Washington, DC 20416
(202) 205-6734

Description: Provides direct loans to small businesses suffering economic damage under Small Business Administration, Department of Agriculture, and/or presidentially declared disaster. Must be a small business or agricultural concern, located within declared disaster area and unable to obtain credit elsewhere.
$ Given: $78,209,000 est. FY 95; range: up to $1,500,000; average assistance: $50,725
Application Information: Applications are filed with nearest available SBA disaster area or special disaster office.
Deadline: Established for each declaration of disaster.

Contact: Small Business Administration, Region I
           155 Federal Street
           Ninth Floor
           Boston, MA 02110
           (617) 451-2023

DELAWARE

EMPLOYMENT SERVICE

United States Employment Service
Employment and Training Administration, Department of Labor
Washington, DC 20210
(202) 219-5257

Description: Provides placement services for job seekers and
employers. These include services to special applicant groups, such
as veterans, the handicapped, youth, minorities, and older workers;
a computerized interstate job listing; and other labor market
information.
$ Given: $847,220,000 est. FY 95
Application Information: Contact your state office.
Deadline: Established each year (contact federal agency for deadline
for application submission).
Contact: Darnell J. Minott, Secretary of Labor
           Department of Labor
           State Office Building
           820 North French Street
           Wilmington, DE 19801
           (302) 577-2710
           Fax: (302) 577-2735

UNEMPLOYMENT INSURANCE

Unemployment Insurance Service
Employment and Training Administration, Department of Labor
Washington, DC 20210
(202) 219-7831

Description: Provides unemployment insurance for workers whose
employers have contributed to state unemployment funds, federal
civilian employees, ex–service persons, those who have become
unemployed as a result of product imports, and those whose

unemployment comes under the purview of a presidentially declared disaster.
$ Given: $23.7 billion est. FY 95
Application Information: Contact the Employment Security Department for your state.
Deadline: Not available
Contact: Darnell J. Minott, Secretary of Labor
                Department of Labor
                State Office Building
                820 North French Street
                Wilmington, DE 19801
                (302) 577-2710
                Fax: (302) 577-2735

EMPLOYMENT AND TRAINING ASSISTANCE— DISLOCATED WORKERS

Employment and Training Administration, Department of Labor
200 Constitution Avenue, NW
Washington, DC 20210
(202) 219-5577

Description: Federal grants given to state and local programs to assist workers through training and employment services. These are workers who have been terminated or laid off or received notice of such and are not likely to return to their previous occupation or industry or who are long-term unemployed. Targeted individuals include those affected by mass layoffs and natural disasters.
$ Given: $571.1 million total nationwide for FY 93
Application Information: Inquire at Employment Security office listed below.
Deadline: Not available
Contact: Darnell J. Minott, Secretary of Labor
                Department of Labor
                State Office Building
                820 North French Street
                Wilmington, DE 19801
                (302) 577-2710
                Fax: (302) 577-2735

WOMEN'S SPECIAL EMPLOYMENT ASSISTANCE

Office of Administrative Management
Women's Bureau
Office of the Secretary
Department of Labor
Washington, DC 20210
(202) 219-6611

Description: Makes referrals as to sources for counseling and disseminates technical information to aid in the employment of women—especially in the realm of nontraditional women's jobs and jobs in new technologies.
$ Given: $8,054,000 est. FY 95
Application Information: Write to Women's Bureau in your region.
Deadline: None
Contact: Region III, Women's Bureau
                Department of Labor
                Gateway Building
                Room 2450
                3535 Market Street
                Philadelphia, PA 19104
                (215) 596-1184

EMERGENCY LOANS

Farmers Home Administration
Department of Agriculture
14th Street and Independence Avenue, SW
Washington, DC 20250
(202) 720-1632

Description: Provides loans to family farmers (either owner or tenant), ranchers, and aquaculture operators to cover losses resulting from natural or other major disasters. Recipients must be unable to obtain credit from other sources.
$ Given: $180 million est. FY 95; average range: $500–$500,000; average assistance: $66,200
Application Information: Consult local telephone directory under United States Government, Department of Agriculture, for Farmers Home Administration Office.
Deadline: Not available

Contact: Farmers Home Administration
          4611 South Dupont Highway
          P.O. Box 400
          Camden, DE 19934-9998
          (302) 697-4300

ECONOMIC INJURY DISASTER LOANS

Office of Disaster Assistance
Small Business Administration (SBA)
409 Third Street, SW
Washington, DC 20416
(202) 205-6734

Description: Provides direct loans to small businesses suffering
economic damage under Small Business Administration, Department of Agriculture, and/or presidentially declared disaster. Must be
a small business or agricultural concern, located within declared
disaster area and unable to obtain credit elsewhere.
$ Given: $78,209,000 est. FY 95; range: up to $1,500,000; average
assistance: $50,725
Application Information: Applications are filed with nearest
available SBA disaster area or special disaster office.
Deadline: Established for each declaration of disaster.
Contact: Small Business Administration, Region I
          475 Allendale Road
          Suite 201
          King of Prussia, PA 19406
          (215) 962-3700

DISTRICT OF COLUMBIA

EMPLOYMENT SERVICE

United States Employment Service
Employment and Training Administration, Department of Labor
Washington, DC 20210
(202) 219-5257

Description: Provides placement services for job seekers and
employers. These include services to special applicant groups, such
as veterans, the handicapped, youth, minorities, and older workers;

a computerized interstate job listing; and other labor market information.

$ Given: $847,220,000 est. FY 95

Application Information: Contact your state office.

Deadline: Established each year (contact federal agency for deadline for application submission).

Contact: Joseph Yedell, Acting Director
Department of Employment Services
Department of Labor
500 C Street, NW
Room 600
Washington, DC 20001
(202) 724-7185
Fax: (202) 724-7112

UNEMPLOYMENT INSURANCE

Unemployment Insurance Service
Employment and Training Administration, Department of Labor
Washington, DC 20210
(202) 219-7831

Description: Provides unemployment insurance for workers whose employers have contributed to state unemployment funds, federal civilian employees, ex–service persons, those who have become unemployed as a result of product imports, and those whose unemployment comes under the purview of a presidentially declared disaster.

$ Given: $23.7 billion est. FY 95

Application Information: Contact the Employment Security Department for your state.

Deadline: Not available

Contact: Joseph Yedell, Acting Director
Department of Employment Services
Department of Labor
500 C Street, NW
Room 600
Washington, DC 20001
(202) 724-7185
Fax: (202) 724-7112

EMPLOYMENT AND TRAINING ASSISTANCE— DISLOCATED WORKERS

Employment and Training Administration, Department of Labor
200 Constitution Avenue, NW
Washington, DC 20210
(202) 219-5577

Description: Federal grants given to state and local programs to assist workers through training and employment services. These are workers who have been terminated or laid off or received notice of such and are not likely to return to their previous occupation or industry or who are long-term unemployed. Targeted individuals include those affected by mass layoffs and natural disasters.
$ Given: $571.1 million total nationwide for FY 93
Application Information: Inquire at Employment Security office listed below.
Deadline: Not available
Contact: Joseph Yedell, Acting Director
            Department of Employment Services
            Department of Labor
            500 C Street, NW
            Room 600
            Washington, DC 20001
            (202) 724-7185
            Fax: (202) 724-7112

WOMEN'S SPECIAL EMPLOYMENT ASSISTANCE

Office of Administrative Management
Women's Bureau
Office of the Secretary
Department of Labor
Washington, DC 20210
(202) 219-6611

Description: Makes referrals as to sources for counseling and disseminates technical information to aid in the employment of women—especially in the realm of nontraditional women's jobs and jobs in new technologies.
$ Given: $8,054,000 est. FY 95
Application Information: Write to Women's Bureau in your region.
Deadline: None

Contact: Region III, Women's Bureau
          Department of Labor
          Gateway Building
          Room 2450
          3535 Market Street
          Philadelphia, PA 19104
          (215) 596-1184

EMERGENCY LOANS

Farmers Home Administration
Department of Agriculture
14th Street and Independence Avenue, SW
Washington, DC 20250
(202) 720-1632

Description: Provides loans to family farmers (either owner or
tenant), ranchers, and aquaculture operators to cover losses resulting from natural or other major disasters. Recipients must be
unable to obtain credit from other sources.
$ Given: $180 million est. FY 95; average range: $500–$500,000;
average assistance: $66,200
Application Information: Consult local telephone directory under
United States Government, Department of Agriculture, for Farmers
Home Administration Office.
Deadline: Not available
Contact: Farmers Home Administration
          4611 South Dupont Highway
          P.O. Box 400
          Camden, DE 19934-9998
          (302) 697-4300

ECONOMIC INJURY DISASTER LOANS

Office of Disaster Assistance
Small Business Administration (SBA)
409 Third Street, SW
Washington, DC 20416
(202) 205-6734

Description: Provides direct loans to small businesses suffering
economic damage under Small Business Administration, Department of Agriculture, and/or presidentially declared disaster. Must be

a small business or agricultural concern, located within declared disaster area and unable to obtain credit elsewhere.
$ Given: $78,209,000 est. FY 95; range: up to $1,500,000; average assistance: $50,725
Application Information: Applications are filed with nearest available SBA disaster area or special disaster office.
Deadline: Established for each declaration of disaster.
Contact: Small Business Administration, Region I
               475 Allendale Road
               Suite 201
               King of Prussia, PA 19406
               (215) 962-3700

FLORIDA

EMPLOYMENT SERVICE

United States Employment Service
Employment and Training Administration, Department of Labor
Washington, DC 20210
(202) 219-5257

Description: Provides placement services for job seekers and employers. These include services to special applicant groups, such as veterans, the handicapped, youth, minorities, and older workers; a computerized interstate job listing; and other labor market information.
$ Given: $847,220,000 est. FY 95
Application Information: Contact your state office.
Deadline: Established each year (contact federal agency for deadline for application submission).
Contact: Shirley Gooding, Secretary
               Department of Labor and Employment Security
               2012 Capitol Circle, SE
               Hartman Building
               Suite 303
               Tallahassee, FL 32399-2152
               (904) 488-8930
               Fax: (904) 488-8930

UNEMPLOYMENT INSURANCE

Unemployment Insurance Service
Employment and Training Administration, Department of Labor
Washington, DC 20210
(202) 219-7831

Description: Provides unemployment insurance for workers whose employers have contributed to state unemployment funds, federal civilian employees, ex–service persons, those who have become unemployed as a result of product imports, and those whose unemployment comes under the purview of a presidentially declared disaster.
$ Given: $23.7 billion est. FY 95
Application Information: Contact the Employment Security Department for your state.
Deadline: Not available
Contact: Shirley Gooding, Secretary
Department of Labor and Employment Security
2012 Capitol Circle, SE
Hartman Building
Suite 303
Tallahassee, FL 32399-2152
(904) 488-8930
Fax: (904) 488-8930

EMPLOYMENT AND TRAINING ASSISTANCE—DISLOCATED WORKERS

Employment and Training Administration, Department of Labor
200 Constitution Avenue, NW
Washington, DC 20210
(202) 219-5577

Description: Federal grants given to state and local programs to assist workers through training and employment services. These are workers who have been terminated or laid off or received notice of such and are not likely to return to their previous occupation or industry or who are long-term unemployed. Targeted individuals include those affected by mass layoffs and natural disasters.
$ Given: $571.1 million total nationwide for FY 93
Application Information: Inquire at Employment Security office listed below.
Deadline: Not available

Contact: Shirley Gooding, Secretary
Department of Labor and Employment Security
2012 Capitol Circle, SE
Hartman Building
Suite 303
Tallahassee, FL 32399-2152
(904) 488-8930
Fax: (904) 488-8930

WOMEN'S SPECIAL EMPLOYMENT ASSISTANCE

Office of Administrative Management
Women's Bureau
Office of the Secretary
Department of Labor
Washington, DC 20210
(202) 219-6611

Description: Makes referrals as to sources for counseling and disseminates technical information to aid in the employment of women—especially in the realm of nontraditional women's jobs and jobs in new technologies.
$ Given: $8,054,000 est. FY 95
Application Information: Write to Women's Bureau in your region.
Deadline: None
Contact: Delores L. Crockett, Regional Administrator
Region IV, Women's Bureau
Department of Labor
1371 Peachtree Street, NE
Room 323
Atlanta, GA 30367
(404) 347-4461

EMERGENCY LOANS

Farmers Home Administration
Department of Agriculture
14th Street and Independence Avenue, SW
Washington, DC 20250
(202) 720-1632

Description: Provides loans to family farmers (either owner or tenant), ranchers, and aquaculture operators to cover losses result-

ing from natural or other major disasters. Recipients must be unable to obtain credit from other sources.

$ Given: $180 million est. FY 95; average range: $500–$500,000; average assistance: $66,200

Application Information: Consult local telephone directory under United States Government, Department of Agriculture, for Farmers Home Administration office.

Deadline: Not available

Contact: Farmers Home Administration
              Federal Building
              4440 NW 25th Place
              P.O. Box 147010
              Gainesville, FL 32614-7010
              (904) 338-3400

ECONOMIC INJURY DISASTER LOANS

Office of Disaster Assistance
Small Business Administration (SBA)
409 Third Street, SW
Washington, DC 20416
(202) 205-6734

Description: Provides direct loans to small businesses suffering economic damage under Small Business Administration, Department of Agriculture, and/or presidentially declared disaster. Must be a small business or agricultural concern, located within declared disaster area and unable to obtain credit elsewhere.

$ Given: $78,209,000 est. FY 95; range: up to $1,500,000; average assistance: $50,725

Application Information: Applications are filed with nearest available SBA disaster area or special disaster office.

Deadline: Established for each declaration of disaster.

Contact: Small Business Administration, Region IV
              1375 Peachtree Street, NE
              Fifth Floor
              Atlanta, GA 30367-8102
              (404) 347-2797

GEORGIA

EMPLOYMENT SERVICE

United States Employment Service
Employment and Training Administration, Department of Labor
Washington, DC 20210
(202) 219-5257

Description: Provides placement services for job seekers and employers. These include services to special applicant groups, such as veterans, the handicapped, youth, minorities, and older workers; a computerized interstate job listing; and other labor market information.
$ Given: $847,220,000 est. FY 95
Application Information: Contact your state office.
Deadline: Established each year (contact federal agency for deadline for application submission).
Contact: David B. Poythress
               Department of Labor
               Employment Security Agency
               Sussex Place
               148 International Boulevard, NE
               Atlanta, GA 30303
               (404) 545-3011
               Fax: (404) 651-9377

UNEMPLOYMENT INSURANCE

Unemployment Insurance Service
Employment and Training Administration, Department of Labor
Washington, DC 20210
(202) 219-7831

Description: Provides unemployment insurance for workers whose employers have contributed to state unemployment funds, federal civilian employees, ex–service persons, those who have become unemployed as a result of product imports, and those whose unemployment comes under the purview of a presidentially declared disaster.
$ Given: $23.7 billion est. FY 95
Application Information: Contact the Employment Security Department for your state.
Deadline: Not available

Contact: David B. Poythress
           Department of Labor
           Employment Security Agency
           Sussex Place
           148 International Boulevard, NE
           Atlanta, GA 30303
           (404) 545-3011
           Fax: (404) 651-9377

EMPLOYMENT AND TRAINING ASSISTANCE— DISLOCATED WORKERS

Employment and Training Administration, Department of Labor
200 Constitution Avenue, NW
Washington, DC 20210
(202) 219-5577

Description: Federal grants given to state and local programs to assist workers through training and employment services. These are workers who have been terminated or laid off or received notice of such and are not likely to return to their previous occupation or industry or who are long-term unemployed. Targeted individuals include those affected by mass layoffs and natural disasters.
$ Given: $571.1 million total nationwide for FY 93
Application Information: Inquire at Employment Security office listed below.
Deadline: Not available
Contact: David B. Poythress
           Department of Labor
           Employment Security Agency
           Sussex Place
           148 International Boulevard, NE
           Atlanta, GA 30303
           (404) 545-3011
           Fax: (404) 651-9377

WOMEN'S SPECIAL EMPLOYMENT ASSISTANCE

Office of Administrative Management
Women's Bureau
Office of the Secretary, Department of Labor
Washington, DC 20210
(202) 219-6611

Description: Makes referrals as to sources for counseling and
disseminates technical information to aid in the employment of
women—especially in the realm of nontraditional women's jobs and
jobs in new technologies.
$ Given: $8,054,000 est. FY 95
Application Information: Write to Women's Bureau in your region.
Deadline: None
Contact: Delores L. Crockett, Regional Administrator
           Region IV, Women's Bureau
           Department of Labor
           1371 Peachtree Street, NE
           Room 323
           Atlanta, GA 30367
           (404) 347-4461

EMERGENCY LOANS

Farmers Home Administration
Department of Agriculture
14th Street and Independence Avenue, SW
Washington, DC 20250
(202) 720-1632

Description: Provides loans to family farmers (either owner or
tenant), ranchers, and aquaculture operators to cover losses resulting from natural or other major disasters. Recipients must be
unable to obtain credit from other sources.
$ Given: $180 million est. FY 95; average range: $500–$500,000;
average assistance: $66,200
Application Information: Consult local telephone directory under
United States Government, Department of Agriculture, for Farmers
Home Administration office.
Deadline: Not available
Contact: Farmers Home Administration
           355 East Hancock Avenue
           Stephens Federal Building
           Athens, GA 30610
           (404) 546-2152

ECONOMIC INJURY DISASTER LOANS

Office of Disaster Assistance
Small Business Administration (SBA)
409 Third Street, SW
Washington, DC 20416
(202) 205-6734

Description: Provides direct loans to small businesses suffering economic damage under Small Business Administration, Department of Agriculture, and/or presidentially declared disaster. Must be a small business or agricultural concern, located within declared disaster area and unable to obtain credit elsewhere.
$ Given: $78,209,000 est. FY 95; range: up to $1,500,000; average assistance: $50,725
Application Information: Applications are filed with nearest available SBA disaster area or special disaster office.
Deadline: Established for each declaration of disaster.
Contact: Small Business Administration, Region VI
1375 Peachtree Street, NE
Fifth Floor
Atlanta, GA 30367-8102
(404) 347-2797

GUAM

EMPLOYMENT SERVICE

United States Employment Service
Employment and Training Administration, Department of Labor
Washington, DC 20210
(202) 219-5257

Description: Provides placement services for job seekers and employers. These include services to special applicant groups, such as veterans, the handicapped, youth, minorities, and older workers; a computerized interstate job listing; and other labor market information.
$ Given: $847,220,000 est. FY 95
Application Information: Contact your state office.
Deadline: Established each year (contact federal agency for deadline for application submission).

Contact: Juan M. Tajito, Director
Department of Labor
P.O. Box 9970
Tamunning, GU 96911
(671) 646-9241
Fax: 9-011-671-646-9004

UNEMPLOYMENT INSURANCE

Unemployment Insurance Service
Employment and Training Administration, Department of Labor
Washington, DC 20210
(202) 219-7831

Description: Provides unemployment insurance for workers whose
employers have contributed to state unemployment funds, federal
civilian employees, ex–service persons, those who have become
unemployed as a result of product imports, and those whose
unemployment comes under the purview of a presidentially declared
disaster.
$ Given: $23.7 billion est. FY 95
Application Information: Contact the Employment Security Department for your state.
Deadline: Not available
Contact: Juan M. Tajito, Director
Department of Labor
P.O. Box 9970
Tamunning, GU 96911
(671) 646-9241
Fax: 9-011-671-646-9004

EMPLOYMENT AND TRAINING ASSISTANCE— DISLOCATED WORKERS

Employment and Training Administration, Department of Labor
200 Constitution Avenue, NW
Washington, DC 20210
(202) 219-5577

Description: Federal grants given to state and local programs to
assist workers through training and employment services. These are
workers who have been terminated or laid off or received notice of
such and are not likely to return to their previous occupation or
industry or who are long-term unemployed. Targeted individuals

include those affected by mass layoffs and natural disasters.
$ Given: $571.1 million total nationwide for FY 93
Application Information: Inquire at Employment Security office
listed below.
Deadline: Not available
Contact: Juan M. Tajito, Director
              Department of Labor
              P.O. Box 9970
              Tamunning, GU 96911
              (671) 646-9241
              Fax: 9-011-671-646-9004

WOMEN'S SPECIAL EMPLOYMENT ASSISTANCE

Office of Administrative Management
Women's Bureau
Office of the Secretary
Department of Labor
Washington, DC 20210
(202) 219-6611

Description: Makes referrals as to sources for counseling and
disseminates technical information to aid in the employment of
women—especially in the realm of nontraditional women's jobs and
jobs in new technologies.
$ Given: $8,054,000 est. FY 95
Application Information: Write to Women's Bureau in your region.
Deadline: None
Contact: Women's Bureau
              Room S3305
              Office of the Secretary
              Department of Labor
              Washington, DC 20210
              (202) 523-6606

EMERGENCY LOANS

Farmers Home Administration
Department of Agriculture
14th Street and Independence Avenue, SW
Washington, DC 20250
(202) 720-1632

Description: Provides loans to family farmers (either owner or tenant), ranchers, and aquaculture operators to cover losses resulting from natural or other major disasters. Recipients must be unable to obtain credit from other sources.
$ Given: $180 million est. FY 95; average range: $500–$500,000; average assistance: $66,200
Application Information: Consult local telephone directory under United States Government, Department of Agriculture, for Farmers Home Administration office.
Deadline: Not available
Contact: Farmers Home Administration
              Department of Agriculture
              14th Street and Independence Avenue, SW
              Washington, DC 20250
              (202) 720-1632

ECONOMIC INJURY DISASTER LOANS

Office of Disaster Assistance
Small Business Administration (SBA)
409 Third Street, SW
Washington, DC 20416
(202) 205-6734

Description: Provides direct loans to small businesses suffering economic damage under Small Business Administration, Department of Agriculture, and/or presidentially declared disaster. Must be a small business or agricultural concern, located within declared disaster area and unable to obtain credit elsewhere.
$ Given: $78,209,000 est. FY 95; range: up to $1,500,000; average assistance: $50,725
Application Information: Applications are filed with nearest available SBA disaster area or special disaster office.
Deadline: Established for each declaration of disaster.
Contact: Small Business Administration, Region IX
              71 Stevenson Street
              20th Floor
              San Francisco, CA 94105-2939
              (415) 744-6402

HAWAII

EMPLOYMENT SERVICE

United States Employment Service
Employment and Training Administration, Department of Labor
Washington, DC 20210
(202) 219-5257

Description: Provides placement services for job seekers and employers. These include services to special applicant groups, such as veterans, the handicapped, youth, minorities, and older workers; a computerized interstate job listing; and other labor market information.
$ Given: $847,220,000 est. FY 95
Application Information: Contact your state office.
Deadline: Established each year (contact federal agency for deadline for application submission).
Contact: Dayton M. Nakalua, Director
              Department of Labor and Industrial Relations
              830 Punchbowl Street
              Room 321
              Honolulu, HI 96813
              (808) 586-8844
              Fax: (808) 586-9099

UNEMPLOYMENT INSURANCE

Unemployment Insurance Service
Employment and Training Administration, Department of Labor
Washington, DC 20210
(202) 219-7831

Description: Provides unemployment insurance for workers whose employers have contributed to state unemployment funds, federal civilian employees, ex–service persons, those who have become unemployed as a result of product imports, and those whose unemployment comes under the purview of a presidentially declared disaster.
$ Given: $23.7 billion est. FY 95
Application Information: Contact the Employment Security Department for your state.
Deadline: Not available

Contact: Dayton M. Nakalua, Director
          Department of Labor and Industrial Relations
          830 Punchbowl Street
          Room 321
          Honolulu, HI 96813
          (808) 586-8844
          Fax: (808) 586-9099

EMPLOYMENT AND TRAINING ASSISTANCE— DISLOCATED WORKERS

Employment and Training Administration, Department of Labor
200 Constitution Avenue, NW
Washington, DC 20210
(202) 219-5577

Description: Federal grants given to state and local programs to assist workers through training and employment services. These are workers who have been terminated or laid off or received notice of such and are not likely to return to their previous occupation or industry or who are long-term unemployed. Targeted individuals include those affected by mass layoffs and natural disasters.
$ Given: $571.1 million total nationwide for FY 93
Application Information: Inquire at Employment Security office listed below.
Deadline: Not available
Contact: Dayton M. Nakalua, Director
          Department of Labor and Industrial Relations
          830 Punchbowl Street
          Room 321
          Honolulu, HI 96813
          (808) 586-8844
          Fax: (808) 586-9099

WOMEN'S SPECIAL EMPLOYMENT ASSISTANCE

Office of Administrative Management
Women's Bureau
Office of the Secretary
Department of Labor
Washington, DC 20210
(202) 219-6611

Description: Makes referrals as to sources for counseling and disseminates technical information to aid in the employment of women—especially in the realm of nontraditional women's jobs and jobs in new technologies.
$ Given: $8,054,000 est. FY 95
Application Information: Write to Women's Bureau in your region.
Deadline: None
Contact: Madeline Mixer, Regional Administrator
                Region IX, Women's Bureau
                Department of Labor
                71 Stevenson Street
                Room 927
                San Francisco, CA 94105
                (415) 774-6679

EMERGENCY LOANS

Farmers Home Administration
Department of Agriculture
14th Street and Independence Avenue, SW
Washington, DC 20250
(202) 720-1632

Description: Provides loans to family farmers (either owner or tenant), ranchers, and aquaculture operators to cover losses resulting from natural or other major disasters. Recipients must be unable to obtain credit from other sources.
$ Given: $180 million est. FY 95; average range: $500–$500,000; average assistance: $66,200
Application Information: Consult local telephone directory under United States Government, Department of Agriculture, for Farmers Home Administration office.
Deadline: Not available
Contact: Farmers Home Administration
                Federal Building
                Room 311
                154 Waianuenue Avenue
                Hilo, HI 96720
                (808) 933-3000

ECONOMIC INJURY DISASTER LOANS

Office of Disaster Assistance
Small Business Administration (SBA)
409 Third Street, SW
Washington, DC 20416
(202) 205-6734

Description: Provides direct loans to small businesses suffering
economic damage under Small Business Administration, Department of Agriculture, and/or presidentially declared disaster. Must be
a small business or agricultural concern, located within declared
disaster area and unable to obtain credit elsewhere.
$ Given: $78,209,000 est. FY 95; range: up to $1,500,000; average
assistance: $50,725
Application Information: Applications are filed with nearest
available SBA disaster area or special disaster office.
Deadline: Established for each declaration of disaster.
Contact: Small Business Administration, Region IX
　　　　　71 Stevenson Street
　　　　　20th Floor
　　　　　San Francisco, CA 94105-2939
　　　　　(415) 744-6402

IDAHO

EMPLOYMENT SERVICE

United States Employment Service
Employment and Training Administration, Department of Labor
Washington, DC 20210
(202) 219-5257

Description: Provides placement services for job seekers and
employers. These include services to special applicant groups, such
as veterans, the handicapped, youth, minorities, and older workers;
a computerized interstate job listing; and other labor market
information.
$ Given: $847,220,000 est. FY 95
Application Information: Contact your state office.
Deadline: Established each year (contact federal agency for deadline
for application submission).

Contact: Connie Ryals, Director
Department of Employment
P.O. Box 35
317 Main Street
Boise, ID 83735-0001
(208) 334-6110
Fax: (208) 334-6430

UNEMPLOYMENT INSURANCE

Unemployment Insurance Service
Employment and Training Administration, Department of Labor
Washington, DC 20210
(202) 219-7831

Description: Provides unemployment insurance for workers whose employers have contributed to state unemployment funds, federal civilian employees, ex–service persons, those who have become unemployed as a result of product imports, and those whose unemployment comes under the purview of a presidentially declared disaster.
$ Given: $23.7 billion est. FY 95
Application Information: Contact the Employment Security Department for your state.
Deadline: Not available
Contact: Connie Ryals, Director
Department of Employment
P.O. Box 35
317 Main Street
Boise, ID 83735-0001
(208) 334-6110
Fax: (208) 334-6430

EMPLOYMENT AND TRAINING ASSISTANCE— DISLOCATED WORKERS

Employment and Training Administration, Department of Labor
200 Constitution Avenue, NW
Washington, DC 20210
(202) 219-5577

Description: Federal grants given to state and local programs to assist workers through training and employment services. These are

workers who have been terminated or laid off or received notice of such and are not likely to return to their previous occupation or industry or who are long-term unemployed. Targeted individuals include those affected by mass layoffs and natural disasters.
$ Given: $571.1 million total nationwide for FY 93
Application Information: Inquire at Employment Security office listed below.
Deadline: Not available
Contact: Connie Ryals, Director
                Department of Employment
                P.O. Box 35
                317 Main Street
                Boise, ID 83735-0001
                (208) 334-6110
                Fax: (208) 334-6430

WOMEN'S SPECIAL EMPLOYMENT ASSISTANCE

Office of Administrative Management
Women's Bureau
Office of the Secretary
Department of Labor
Washington, DC 20210
(202) 219-6611

Description: Makes referrals as to sources for counseling and disseminates technical information to aid in the employment of women—especially in the realm of nontraditional women's jobs and jobs in new technologies.
$ Given: $8,054,000 est. FY 95
Application Information: Write to Women's Bureau in your region.
Deadline: None
Contact: Regional Administrator
                Region X, Women's Bureau
                Department of Labor
                111 Third Avenue
                Room 885
                Seattle, WA 98101-3211
                (206) 553-1534

EMERGENCY LOANS

Farmers Home Administration
Department of Agriculture
14th Street and Independence Avenue, SW
Washington, DC 20250
(202) 720-1632

Description: Provides loans to family farmers (either owner or tenant), ranchers, and aquaculture operators to cover losses resulting from natural or other major disasters. Recipients must be unable to obtain credit from other sources.
$ Given: $180 million est. FY 95; average range: $500–$500,000; average assistance: $66,200
Application Information: Consult local telephone directory under United States Government, Department of Agriculture, for Farmers Home Administration office.
Deadline: Not available
Contact: Farmers Home Administration
        3232 Elder Street
        Boise, ID 83705
        (208) 334-1301

ECONOMIC INJURY DISASTER LOANS

Office of Disaster Assistance
Small Business Administration (SBA)
409 Third Street, SW
Washington, DC 20416
(202) 205-6734

Description: Provides direct loans to small businesses suffering economic damage under Small Business Administration, Department of Agriculture, and/or presidentially declared disaster. Must be a small business or agricultural concern, located within declared disaster area and unable to obtain credit elsewhere.
$ Given: $78,209,000 est. FY 95; range: up to $1,500,000; average assistance: $50,725
Application Information: Applications are filed with nearest available SBA disaster area or special disaster office.
Deadline: Established for each declaration of disaster.

Contact: Small Business Administration, Region X
          2615 Fourth Avenue
          Room 440
          Seattle, WA 98121
          (206) 442-5676

ILLINOIS

EMPLOYMENT SERVICE

United States Employment Service
Employment and Training Administration, Department of Labor
Washington, DC 20210
(202) 219-5257

Description: Provides placement services for job seekers and
employers. These include services to special applicant groups, such
as veterans, the handicapped, youth, minorities, and older workers;
a computerized interstate job listing; and other labor market
information.
$ Given: $847,220,000 est. FY 95
Application Information: Contact your state office.
Deadline: Established each year (contact federal agency for deadline
for application submission).
Contact: Sally A. Jackson, Director
          Bureau of Employment Security
          401 South State Street
          Suite 615 South
          Chicago, IL 60605
          (312) 793-5700

UNEMPLOYMENT INSURANCE

Unemployment Insurance Service
Employment and Training Administration, Department of Labor
Washington, DC 20210
(202) 219-7831

Description: Provides unemployment insurance for workers whose
employers have contributed to state unemployment funds, federal
civilian employees, ex–service persons, those who have become
unemployed as a result of product imports, and those whose

unemployment comes under the purview of a presidentially declared disaster.

$ Given: $23.7 billion est. FY 95

Application Information: Contact the Employment Security Department for your state.

Deadline: Not available

Contact: Sally A. Jackson, Director
Bureau of Employment Security
401 South State Street
Suite 615 South
Chicago, IL 60605
(312) 793-5700

EMPLOYMENT AND TRAINING ASSISTANCE— DISLOCATED WORKERS

Employment and Training Administration, Department of Labor
200 Constitution Avenue, NW
Washington, DC 20210
(202) 219-5577

Description: Federal grants given to state and local programs to assist workers through training and employment services. These are workers who have been terminated or laid off or received notice of such and are not likely to return to their previous occupation or industry or who are long-term unemployed. Targeted individuals include those affected by mass layoffs and natural disasters.

$ Given: $571.1 million total nationwide for FY 93

Application Information: Inquire at Employment Security office listed below.

Deadline: Not available

Contact: Sally A. Jackson, Director
Bureau of Employment Security
401 South State Street
Suite 615 South
Chicago, IL 60605
(312) 793-5700

WOMEN'S SPECIAL EMPLOYMENT ASSISTANCE

Office of Administrative Management
Women's Bureau
Office of the Secretary
Department of Labor
Washington, DC 20210
(202) 219-6611

Description: Makes referrals as to sources for counseling and disseminates technical information to aid in the employment of women—especially in the realm of nontraditional women's jobs and jobs in new technologies.
$ Given: $8,054,000 est. FY 95
Application Information: Write to Women's Bureau in your region.
Deadline: None
Contact: Sandra K. Frank, Regional Administrator
              Region V, Women's Bureau
              Department of Labor
              230 South Dearborn Street
              Room 1022
              Chicago, IL 60604
              (312) 353-6985

EMERGENCY LOANS

Farmers Home Administration
Department of Agriculture
14th Street and Independence Avenue, SW
Washington, DC 20250
(202) 720-1632

Description: Provides loans to family farmers (either owner or tenant), ranchers, and aquaculture operators to cover losses resulting from natural or other major disasters. Recipients must be unable to obtain credit from other sources.
$ Given: $180 million est. FY 95; average range: $500–$500,000; average assistance: $66,200
Application Information: Consult local telephone directory under United States Government, Department of Agriculture, for Farmers Home Administration office.
Deadline: Not available

Contact: Farmers Home Administration
            Illini Plaza
            Suite 103
            1817 South Neil Street
            Champaign, IL 61820
            (217) 398-5235

ECONOMIC INJURY DISASTER LOANS

Office of Disaster Assistance
Small Business Administration (SBA)
409 Third Street, SW
Washington, DC 20416
(202) 205-6734

Description: Provides direct loans to small businesses suffering economic damage under Small Business Administration, Department of Agriculture, and/or presidentially declared disaster. Must be a small business or agricultural concern, located within declared disaster area and unable to obtain credit elsewhere.
$ Given: $78,209,000 est. FY 95; range: up to $1,500,000; average assistance: $50,725
Application Information: Applications are filed with nearest available SBA disaster area or special disaster office.
Deadline: Established for each declaration of disaster.
Contact: Small Business Administration, Region V
            Federal Building
            300 South Riverside Plaza
            Room 1975
            Chicago, IL 60606-6611
            (312) 353-0359

INDIANA

EMPLOYMENT SERVICE

United States Employment Service
Employment and Training Administration, Department of Labor
Washington, DC 20210
(202) 219-5257

Description: Provides placement services for job seekers and employers. These include services to special applicant groups, such

as veterans, the handicapped, youth, minorities, and older workers;
a computerized interstate job listing; and other labor market
information.
$ Given: $847,220,000 est. FY 95
Application Information: Contact your state office.
Deadline: Established each year (contact federal agency for deadline
for application submission).
Contact: Bruce Kimery, Acting Commissioner
          Indiana Department of Workforce Development
          10 North Senate Avenue
          Indianapolis, IN 46204
          (317) 233-5661
          Fax: (317) 232-6950

UNEMPLOYMENT INSURANCE

Unemployment Insurance Service
Employment and Training Administration, Department of Labor
Washington, DC 20210
(202) 219-7831

Description: Provides unemployment insurance for workers whose
employers have contributed to state unemployment funds, federal
civilian employees, ex–service persons, those who have become
unemployed as a result of product imports, and those whose
unemployment comes under the purview of a presidentially declared
disaster.
$ Given: $23.7 billion est. FY 95
Application Information: Contact the Employment Security Department for your state.
Deadline: Not available
Contact: Bruce Kimery, Acting Commissioner
          Indiana Department of Workforce Development
          10 North Senate Avenue
          Indianapolis, IN 46204
          (317) 233-5661
          Fax: (317) 232-6950

EMPLOYMENT AND TRAINING ASSISTANCE— DISLOCATED WORKERS

Employment and Training Administration, Department of Labor
200 Constitution Avenue, NW
Washington, DC 20210
(202) 219-5577

Description: Federal grants given to state and local programs to assist workers through training and employment services. These are workers who have been terminated or laid off or received notice of such and are not likely to return to their previous occupation or industry or who are long-term unemployed. Targeted individuals include those affected by mass layoffs and natural disasters.
$ Given: $571.1 million total nationwide for FY 93
Application Information: Inquire at Employment Security office listed below.
Deadline: Not available
Contact: Bruce Kimery, Acting Commissioner
             Indiana Department of Workforce Development
             10 North Senate Avenue
             Indianapolis, IN 46204
             (317) 233-5661
             Fax: (317) 232-6950

WOMEN'S SPECIAL EMPLOYMENT ASSISTANCE

Office of Administrative Management
Women's Bureau
Office of the Secretary
Department of Labor
Washington, DC 20210
(202) 219-6611

Description: Makes referrals as to sources for counseling and disseminates technical information to aid in the employment of women—especially in the realm of nontraditional women's jobs and jobs in new technologies.
$ Given: $8,054,000 est. FY 95
Application Information: Write to Women's Bureau in your region.
Deadline: None

Contact: Sandra K. Frank, Regional Administrator
Region V, Women's Bureau
Department of Labor
230 South Dearborn Street
Room 1022
Chicago, IL 60604
(312) 353-6985

EMERGENCY LOANS

Farmers Home Administration
Department of Agriculture
14th Street and Independence Avenue, SW
Washington, DC 20250
(202) 720-1632

Description: Provides loans to family farmers (either owner or
tenant), ranchers, and aquaculture operators to cover losses resulting from natural or other major disasters. Recipients must be
unable to obtain credit from other sources.
$ Given: $180 million est. FY 95; average range: $500–$500,000;
average assistance: $66,200
Application Information: Consult local telephone directory under
United States Government, Department of Agriculture, for Farmers
Home Administration office.
Deadline: Not available
Contact: Farmers Home Administration
5975 Lakeside Boulevard
Indianapolis, IN 46278
(317) 290-3100

ECONOMIC INJURY DISASTER LOANS

Office of Disaster Assistance
Small Business Administration (SBA)
409 Third Street, SW
Washington, DC 20416
(202) 205-6734

Description: Provides direct loans to small businesses suffering
economic damage under Small Business Administration, Department of Agriculture, and/or presidentially declared disaster. Must be
a small business or agricultural concern, located within declared

disaster area and unable to obtain credit elsewhere.
$ Given: $78,209,000 est. FY 95; range: up to $1,500,000; average
assistance: $50,725
Application Information: Applications are filed with nearest
available SBA disaster area or special disaster office.
Deadline: Established for each declaration of disaster.
Contact: Small Business Administration, Region V
             Federal Building
             300 South Riverside Plaza
             Room 1975
             Chicago, IL 60606-6611
             (312) 353-0359

IOWA

EMPLOYMENT SERVICE

United States Employment Service
Employment and Training Administration, Department of Labor
Washington, DC 20210
(202) 219-5257

Description: Provides placement services for job seekers and
employers. These include services to special applicant groups, such
as veterans, the handicapped, youth, minorities, and older workers;
a computerized interstate job listing; and other labor market
information.
$ Given: $847,220,000 est. FY 95
Application Information: Contact your state office.
Deadline: Established each year (contact federal agency for deadline
for application submission).
Contact: Cynthia P. Eisenhower, Director
             Job Service of Iowa
             Iowa Department of Employment Services
             1000 East Grand Avenue
             Des Moines, IA 50319
             (515) 281-5361
             Fax: (515) 242-5144

UNEMPLOYMENT INSURANCE

Unemployment Insurance Service
Employment and Training Administration, Department of Labor
Washington, DC 20210
(202) 219-7831

Description: Provides unemployment insurance for workers whose
employers have contributed to state unemployment funds, federal
civilian employees, ex–service persons, those who have become
unemployed as a result of product imports, and those whose
unemployment comes under the purview of a presidentially declared
disaster.
$ Given: $23.7 billion est. FY 95
Application Information: Contact the Employment Security Department for your state.
Deadline: Not available
Contact: Cynthia P. Eisenhower, Director
            Job Service of Iowa
            Iowa Department of Employment Services
            1000 East Grand Avenue
            Des Moines, IA 50319
            (515) 281-5361
            Fax: (515) 242-5144

EMPLOYMENT AND TRAINING ASSISTANCE— DISLOCATED WORKERS

Employment and Training Administration, Department of Labor
200 Constitution Avenue, NW
Washington, DC 20210
(202) 219-5577

Description: Federal grants given to state and local programs to
assist workers through training and employment services. These are
workers who have been terminated or laid off or received notice of
such and are not likely to return to their previous occupation or
industry or who are long-term unemployed. Targeted individuals
include those affected by mass layoffs and natural disasters.
$ Given: $571.1 million total nationwide for FY 93
Application Information: Inquire at Employment Security office
listed below.
Deadline: Not available

Contact: Cynthia P. Eisenhower, Director
           Job Service of Iowa
           Iowa Department of Employment Services
           1000 East Grand Avenue
           Des Moines, IA 50319
           (515) 281-5361
           Fax: (515) 242-5144

WOMEN'S SPECIAL EMPLOYMENT ASSISTANCE

Office of Administrative Management
Women's Bureau
Office of the Secretary
Department of Labor
Washington, DC 20210
(202) 219-6611

Description: Makes referrals as to sources for counseling and disseminates technical information to aid in the employment of women—especially in the realm of nontraditional women's jobs and jobs in new technologies.
$ Given: $8,054,000 est. FY 95
Application Information: Write to Women's Bureau in your region.
Deadline: None
Contact: Rose A. Kemp, Regional Administrator
           Region VII, Women's Bureau
           Department of Labor
           Federal Building
           Room 2511
           911 Walnut Street
           Kansas City, MO 64106
           (816) 426-6108

EMERGENCY LOANS

Farmers Home Administration
Department of Agriculture
14th Street and Independence Avenue, SW
Washington, DC 20250
(202) 720-1632

Description: Provides loans to family farmers (either owner or tenant), ranchers, and aquaculture operators to cover losses result-

ing from natural or other major disasters. Recipients must be
unable to obtain credit from other sources.
$ Given: $180 million est. FY 95; average range: $500–$500,000;
average assistance: $66,200
Application Information: Consult local telephone directory under
United States Government, Department of Agriculture, for Farmers
Home Administration office.
Deadline: Not available
Contact: Farmers Home Administration
            Federal Building
            Room 873
            210 Walnut Street
            13th floor
            Des Moines, IA 50309
            (515) 284-4663

ECONOMIC INJURY DISASTER LOANS

Office of Disaster Assistance
Small Business Administration (SBA)
409 Third Street, SW
Washington, DC 20416
(202) 205-6734

Description: Provides direct loans to small businesses suffering
economic damage under Small Business Administration, Department of Agriculture, and/or presidentially declared disaster. Must be
a small business or agricultural concern, located within declared
disaster area and unable to obtain credit elsewhere.
$ Given: $78,209,000 est. FY 95; range: up to $1,500,000; average
assistance: $50,725
Application Information: Applications are filed with nearest
available SBA disaster area or special disaster office.
Deadline: Established for each declaration of disaster.
Contact: Small Business Administration, Region VII
            911 Walnut Street
            13th Floor
            Kansas City, MO 64106
            (816) 426-3609

KANSAS

EMPLOYMENT SERVICE

United States Employment Service
Employment and Training Administration, Department of Labor
Washington, DC 20210
(202) 219-5257

Description: Provides placement services for job seekers and employers. These include services to special applicant groups, such as veterans, the handicapped, youth, minorities, and older workers; a computerized interstate job listing; and other labor market information.
$ Given: $847,220,000 est. FY 95
Application Information: Contact your state office.
Deadline: Established each year (contact federal agency for deadline for application submission).
Contact: Joe Dick, Secretary
            Department of Human Resources
            401 SW Topeka Avenue
            Topeka, KS 66603
            (913) 296-7474
            Fax: (913) 296-0179

UNEMPLOYMENT INSURANCE

Unemployment Insurance Service
Employment and Training Administration, Department of Labor
Washington, DC 20210
(202) 219-7831

Description: Provides unemployment insurance for workers whose employers have contributed to state unemployment funds, federal civilian employees, ex–service persons, those who have become unemployed as a result of product imports, and those whose unemployment comes under the purview of a presidentially declared disaster.
$ Given: $23.7 billion est. FY 95
Application Information: Contact the Employment Security Department for your state.
Deadline: Not available

Contact: Joe Dick, Secretary
          Department of Human Resources
          401 SW Topeka Avenue
          Topeka, KS 66603
          (913) 296-7474
          Fax: (913) 296-0179

EMPLOYMENT AND TRAINING ASSISTANCE—DISLOCATED WORKERS

Employment and Training Administration, Department of Labor
200 Constitution Avenue, NW
Washington, DC 20210
(202) 219-5577

Description: Federal grants given to state and local programs to assist workers through training and employment services. These are workers who have been terminated or laid off or received notice of such and are not likely to return to their previous occupation or industry or who are long-term unemployed. Targeted individuals include those affected by mass layoffs and natural disasters.
$ Given: $571.1 million total nationwide for FY 93
Application Information: Inquire at Employment Security office listed below.
Deadline: Not available
Contact: Joe Dick, Secretary
          Department of Human Resources
          401 SW Topeka Avenue
          Topeka, KS 66603
          (913) 296-7474
          Fax: (913) 296-0179

WOMEN'S SPECIAL EMPLOYMENT ASSISTANCE

Office of Administrative Management
Women's Bureau
Office of the Secretary
Department of Labor
Washington, DC 20210
(202) 219-6611

Description: Makes referrals as to sources for counseling and disseminates technical information to aid in the employment of women—especially in the realm of nontraditional women's jobs and jobs in new technologies.

$ **Given:** $8,054,000 est. FY 95
Application Information: Write to Women's Bureau in your region.
Deadline: None
Contact: Rose A. Kemp, Regional Administrator
          Region VII, Women's Bureau
          Department of Labor
          Federal Building
          Room 2511
          911 Walnut Street
          Kansas City, MO 64106
          (816) 426-6108

EMERGENCY LOANS

Farmers Home Administration
Department of Agriculture
14th Street and Independence Avenue, SW
Washington, DC 20250
(202) 720-1632

Description: Provides loans to family farmers (either owner or tenant), ranchers, and aquaculture operators to cover losses resulting from natural or other major disasters. Recipients must be unable to obtain credit from other sources.
$ **Given:** $180 million est. FY 95; average range: $500–$500,000; average assistance: $66,200
Application Information: Consult local telephone directory under United States Government, Department of Agriculture, for Farmers Home Administration office.
Deadline: Not available
Contact: Farmers Home Administration
          1201 SW Summit Executive Court
          P.O. Box 4653
          Topeka, KS 66604
          (913) 271-7300

ECONOMIC INJURY DISASTER LOANS

Office of Disaster Assistance
Small Business Administration (SBA)
409 Third Street, SW
Washington, DC 20416
(202) 205-6734

Description: Provides direct loans to small businesses suffering economic damage under Small Business Administration, Department of Agriculture, and/or presidentially declared disaster. Must be a small business or agricultural concern, located within declared disaster area and unable to obtain credit elsewhere.
$ Given: $78,209,000 est. FY 95; range: up to $1,500,000; average assistance: $50,725
Application Information: Applications are filed with nearest available SBA disaster area or special disaster office.
Deadline: Established for each declaration of disaster.
Contact: Small Business Administration, Region VII
              911 Walnut Street
              13th Floor
              Kansas City, MO 64106
              (816) 426-3609

KENTUCKY

EMPLOYMENT SERVICE

United States Employment Service
Employment and Training Administration, Department of Labor
Washington, DC 20210
(202) 219-5257

Description: Provides placement services for job seekers and employers. These include services to special applicant groups, such as veterans, the handicapped, youth, minorities, and older workers; a computerized interstate job listing; and other labor market information.
$ Given: $847,220,000 est. FY 95
Application Information: Contact your state office.
Deadline: Established each year (contact federal agency for deadline for application submission).
Contact: Masten Childers II, Secretary
              Cabinet for Human Resources
              275 East Main Street
              Second Floor West
              Frankfort, KY 40621
              (502) 564-7130
              Fax: (502) 564-7452

UNEMPLOYMENT INSURANCE

Unemployment Insurance Service
Employment and Training Administration, Department of Labor
Washington, DC 20210
(202) 219-7831

Description: Provides unemployment insurance for workers whose employers have contributed to state unemployment funds, federal civilian employees, ex–service persons, those who have become unemployed as a result of product imports, and those whose unemployment comes under the purview of a presidentially declared disaster.
$ Given: $23.7 billion est. FY 95
Application Information: Contact the Employment Security Department for your state.
Deadline: Not available
Contact: Masten Childers II, Secretary
Cabinet for Human Resources
275 East Main Street
Second Floor West
Frankfort, KY 40621
(502) 564-7130
Fax: (502) 564-7452

EMPLOYMENT AND TRAINING ASSISTANCE— DISLOCATED WORKERS

Employment and Training Administration, Department of Labor
200 Constitution Avenue, NW
Washington, DC 20210
(202) 219-5577

Description: Federal grants given to state and local programs to assist workers through training and employment services. These are workers who have been terminated or laid off or received notice of such and are not likely to return to their previous occupation or industry or who are long-term unemployed. Targeted individuals include those affected by mass layoffs and natural disasters.
$ Given: $571.1 million total nationwide for FY 93
Application Information: Inquire at Employment Security office listed below.
Deadline: Not available

Contact: Masten Childers II, Secretary
          Cabinet for Human Resources
          275 East Main Street
          Second Floor West
          Frankfort, KY 40621
          (502) 564-7130
          Fax: (502) 564-7452

WOMEN'S SPECIAL EMPLOYMENT ASSISTANCE

Office of Administrative Management
Women's Bureau
Office of the Secretary
Department of Labor
Washington, DC 20210
(202) 219-6611

Description: Makes referrals as to sources for counseling and
disseminates technical information to aid in the employment of
women—especially in the realm of nontraditional women's jobs and
jobs in new technologies.
$ Given: $8,054,000 est. FY 95
Application Information: Write to Women's Bureau in your region.
Deadline: None
Contact: Delores L. Crockett, Regional Administrator
          Region IV, Women's Bureau
          Department of Labor
          1371 Peachtree Street, NE
          Room 323
          Atlanta, GA 30367
          (404) 347-4461

EMERGENCY LOANS

Farmers Home Administration
Department of Agriculture
14th Street and Independence Avenue, SW
Washington, DC 20250
(202) 720-1632

Description: Provides loans to family farmers (either owner or
tenant), ranchers, and aquaculture operators to cover losses resulting from natural or other major disasters. Recipients must be
unable to obtain credit from other sources.

$ Given: $180 million est. FY 95; average range: $500-$500,000; average assistance: $66,200

Application Information: Consult local telephone directory under United States Government, Department of Agriculture, for Farmers Home Administration office.

Deadline: Not available

Contact: Farmers Home Administration
771 Corporate Plaza
Suite 200
Lexington, KY 4503
(606) 224-7300

ECONOMIC INJURY DISASTER LOANS

Office of Disaster Assistance
Small Business Administration (SBA)
409 Third Street, SW
Washington, DC 20416
(202) 205-6734

Description: Provides direct loans to small businesses suffering economic damage under Small Business Administration, Department of Agriculture, and/or presidentially declared disaster. Must be a small business or agricultural concern, located within declared disaster area and unable to obtain credit elsewhere.

$ Given: $78,209,000 est. FY 95; range: up to $1,500,000; average assistance: $50,725

Application Information: Applications are filed with nearest available SBA disaster area or special disaster office.

Deadline: Established for each declaration of disaster.

Contact: Small Business Administration, Region VII
1375 Peachtree Street, NE
Fifth Floor
Atlanta, GA 30367-8102
(404) 347-2797

LOUISIANA

EMPLOYMENT SERVICE

United States Employment Service
Employment and Training Administration, Department of Labor
Washington, DC 20210
(202) 219-5257

Description: Provides placement services for job seekers and employers. These include services to special applicant groups, such as veterans, the handicapped, youth, minorities, and older workers; a computerized interstate job listing; and other labor market information.
$ Given: $847,220,000 est. FY 95
Application Information: Contact your state office.
Deadline: Established each year (contact federal agency for deadline for application submission).
Contact: Joseph R. Gerace, Assistant Secretary
           Louisiana Department of Labor
           Office of Employment Security
           Employment Security Building
           1001 North 23rd Street
           P.O. Box 94094
           Capitol Station
           Baton Rouge, LA 70804-9094
           (504) 342-3013
           Fax: (504) 342-3778

UNEMPLOYMENT INSURANCE

Unemployment Insurance Service
Employment and Training Administration, Department of Labor
Washington, DC 20210
(202) 219-7831

Description: Provides unemployment insurance for workers whose employers have contributed to state unemployment funds, federal civilian employees, ex–service persons, those who have become unemployed as a result of product imports, and those whose unemployment comes under the purview of a presidentially declared disaster.
$ Given: $23.7 billion est. FY 95

Application Information: Contact the Employment Security Department for your state.
Deadline: Not available
Contact: Joseph R. Gerace, Assistant Secretary
Louisiana Department of Labor
Office of Employment Security
Employment Security Building
1001 North 23rd Street
P.O. Box 94094
Capitol Station
Baton Rouge, LA 70804-9094
(504) 342-3013
Fax: (504) 342-3778

EMPLOYMENT AND TRAINING ASSISTANCE— DISLOCATED WORKERS

Employment and Training Administration, Department of Labor
200 Constitution Avenue, NW
Washington, DC 20210
(202) 219-5577

Description: Federal grants given to state and local programs to assist workers through training and employment services. These are workers who have been terminated or laid off or received notice of such and are not likely to return to their previous occupation or industry or who are long-term unemployed. Targeted individuals include those affected by mass layoffs and natural disasters.
$ Given: $571.1 million total nationwide for FY 93
Application Information: Inquire at Employment Security office listed below.
Deadline: Not available
Contact: Joseph R. Gerace, Assistant Secretary
Louisiana Department of Labor
Office of Employment Security
Employment Security Building
1001 North 23rd Street
P.O. Box 94094
Capitol Station
Baton Rouge, LA 70804-9094
(504) 342-3013
Fax: (504) 342-3778

WOMEN'S SPECIAL EMPLOYMENT ASSISTANCE

Office of Administrative Management
Women's Bureau
Office of the Secretary
Department of Labor
Washington, DC 20210
(202) 219-6611

Description: Makes referrals as to sources for counseling and
disseminates technical information to aid in the employment of
women—especially in the realm of nontraditional women's jobs and
jobs in new technologies.
$ Given: $8,054,000 est. FY 95
Application Information: Write to Women's Bureau in your region.
Deadline: None
Contact: Evelyn Smith, Regional Administrator
                Region VI, Women's Bureau
                Department of Labor
                Federal Building
                Suite 731
                Griffin Street
                Dallas, TX 75202
                (214) 767-6985

EMERGENCY LOANS

Farmers Home Administration
Department of Agriculture
14th Street and Independence Avenue, SW
Washington, DC 20250
(202) 720-1632

Description: Provides loans to family farmers (either owner or
tenant), ranchers, and aquaculture operators to cover losses resulting from natural or other major disasters. Recipients must be
unable to obtain credit from other sources.
$ Given: $180 million est. FY 95; average range: $500–$500,000;
average assistance: $66,200
Application Information: Consult local telephone directory under
United States Government, Department of Agriculture, for Farmers
Home Administration office.
Deadline: Not available

Contact: Farmers Home Administration
          3727 Government Street
          Alexandria, LA 71302
          (318) 473-7920

ECONOMIC INJURY DISASTER LOANS

Office of Disaster Assistance
Small Business Administration (SBA)
409 Third Street, SW
Washington, DC 20416
(202) 205-6734

Description: Provides direct loans to small businesses suffering
economic damage under Small Business Administration, Department of Agriculture, and/or presidentially declared disaster. Must be
a small business or agricultural concern, located within declared
disaster area and unable to obtain credit elsewhere.
$ Given: $78,209,000 est. FY 95; range: up to $1,500,000; average
assistance: $50,725
Application Information: Applications are filed with nearest
available SBA disaster area or special disaster office.
Deadline: Established for each declaration of disaster.
Contact: Small Business Administration, Region VI
          8625 King George Drive
          Building C
          Dallas, TX 75235-3391
          (214) 767-7633

MAINE

EMPLOYMENT SERVICE

United States Employment Service
Employment and Training Administration, Department of Labor
Washington, DC 20210
(202) 219-5257

Description: Provides placement services for job seekers and
employers. These include services to special applicant groups, such
as veterans, the handicapped, youth, minorities, and older workers;
a computerized interstate job listing; and other labor market
information.

$ **Given:** $847,220,000 est. FY 95
Application Information: Contact your state office.
Deadline: Established each year (contact federal agency for deadline for application submission).
Contact: Charles Morrison, Commissioner
               Department of Labor
               20 Union Street
               P.O. Box 309
               Augusta, ME 04330
               (207) 287-3788
               Fax: (207) 287-5292

UNEMPLOYMENT INSURANCE

Unemployment Insurance Service
Employment and Training Administration, Department of Labor
Washington, DC 20210
(202) 219-7831

Description: Provides unemployment insurance for workers whose employers have contributed to state unemployment funds, federal civilian employees, ex–service persons, those who have become unemployed as a result of product imports, and those whose unemployment comes under the purview of a presidentially declared disaster.
$ **Given:** $23.7 billion est. FY 95
Application Information: Contact the Employment Security Department for your state.
Deadline: Not available
Contact: Charles Morrison, Commissioner
               Department of Labor
               20 Union Street
               P.O. Box 309
               Augusta, ME 04330
               (207) 287-3788
               Fax: (207) 287-5292

EMPLOYMENT AND TRAINING ASSISTANCE— DISLOCATED WORKERS

Employment and Training Administration, Department of Labor
200 Constitution Avenue, NW
Washington, DC 20210
(202) 219-5577

Description: Federal grants given to state and local programs to assist workers through training and employment services. These are workers who have been terminated or laid off or received notice of such and are not likely to return to their previous occupation or industry or who are long-term unemployed. Targeted individuals include those affected by mass layoffs and natural disasters.
$ Given: $571.1 million total nationwide for FY 93
Application Information: Inquire at Employment Security office listed below.
Deadline: Not available
Contact: Charles Morrison, Commissioner
                 Department of Labor
                 20 Union Street
                 P.O. Box 309
                 Augusta, ME 04330
                 (207) 287-3788
                 Fax: (207) 287-5292

WOMEN'S SPECIAL EMPLOYMENT ASSISTANCE

Office of Administrative Management
Women's Bureau
Office of the Secretary
Department of Labor
Washington, DC 20210
(202) 219-6611

Description: Makes referrals as to sources for counseling and disseminates technical information to aid in the employment of women—especially in the realm of nontraditional women's jobs and jobs in new technologies.
$ Given: $8,054,000 est. FY 95
Application Information: Write to Women's Bureau in your region.
Deadline: None
Contact: Martha Izzi, Regional Administrator
                 Region I, Women's Bureau
                 Department of Labor
                 One Congress Street
                 Boston, MA 02214
                 (617) 565-1988

EMERGENCY LOANS

Farmers Home Administration
Department of Agriculture
14th Street and Independence Avenue, SW
Washington, DC 20250
(202) 720-1632

Description: Provides loans to family farmers (either owner or tenant), ranchers, and aquaculture operators to cover losses resulting from natural or other major disasters. Recipients must be unable to obtain credit from other sources.
$ Given: $180 million est. FY 95; average range: $500–$500,000; average assistance: $66,200
Application Information: Consult local telephone directory under United States Government, Department of Agriculture, for Farmers Home Administration office.
Deadline: Not available
Contact: Farmers Home Administration
                444 Stillwater Avenue
                Suite 2
                P.O. Box 405
                Bangor, ME 04402-0405
                (207) 990-9106

ECONOMIC INJURY DISASTER LOANS

Office of Disaster Assistance
Small Business Administration (SBA)
409 Third Street, SW
Washington, DC 20416
(202) 205-6734

Description: Provides direct loans to small businesses suffering economic damage under Small Business Administration, Department of Agriculture, and/or presidentially declared disaster. Must be a small business or agricultural concern, located within declared disaster area and unable to obtain credit elsewhere.
$ Given: $78,209,000 est. FY 95; range: up to $1,500,000; average assistance: $50,725
Application Information: Applications are filed with nearest available SBA disaster area or special disaster office.
Deadline: Established for each declaration of disaster.

Contact: Small Business Administration, Region I
           155 Federal Street
           Ninth Floor
           Boston, MA 02110
           (617) 451-2023

MARYLAND

EMPLOYMENT SERVICE

United States Employment Service
Employment and Training Administration, Department of Labor
Washington, DC 20210
(202) 219-5257

Description: Provides placement services for job seekers and
employers. These include services to special applicant groups, such
as veterans, the handicapped, youth, minorities, and older workers;
a computerized interstate job listing; and other labor market
information.
$ Given: $847,220,000 est. FY 95
Application Information: Contact your state office.
Deadline: Established each year (contact federal agency for deadline
for application submission).
Contact: Charles O. Middlebrooks, Assistant Secretary
           Division of Employment and Training
           Department of Economic and Employment Development
           State Office Building
           1100 North Eutaw Street
           Room 600
           Baltimore, MD 21201
           (410) 333-5070
           Fax: (410) 333-5608

UNEMPLOYMENT INSURANCE

Unemployment Insurance Service
Employment and Training Administration, Department of Labor
Washington, DC 20210
(202) 219-7831

Description: Provides unemployment insurance for workers whose
employers have contributed to state unemployment funds, federal
civilian employees, ex–service persons, those who have become

unemployed as a result of product imports, and those whose unemployment comes under the purview of a presidentially declared disaster.
$ Given: $23.7 billion est. FY 95
Application Information: Contact the Employment Security Department for your state.
Deadline: Not available
Contact: Charles O. Middlebrooks, Assistant Secretary
         Division of Employment and Training
         Department of Economic and Employment Development
         State Office Building
         1100 North Eutaw Street
         Room 600
         Baltimore, MD 21201
         (410) 333-5070
         Fax: (410) 333-5608

EMPLOYMENT AND TRAINING ASSISTANCE— DISLOCATED WORKERS

Employment and Training Administration, Department of Labor
200 Constitution Avenue, NW
Washington, DC 20210
(202) 219-5577

Description: Federal grants given to state and local programs to assist workers through training and employment services. These are workers who have been terminated or laid off or received notice of such and are not likely to return to their previous occupation or industry or who are long-term unemployed. Targeted individuals include those affected by mass layoffs and natural disasters.
$ Given: $571.1 million total nationwide for FY 93
Application Information: Inquire at Employment Security office listed below.
Deadline: Not available
Contact: Charles O. Middlebrooks, Assistant Secretary
         Division of Employment and Training
         Department of Economic and Employment Development
         State Office Building
         1100 North Eutaw Street
         Room 600
         Baltimore, MD 21201
         (410) 333-5070
         Fax: (410) 333-5608

WOMEN'S SPECIAL EMPLOYMENT ASSISTANCE

Office of Administrative Management
Women's Bureau
Office of the Secretary
Department of Labor
Washington, DC 20210
(202) 219-6611

Description: Makes referrals as to sources for counseling and
disseminates technical information to aid in the employment of
women—especially in the realm of nontraditional women's jobs and
jobs in new technologies.
$ Given: $8,054,000 est. FY 95
Application Information: Write to Women's Bureau in your region.
Deadline: None
Contact: Regional Administrator
              Region III, Women's Bureau
              Department of Labor
              Gateway Building
              Room 13280
              3535 Market Street
              Philadelphia, PA 19104
              (215) 596-1184

EMERGENCY LOANS

Farmers Home Administration
Department of Agriculture
14th Street and Independence Avenue, SW
Washington, DC 20250
(202) 720-1632

Description: Provides loans to family farmers (either owner or
tenant), ranchers, and aquaculture operators to cover losses resulting from natural or other major disasters. Recipients must be
unable to obtain credit from other sources.
$ Given: $180 million est. FY 95; average range: $500–$500,000;
average assistance: $66,200
Application Information: Consult local telephone directory under
United States Government, Department of Agriculture, for Farmers
Home Administration office.
Deadline: Not available

Contact: Farmers Home Administration
           4611 South Dupont Highway
           P.O. Box 400
           Camden, DE 19934-9998
           (302) 697-4300

ECONOMIC INJURY DISASTER LOANS

Office of Disaster Assistance
Small Business Administration (SBA)
409 Third Street, SW
Washington, DC 20416
(202) 205-6734

Description: Provides direct loans to small businesses suffering
economic damage under Small Business Administration, Department of Agriculture, and/or presidentially declared disaster. Must be
a small business or agricultural concern, located within declared
disaster area and unable to obtain credit elsewhere.
$ Given: $78,209,000 est. FY 95; range: up to $1,500,000; average
assistance: $50,725
Application Information: Applications are filed with nearest
available SBA disaster area or special disaster office.
Deadline: Established for each declaration of disaster.
Contact: Small Business Administration, Region III
           475 Allendale Road
           Suite 201
           King of Prussia, PA 19406
           (215) 962-3700

MASSACHUSETTS

EMPLOYMENT SERVICE

United States Employment Service
Employment and Training Administration, Department of Labor
Washington, DC 20210
(202) 219-5257

Description: Provides placement services for job seekers and
employers. These include services to special applicant groups, such

as veterans, the handicapped, youth, minorities, and older workers;
a computerized interstate job listing; and other labor market
information.

$ Given: $847,220,000 est. FY 95

Application Information: Contact your state office.

Deadline: Established each year (contact federal agency for deadline
for application submission).

Contact: Nils L. Nordberg, Commissioner
Department of Employment and Training
Charles F. Hurley Building
Third Floor
Government Center
Boston, MA 02114
(617) 626-6600
Fax: (617) 626-0315

UNEMPLOYMENT INSURANCE

Unemployment Insurance Service
Employment and Training Administration, Department of Labor
Washington, DC 20210
(202) 219-7831

Description: Provides unemployment insurance for workers whose
employers have contributed to state unemployment funds, federal
civilian employees, ex–service persons, those who have become
unemployed as a result of product imports, and those whose
unemployment comes under the purview of a presidentially declared
disaster.

$ Given: $23.7 billion est. FY 95

Application Information: Contact the Employment Security Department for your state.

Deadline: Not available

Contact: Nils L. Nordberg, Commissioner
Department of Employment and Training
Charles F. Hurley Building
Third Floor
Government Center
Boston, MA 02114
(617) 626-6600
Fax: (617) 626-0315

EMPLOYMENT AND TRAINING ASSISTANCE— DISLOCATED WORKERS

Employment and Training Administration, Department of Labor
200 Constitution Avenue, NW
Washington, DC 20210
(202) 219-5577

Description: Federal grants given to state and local programs to assist workers through training and employment services. These are workers who have been terminated or laid off or received notice of such and are not likely to return to their previous occupation or industry or who are long-term unemployed. Targeted individuals include those affected by mass layoffs and natural disasters.
$ Given: $571.1 million total nationwide for FY 93
Application Information: Inquire at Employment Security office listed below.
Deadline: Not available
Contact: Nils L. Nordberg, Commissioner
Department of Employment and Training
Charles F. Hurley Building
Third Floor
Government Center
Boston, MA 02114
(617) 626-6600
Fax: (617) 626-0315

WOMEN'S SPECIAL EMPLOYMENT ASSISTANCE

Office of Administrative Management
Women's Bureau
Office of the Secretary
Department of Labor
Washington, DC 20210
(202) 219-6611

Description: Makes referrals as to sources for counseling and disseminates technical information to aid in the employment of women—especially in the realm of nontraditional women's jobs and jobs in new technologies.
$ Given: $8,054,000 est. FY 95
Application Information: Write to Women's Bureau in your region.
Deadline: None

Contact: Martha Izzi, Regional Administrator
          Region I, Women's Bureau
          Department of Labor
          One Congress Street
          Boston, MA 02214
          (617) 565-1988

EMERGENCY LOANS

Farmers Home Administration
Department of Agriculture
14th Street and Independence Avenue, SW
Washington, DC 20250
(202) 720-1632

Description: Provides loans to family farmers (either owner or
tenant), ranchers, and aquaculture operators to cover losses resulting from natural or other major disasters. Recipients must be
unable to obtain credit from other sources.
$ Given: $180 million est. FY 95; average range: $500–$500,000;
average assistance: $66,200
Application Information: Consult local telephone directory under
United States Government, Department of Agriculture, for Farmers
Home Administration office.
Deadline: Not available
Contact: Farmers Home Administration
          451 West Street
          Amherst, MA 01002
          (413) 253-4300

ECONOMIC INJURY DISASTER LOANS

Office of Disaster Assistance
Small Business Administration (SBA)
409 Third Street, SW
Washington, DC 20416
(202) 205-6734

Description: Provides direct loans to small businesses suffering
economic damage under Small Business Administration, Department of Agriculture, and/or presidentially declared disaster. Must be
a small business or agricultural concern, located within declared
disaster area and unable to obtain credit elsewhere.

$ Given: $78,209,000 est. FY 95; range: up to $1,500,000; average assistance: $50,725
Application Information: Applications are filed with nearest available SBA disaster area or special disaster office.
Deadline: Established for each declaration of disaster.
Contact: Small Business Administration, Region I
155 Federal Street
Ninth Floor
Boston, MA 02110
(617) 451-2023

MICHIGAN

EMPLOYMENT SERVICE

United States Employment Service
Employment and Training Administration, Department of Labor
Washington, DC 20210
(202) 219-5257

Description: Provides placement services for job seekers and employers. These include services to special applicant groups, such as veterans, the handicapped, youth, minorities, and older workers; a computerized interstate job listing; and other labor market information.
$ Given: $847,220,000 est. FY 95
Application Information: Contact your state office.
Deadline: Established each year (contact federal agency for deadline for application submission).
Contact: F. Robert Edwards, Director
Department of Labor
Michigan Employment Security Commission
7310 Woodward Avenue
Detroit, MI 48202
(313) 876-5901
Fax: (313) 876-5587

UNEMPLOYMENT INSURANCE

Unemployment Insurance Service
Employment and Training Administration, Department of Labor
Washington, DC 20210
(202) 219-7831

Description: Provides unemployment insurance for workers whose employers have contributed to state unemployment funds, federal civilian employees, ex–service persons, those who have become unemployed as a result of product imports, and those whose unemployment comes under the purview of a presidentially declared disaster.
$ Given: $23.7 billion est. FY 95
Application Information: Contact the Employment Security Department for your state.
Deadline: Not available
Contact: F. Robert Edwards, Director
          Department of Labor
          Michigan Employment Security Commission
          7310 Woodward Avenue
          Detroit, MI 48202
          (313) 876-5901
          Fax: (313) 876-5587

EMPLOYMENT AND TRAINING ASSISTANCE— DISLOCATED WORKERS

Employment and Training Administration, Department of Labor
200 Constitution Avenue, NW
Washington, DC 20210
(202) 219-5577

Description: Federal grants given to state and local programs to assist workers through training and employment services. These are workers who have been terminated or laid off or received notice of such and are not likely to return to their previous occupation or industry or who are long-term unemployed. Targeted individuals include those affected by mass layoffs and natural disasters.
$ Given: $571.1 million total nationwide for FY 93
Application Information: Inquire at Employment Security office listed below.
Deadline: Not available
Contact: F. Robert Edwards, Director
          Department of Labor
          Michigan Employment Security Commission
          7310 Woodward Avenue
          Detroit, MI 48202
          (313) 876-5901
          Fax: (313) 876-5587

WOMEN'S SPECIAL EMPLOYMENT ASSISTANCE

Office of Administrative Management
Women's Bureau
Office of the Secretary
Department of Labor
Washington, DC 20210
(202) 219-6611

Description: Makes referrals as to sources for counseling and disseminates technical information to aid in the employment of women—especially in the realm of nontraditional women's jobs and jobs in new technologies.
$ Given: $8,054,000 est. FY 95
Application Information: Write to Women's Bureau in your region.
Deadline: None
Contact: Sandra K. Frank, Regional Administrator
Region V, Women's Bureau
Department of Labor
230 South Dearborn Street
Room 1022
Chicago, IL 60604
(312) 353-6985

EMERGENCY LOANS

Farmers Home Administration
Department of Agriculture
14th Street and Independence Avenue, SW
Washington, DC 20250
(202) 720-1632

Description: Provides loans to family farmers (either owner or tenant), ranchers, and aquaculture operators to cover losses resulting from natural or other major disasters. Recipients must be unable to obtain credit from other sources.
$ Given: $180 million est. FY 95; average range: $500–$500,000; average assistance: $66,200
Application Information: Consult local telephone directory under United States Government, Department of Agriculture, for Farmers Home Administration office.
Deadline: Not available

Contact: Farmers Home Administration
          3001 Coolidge Road
          Suite 200
          East Lansing, MI 48823
          (517) 337-6635

ECONOMIC INJURY DISASTER LOANS

Office of Disaster Assistance
Small Business Administration (SBA)
409 Third Street, SW
Washington, DC 20416
(202) 205-6734

Description: Provides direct loans to small businesses suffering
economic damage under Small Business Administration, Department of Agriculture, and/or presidentially declared disaster. Must be
a small business or agricultural concern, located within declared
disaster area and unable to obtain credit elsewhere.
$ Given: $78,209,000 est. FY 95; range: up to $1,500,000; average
assistance: $50,725
Application Information: Applications are filed with nearest
available SBA disaster area or special disaster office.
Deadline: Established for each declaration of disaster.
Contact: Small Business Administration, Region V
          Federal Building
          300 South Riverside Plaza
          Room 1975
          Chicago, IL 60606-6611
          (312) 353-5000

MINNESOTA

EMPLOYMENT SERVICE

United States Employment Service
Employment and Training Administration, Department of Labor
Washington, DC 20210
(202) 219-5257

Description: Provides placement services for job seekers and
employers. These include services to special applicant groups, such

as veterans, the handicapped, youth, minorities, and older workers; a computerized interstate job listing; and other labor market information.

$ Given: $847,220,000 est. FY 95

Application Information: Contact your state office.

Deadline: Established each year (contact federal agency for deadline for application submission).

Contact: R. Jane Brown, Commissioner
Department of Economic Security
390 North Robert Street
St. Paul, MN 55101
(612) 296-5901
Fax: (612) 296-0994

UNEMPLOYMENT INSURANCE

Unemployment Insurance Service
Employment and Training Administration, Department of Labor
Washington, DC 20210
(202) 219-7831

Description: Provides unemployment insurance for workers whose employers have contributed to state unemployment funds, federal civilian employees, ex–service persons, those who have become unemployed as a result of product imports, and those whose unemployment comes under the purview of a presidentially declared disaster.

$ Given: $23.7 billion est. FY 95

Application Information: Contact the Employment Security Department for your state.

Deadline: Not available

Contact: R. Jane Brown, Commissioner
Department of Economic Security
390 North Robert Street
St. Paul, MN 55101
(612) 296-5901
Fax: (612) 296-0994

EMPLOYMENT AND TRAINING ASSISTANCE— DISLOCATED WORKERS

Employment and Training Administration, Department of Labor
200 Constitution Avenue, NW
Washington, DC 20210
(202) 219-5577

Description: Federal grants given to state and local programs to assist workers through training and employment services. These are workers who have been terminated or laid off or received notice of such and are not likely to return to their previous occupation or industry or who are long-term unemployed. Targeted individuals include those affected by mass layoffs and natural disasters.
$ Given: $571.1 million total nationwide for FY 93
Application Information: Inquire at Employment Security office listed below.
Deadline: Not available
Contact: R. Jane Brown, Commissioner
Department of Economic Security
390 North Robert Street
St. Paul, MN 55101
(612) 296-5901
Fax: (612) 296-0994

WOMEN'S SPECIAL EMPLOYMENT ASSISTANCE

Office of Administrative Management
Women's Bureau
Office of the Secretary
Department of Labor
Washington, DC 20210
(202) 219-6611

Description: Makes referrals as to sources for counseling and disseminates technical information to aid in the employment of women—especially in the realm of nontraditional women's jobs and jobs in new technologies.
$ Given: $8,054,000 est. FY 95
Application Information: Write to Women's Bureau in your region.
Deadline: None

Contact: Sandra K. Frank, Regional Administrator
          Region V, Women's Bureau
          Department of Labor
          230 South Dearborn Street
          Room 1022
          Chicago, IL 60604
          (312) 353-6985

EMERGENCY LOANS

Farmers Home Administration
Department of Agriculture
14th Street and Independence Avenue, SW
Washington, DC 20250
(202) 720-1632

Description: Provides loans to family farmers (either owner or
tenant), ranchers, and aquaculture operators to cover losses resulting from natural or other major disasters. Recipients must be
unable to obtain credit from other sources.
$ Given: $180 million est. FY 95; average range: $500–$500,000;
average assistance: $66,200
Application Information: Consult local telephone directory under
United States Government, Department of Agriculture, for Farmers
Home Administration office.
Deadline: Not available
Contact: Farmers Home Administration
          410 Farm Credit Building
          375 Jackson Street
          St. Paul, MN 55101
          (612) 290-3842

ECONOMIC INJURY DISASTER LOANS

Office of Disaster Assistance
Small Business Administration (SBA)
409 Third Street, SW
Washington, DC 20416
(202) 205-6734

Description: Provides direct loans to small businesses suffering
economic damage under Small Business Administration, Depart-

ment of Agriculture, and/or presidentially declared disaster. Must be a small business or agricultural concern, located within declared disaster area and unable to obtain credit elsewhere.
$ Given: $78,209,000 est. FY 95; range: up to $1,500,000; average assistance: $50,725
Application Information: Applications are filed with nearest available SBA disaster area or special disaster office.
Deadline: Established for each declaration of disaster.
Contact: Small Business Administration, Region V
Federal Building
300 South Riverside Plaza
Room 1975
Chicago, IL 60606-6611
(312) 353-5000

MISSISSIPPI

EMPLOYMENT SERVICE

United States Employment Service
Employment and Training Administration, Department of Labor
Washington, DC 20210
(202) 219-5257

Description: Provides placement services for job seekers and employers. These include services to special applicant groups, such as veterans, the handicapped, youth, minorities, and older workers; a computerized interstate job listing; and other labor market information.
$ Given: $847,220,000 est. FY 95
Application Information: Contact your state office.
Deadline: Established each year (contact federal agency for deadline for application submission).
Contact: Liston L. Thomasson
Employment Security Commission
P.O. Box 1699
1520 West Capitol Street
Jackson, MS 39215-1699
(601) 961-7400

UNEMPLOYMENT INSURANCE

Unemployment Insurance Service
Employment and Training Administration, Department of Labor
Washington, DC 20210
(202) 219-7831

Description: Provides unemployment insurance for workers whose
employers have contributed to state unemployment funds, federal
civilian employees, ex–service persons, those who have become
unemployed as a result of product imports, and those whose
unemployment comes under the purview of a presidentially declared
disaster.
$ Given: $23.7 billion est. FY 95
Application Information: Contact the Employment Security Department for your state.
Deadline: Not available
Contact: Liston L. Thomasson
          Employment Security Commission
          P.O. Box 1699
          1520 West Capitol Street
          Jackson, MS 39215-1699
          (601) 961-7400

EMPLOYMENT AND TRAINING ASSISTANCE— DISLOCATED WORKERS

Employment and Training Administration, Department of Labor
200 Constitution Avenue, NW
Washington, DC 20210
(202) 219-5577

Description: Federal grants given to state and local programs to
assist workers through training and employment services. These are
workers who have been terminated or laid off or received notice of
such and are not likely to return to their previous occupation or
industry or who are long-term unemployed. Targeted individuals
include those affected by mass layoffs and natural disasters.
$ Given: $571.1 million total nationwide for FY 93
Application Information: Inquire at Employment Security office
listed below.
Deadline: Not available

Contact: Liston L. Thomasson
           Employment Security Commission
           P.O. Box 1699
           1520 West Capitol Street
           Jackson, MS 39215-1699
           (601) 961-7400

WOMEN'S SPECIAL EMPLOYMENT ASSISTANCE

Office of Administrative Management
Women's Bureau
Office of the Secretary
Department of Labor
Washington, DC 20210
(202) 219-6611

Description: Makes referrals as to sources for counseling and
disseminates technical information to aid in the employment of
women—especially in the realm of nontraditional women's jobs and
jobs in new technologies.
$ Given: $8,054,000 est. FY 95
Application Information: Write to Women's Bureau in your region.
Deadline: None
Contact: Delores L. Crockett, Regional Administrator
           Region IV, Women's Bureau
           Department of Labor
           1371 Peachtree Street, NE
           Room 323
           Atlanta, GA 30367
           (404) 347-4461

EMERGENCY LOANS

Farmers Home Administration
Department of Agriculture
14th Street and Independence Avenue, SW
Washington, DC 20250
(202) 720-1632

Description: Provides loans to family farmers (either owner or
tenant), ranchers, and aquaculture operators to cover losses resulting from natural or other major disasters. Recipients must be
unable to obtain credit from other sources.

$ Given: $180 million est. FY 95; average range: $500–$500,000; average assistance: $66,200
Application Information: Consult local telephone directory under United States Government, Department of Agriculture, for Farmers Home Administration office.
Deadline: Not available
Contact: Farmers Home Administration
         Federal Building
         Suite 831
         100 West Capitol
         Jackson, MS 39269
         (601) 965-4316

ECONOMIC INJURY DISASTER LOANS

Office of Disaster Assistance
Small Business Administration (SBA)
409 Third Street, SW
Washington, DC 20416
(202) 205-6734

Description: Provides direct loans to small businesses suffering economic damage under Small Business Administration, Department of Agriculture, and/or presidentially declared disaster. Must be a small business or agricultural concern, located within declared disaster area and unable to obtain credit elsewhere.
$ Given: $78,209,000 est. FY 95; range: up to $1,500,000; average assistance: $50,725
Application Information: Applications are filed with nearest available SBA disaster area or special disaster office.
Deadline: Established for each declaration of disaster.
Contact: Small Business Administration, Region IV
         1375 Peachtree Street, NE
         Fifth Floor
         Atlanta, GA 30367-8102
         (404) 347-2797

MISSOURI

EMPLOYMENT SERVICE

United States Employment Service
Employment and Training Administration, Department of Labor
Washington, DC 20210
(202) 219-5257

Description: Provides placement services for job seekers and employers. These include services to special applicant groups, such as veterans, the handicapped, youth, minorities, and older workers; a computerized interstate job listing; and other labor market information.
$ Given: $847,220,000 est. FY 95
Application Information: Contact your state office.
Deadline: Established each year (contact federal agency for deadline for application submission).
Contact: Paul Rogers, Director
           Department of Labor and Industrial Relations
           Division of Employment Security
           421 East Dunklin Street
           P.O. Box 59
           Jefferson City, MO 65104
           (314) 751-4945
           Fax: (314) 751-4945

UNEMPLOYMENT INSURANCE

Unemployment Insurance Service
Employment and Training Administration, Department of Labor
Washington, DC 20210
(202) 219-7831

Description: Provides unemployment insurance for workers whose employers have contributed to state unemployment funds, federal civilian employees, ex–service persons, those who have become unemployed as a result of product imports, and those whose unemployment comes under the purview of a presidentially declared disaster.
$ Given: $23.7 billion est. FY 95
Application Information: Contact the Employment Security Department for your state.
Deadline: Not available

Contact: Paul Rogers, Director
          Department of Labor and Industrial Relations
          Division of Employment Security
          421 East Dunklin Street
          P.O. Box 59
          Jefferson City, MO 65104
          (314) 751-4945
          Fax: (314) 751-4945

EMPLOYMENT AND TRAINING ASSISTANCE— DISLOCATED WORKERS

Employment and Training Administration, Department of Labor
200 Constitution Avenue, NW
Washington, DC 20210
(202) 219-5577

Description: Federal grants given to state and local programs to assist workers through training and employment services. These are workers who have been terminated or laid off or received notice of such and are not likely to return to their previous occupation or industry or who are long-term unemployed. Targeted individuals include those affected by mass layoffs and natural disasters.
$ Given: $571.1 million total nationwide for FY 93
Application Information: Inquire at Employment Security office listed below.
Deadline: Not available
Contact: Paul Rogers, Director
          Department of Labor and Industrial Relations
          Division of Employment Security
          421 East Dunklin Street
          P.O. Box 59
          Jefferson City, MO 65104
          (314) 751-4945
          Fax: (314) 751-4945

WOMEN'S SPECIAL EMPLOYMENT ASSISTANCE

Office of Administrative Management
Women's Bureau
Office of the Secretary
Department of Labor
Washington, DC 20210
(202) 219-6611

Description: Makes referrals as to sources for counseling and disseminates technical information to aid in the employment of women—especially in the realm of nontraditional women's jobs and jobs in new technologies.
$ Given: $8,054,000 est. FY 95
Application Information: Write to Women's Bureau in your region.
Deadline: None
Contact: Rose A. Kemp, Regional Administrator
Region VII, Women's Bureau
Department of Labor
Federal Building
Room 2511
911 Walnut Street
Kansas City, MO 64106
(816) 426-6108

EMERGENCY LOANS

Farmers Home Administration
Department of Agriculture
14th Street and Independence Avenue, SW
Washington, DC 20250
(202) 720-1632

Description: Provides loans to family farmers (either owner or tenant), ranchers, and aquaculture operators to cover losses resulting from natural or other major disasters. Recipients must be unable to obtain credit from other sources.
$ Given: $180 million est. FY 95; average range: $500–$500,000; average assistance: $66,200
Application Information: Consult local telephone directory under United States Government, Department of Agriculture, for Farmers Home Administration Office.
Deadline: Not available
Contact: Farmers Home Administration
601 Business Loop
70 West Parkade Center
Suite 235
Columbia, MO 65203
(314) 876-0976

ECONOMIC INJURY DISASTER LOANS

Office of Disaster Assistance
Small Business Administration (SBA)
409 Third Street, SW
Washington, DC 20416
(202) 205-6734

Description: Provides direct loans to small businesses suffering economic damage under Small Business Administration, Department of Agriculture, and/or presidentially declared disaster. Must be a small business or agricultural concern, located within declared disaster area and unable to obtain credit elsewhere.
$ Given: $78,209,000 est. FY 95; range: up to $1,500,000; average assistance: $50,725
Application Information: Applications are filed with nearest available SBA disaster area or special disaster office.
Deadline: Established for each declaration of disaster.
Contact: Small Business Administration, Region VII
          911 Walnut Street
          13th Floor
          Kansas City, MO 64106
          (816) 426-3609

MONTANA

EMPLOYMENT SERVICE

United States Employment Service
Employment and Training Administration, Department of Labor
Washington, DC 20210
(202) 219-5257

Description: Provides placement services for job seekers and employers. These include services to special applicant groups, such as veterans, the handicapped, youth, minorities, and older workers; a computerized interstate job listing; and other labor market information.
$ Given: $847,220,000 est. FY 95
Application Information: Contact your state office.
Deadline: Established each year (contact federal agency for deadline for application submission).

Contact: Laurie Ekanger, Commissioner
Department of Labor and Industry
P.O. Box 1728
Helena, MT 59624
(406) 444-4500

UNEMPLOYMENT INSURANCE

Unemployment Insurance Service
Employment and Training Administration, Department of Labor
Washington, DC 20210
(202) 219-7831

Description: Provides unemployment insurance for workers whose employers have contributed to state unemployment funds, federal civilian employees, ex–service persons, those who have become unemployed as a result of product imports, and those whose unemployment comes under the purview of a presidentially declared disaster.
$ Given: $23.7 billion est. FY 95
Application Information: Contact the Employment Security Department for your state.
Deadline: Not available
Contact: Laurie Ekanger, Commissioner
Department of Labor and Industry
P.O. Box 1728
Helena, MT 59624
(406) 444-4500

EMPLOYMENT AND TRAINING ASSISTANCE— DISLOCATED WORKERS

Employment and Training Administration, Department of Labor
200 Constitution Avenue, NW
Washington, DC 20210
(202) 219-5577

Description: Federal grants given to state and local programs to assist workers through training and employment services. These are workers who have been terminated or laid off or received notice of such and are not likely to return to their previous occupation or industry or who are long-term unemployed. Targeted individuals include those affected by mass layoffs and natural disasters.
$ Given: $571.1 million total nationwide for FY 93

Application Information: Inquire at Employment Security office
listed below.
Deadline: Not available
Contact: Laurie Ekanger, Commissioner
          Department of Labor and Industry
          P.O. Box 1728
          Helena, MT 59624
          (406) 444-4500

WOMEN'S SPECIAL EMPLOYMENT ASSISTANCE

Office of Administrative Management
Women's Bureau
Office of the Secretary
Department of Labor
Washington, DC 20210
(202) 219-6611

Description: Makes referrals as to sources for counseling and
disseminates technical information to aid in the employment of
women—especially in the realm of nontraditional women's jobs and
jobs in new technologies.
$ Given: $8,054,000 est. FY 95
Application Information: Write to Women's Bureau in your region.
Deadline: None
Contact: Oleta Crain, Regional Administrator
          Region VIII, Women's Bureau
          Department of Labor
          Federal Office Building
          Room 1452
          1801 California Street
          Suite 905
          Denver, CO 80202-2614
          (303) 391-6755

EMERGENCY LOANS

Farmers Home Administration
Department of Agriculture
14th Street and Independence Avenue, SW
Washington, DC 20250
(202) 720-1632

Description: Provides loans to family farmers (either owner or tenant), ranchers, and aquaculture operators to cover losses resulting from natural or other major disasters. Recipients must be unable to obtain credit from other sources.
$ Given: $180 million est. FY 95; average range: $500–$500,000; average assistance: $66,200
Application Information: Consult local telephone directory under United States Government, Department of Agriculture, for Farmers Home Administration office.
Deadline: Not available
Contact: Farmers Home Administration
            900 Technology Boulevard
            Suite B
            P.O. Box 850
            Bozeman, MT 59771
            (406) 585-2580

ECONOMIC INJURY DISASTER LOANS

Office of Disaster Assistance
Small Business Administration (SBA)
409 Third Street, SW
Washington, DC 20416
(202) 205-6734

Description: Provides direct loans to small businesses suffering economic damage under Small Business Administration, Department of Agriculture, and/or presidentially declared disaster. Must be a small business or agricultural concern, located within declared disaster area and unable to obtain credit elsewhere.
$ Given: $78,209,000 est. FY 95; range: up to $1,500,000; average assistance: $50,725
Application Information: Applications are filed with nearest available SBA disaster area or special disaster office.
Deadline: Established for each declaration of disaster.
Contact: Small Business Administration, Region VIII
            633 17th Street
            Seventh Floor
            Denver, CO 80202
            (303) 294-7186

NEBRASKA

EMPLOYMENT SERVICE

United States Employment Service
Employment and Training Administration, Department of Labor
Washington, DC 20210
(202) 219-5257

Description: Provides placement services for job seekers and employers. These include services to special applicant groups, such as veterans, the handicapped, youth, minorities, and older workers; a computerized interstate job listing; and other labor market information.
$ Given: $847,220,000 est. FY 95
Application Information: Contact your state office.
Deadline: Established each year (contact federal agency for deadline for application submission).
Contact: Dan Dolan, Commissioner of Labor
Department of Employment
550 South 16th Street
P.O. Box 94600
Lincoln, NE 68509-4600
(402) 471-3405
Fax: (402) 471-2318

UNEMPLOYMENT INSURANCE

Unemployment Insurance Service
Employment and Training Administration, Department of Labor
Washington, DC 20210
(202) 219-7831

Description: Provides unemployment insurance for workers whose employers have contributed to state unemployment funds, federal civilian employees, ex–service persons, those who have become unemployed as a result of product imports, and those whose unemployment comes under the purview of a presidentially declared disaster.
$ Given: $23.7 billion est. FY 95
Application Information: Contact the Employment Security Department for your state.
Deadline: Not available

Contact: Dan Dolan, Commissioner of Labor
         Department of Employment
         550 South 16th Street
         P.O. Box 94600
         Lincoln, NE 68509-4600
         (402) 471-3405
         Fax: (402) 471-2318

EMPLOYMENT AND TRAINING ASSISTANCE— DISLOCATED WORKERS

Employment and Training Administration, Department of Labor
200 Constitution Avenue, NW
Washington, DC 20210
(202) 219-5577

Description: Federal grants given to state and local programs to assist workers through training and employment services. These are workers who have been terminated or laid off or received notice of such and are not likely to return to their previous occupation or industry or who are long-term unemployed. Targeted individuals include those affected by mass layoffs and natural disasters.
$ Given: $571.1 million total nationwide for FY 93
Application Information: Inquire at Employment Security office listed below.
Deadline: Not available
Contact: Dan Dolan, Commissioner of Labor
         Department of Employment
         550 South 16th Street
         P.O. Box 94600
         Lincoln, NE 68509-4600
         (402) 471-3405
         Fax: (402) 471-2318

WOMEN'S SPECIAL EMPLOYMENT ASSISTANCE

Office of Administrative Management
Women's Bureau
Office of the Secretary
Department of Labor
Washington, DC 20210
(202) 219-6611

Description: Makes referrals as to sources for counseling and disseminates technical information to aid in the employment of women—especially in the realm of nontraditional women's jobs and jobs in new technologies.
$ Given: $8,054,000 est. FY 95
Application Information: Write to Women's Bureau in your region.
Deadline: None
Contact: Rose A. Kemp, Regional Administrator
           Region VII, Women's Bureau
           Department of Labor
           Federal Building
           Room 2511
           911 Walnut Street
           Kansas City, MO 64106
           (816) 426-6108

EMERGENCY LOANS

Farmers Home Administration
Department of Agriculture
14th Street and Independence Avenue, SW
Washington, DC 20250
(202) 720-1632

Description: Provides loans to family farmers (either owner or tenant), ranchers, and aquaculture operators to cover losses resulting from natural or other major disasters. Recipients must be unable to obtain credit from other sources.
$ Given: $180 million est. FY 95; average range: $500–$500,000; average assistance: $66,200
Application Information: Consult local telephone directory under United States Government, Department of Agriculture, for Farmers Home Administration office.
Deadline: Not available
Contact: Farmers Home Administration
           Federal Building
           Room 308
           100 Centennial Mall North
           Lincoln, NE 68508
           (402) 437-5551

ECONOMIC INJURY DISASTER LOANS

Office of Disaster Assistance
Small Business Administration (SBA)
409 Third Street, SW
Washington, DC 20416
(202) 205-6734

Description: Provides direct loans to small businesses suffering economic damage under Small Business Administration, Department of Agriculture, and/or presidentially declared disaster. Must be a small business or agricultural concern, located within declared disaster area and unable to obtain credit elsewhere.
$ Given: $78,209,000 est. FY 95; range: up to $1,500,000; average assistance: $50,725
Application Information: Applications are filed with nearest available SBA disaster area or special disaster office.
Deadline: Established for each declaration of disaster.
Contact: Small Business Administration, Region VII
911 Walnut Street
13th Floor
Kansas City, MO 64106
(816) 426-3608

NEVADA

EMPLOYMENT SERVICE

United States Employment Service
Employment and Training Administration, Department of Labor
Washington, DC 20210
(202) 219-5257

Description: Provides placement services for job seekers and employers. These include services to special applicant groups, such as veterans, the handicapped, youth, minorities, and older workers; a computerized interstate job listing; and other labor market information.
$ Given: $847,220,000 est. FY 95
Application Information: Contact your state office.
Deadline: Established each year (contact federal agency for deadline for application submission).

Contact: Carol A. Jackson
          Department of Employment Training and Rehabilitation
          500 East Third Street
          Carson City, NV 89713
          (702) 687-3911
          Fax: (702) 687-8315

UNEMPLOYMENT INSURANCE

Unemployment Insurance Service
Employment and Training Administration, Department of Labor
Washington, DC 20210
(202) 219-7831

Description: Provides unemployment insurance for workers whose
employers have contributed to state unemployment funds, federal
civilian employees, ex–service persons, those who have become
unemployed as a result of product imports, and those whose
unemployment comes under the purview of a presidentially declared
disaster.
$ Given: $23.7 billion est. FY 95
Application Information: Contact the Employment Security Department for your state.
Deadline: Not available
Contact: Carol A. Jackson
          Department of Employment Training and Rehabilitation
          500 East Third Street
          Carson City, NV 89713
          (702) 687-3911
          Fax: (702) 687-8315

EMPLOYMENT AND TRAINING ASSISTANCE—
DISLOCATED WORKERS

Employment and Training Administration, Department of Labor
200 Constitution Avenue, NW
Washington, DC 20210
(202) 219-5577

Description: Federal grants given to state and local programs to
assist workers through training and employment services. These are
workers who have been terminated or laid off or received notice of
such and are not likely to return to their previous occupation or
industry or who are long-term unemployed. Targeted individuals

include those affected by mass layoffs and natural disasters.
$ Given: $571.1 million total nationwide for FY 93
Application Information: Inquire at Employment Security office
listed below.
Deadline: Not available
Contact: Carol A. Jackson
                 Department of Employment Training and Rehabilitation
                 500 East Third Street
                 Carson City, NV 89713
                 (702) 687-3911
                 Fax: (702) 687-8315

WOMEN'S SPECIAL EMPLOYMENT ASSISTANCE

Office of Administrative Management
Women's Bureau
Office of the Secretary
Department of Labor
Washington, DC 20210
(202) 219-6611

Description: Makes referrals as to sources for counseling and
disseminates technical information to aid in the employment of
women—especially in the realm of nontraditional women's jobs and
jobs in new technologies.
$ Given: $8,054,000 est. FY 95
Application Information: Write to Women's Bureau in your region.
Deadline: None
Contact: Madeline Mixer, Regional Administrator
                 Region XI, Women's Bureau
                 71 Stevenson Street
                 Room 927
                 San Francisco, CA 94105
                 (415) 774-6679

EMERGENCY LOANS

Farmers Home Administration
Department of Agriculture
14th Street and Independence Avenue, SW
Washington, DC 20250
(202) 720-1632

Description: Provides loans to family farmers (either owner or tenant), ranchers, and aquaculture operators to cover losses resulting from natural or other major disasters. Recipients must be unable to obtain credit from other sources.
$ Given: $180 million est. FY 95; average range: $500-$500,000; average assistance: $66,200
Application Information: Consult local telephone directory under United States Government, Department of Agriculture, for Farmers Home Administration office.
Deadline: Not available
Contact: Farmers Home Administration
             1390 South Curry Street
             Carson City, NV 89703-5405
             (702) 887-1222

ECONOMIC INJURY DISASTER LOANS

Office of Disaster Assistance
Small Business Administration (SBA)
409 Third Street, SW
Washington, DC 20416
(202) 205-6734

Description: Provides direct loans to small businesses suffering economic damage under Small Business Administration, Department of Agriculture, and/or presidentially declared disaster. Must be a small business or agricultural concern, located within declared disaster area and unable to obtain credit elsewhere.
$ Given: $78,209,000 est. FY 95; range: up to $1,500,000; average assistance: $50,725
Application Information: Applications are filed with nearest available SBA disaster area or special disaster office.
Deadline: Established for each declaration of disaster.
Contact: Small Business Administration, Region IX
             71 Stevenson Street
             20th Floor
             San Francisco, CA 94105-2939
             (415) 744-6402

NEW HAMPSHIRE

EMPLOYMENT SERVICE

United States Employment Service
Employment and Training Administration, Department of Labor
Washington, DC 20210
(202) 219-5257

Description: Provides placement services for job seekers and employers. These include services to special applicant groups, such as veterans, the handicapped, youth, minorities, and older workers; a computerized interstate job listing; and other labor market information.
$ Given: $847,220,000 est. FY 95
Application Information: Contact your state office.
Deadline: Established each year (contact federal agency for deadline for application submission).
Contact: John Ratoff, Commissioner
             Department of Employment Security
             32 South Main Street
             Room 204
             Concord, NH 03301
             (603) 224-3311
             Fax: (603) 224-4145

UNEMPLOYMENT INSURANCE

Unemployment Insurance Service
Employment and Training Administration, Department of Labor
Washington, DC 20210
(202) 219-7831

Description: Provides unemployment insurance for workers whose employers have contributed to state unemployment funds, federal civilian employees, ex–service persons, those who have become unemployed as a result of product imports, and those whose unemployment comes under the purview of a presidentially declared disaster.
$ Given: $23.7 billion est. FY 95
Application Information: Contact the Employment Security Department for your state.
Deadline: Not available

Contact: John Ratoff, Commissioner
           Department of Employment Security
           32 South Main Street
           Room 204
           Concord, NH 03301
           (603) 224-3311
           Fax: (603) 224-4145

EMPLOYMENT AND TRAINING ASSISTANCE— DISLOCATED WORKERS

Employment and Training Administration, Department of Labor
200 Constitution Avenue, NW
Washington, DC 20210
(202) 219-5577

Description: Federal grants given to state and local programs to
assist workers through training and employment services. These are
workers who have been terminated or laid off or received notice of
such and are not likely to return to their previous occupation or
industry or who are long-term unemployed. Targeted individuals
include those affected by mass layoffs and natural disasters.
$ Given: $571.1 million total nationwide for FY 93
Application Information: Inquire at Employment Security office
listed below.
Deadline: Not available
Contact: John Ratoff, Commissioner
           Department of Employment Security
           32 South Main Street
           Room 204
           Concord, NH 03301
           (603) 224-3311
           Fax: (603) 224-4145

WOMEN'S SPECIAL EMPLOYMENT ASSISTANCE

Office of Administrative Management
Women's Bureau
Office of the Secretary
Department of Labor
Washington, DC 20210
(202) 219-6611

Description: Makes referrals as to sources for counseling and disseminates technical information to aid in the employment of women—especially in the realm of nontraditional women's jobs and jobs in new technologies.
$ Given: $8,054,000 est. FY 95
Application Information: Write to Women's Bureau in your region.
Deadline: None
Contact: Martha Izzi, Regional Administrator
                 Region I, Women's Bureau
                 Department of Labor
                 One Congress Street
                 11th Floor
                 Boston, MA 02214
                 (617) 565-1988

EMERGENCY LOANS

Farmers Home Administration
Department of Agriculture
14th Street and Independence Avenue, SW
Washington, DC 20250
(202) 720-1632

Description: Provides loans to family farmers (either owner or tenant), ranchers, and aquaculture operators to cover losses resulting from natural or other major disasters. Recipients must be unable to obtain credit from other sources.
$ Given: $180 million est. FY 95; average range: $500–$500,000; average assistance: $66,200
Application Information: Consult local telephone directory under United States Government, Department of Agriculture, for Farmers Home Administration office.
Deadline: Not available
Contact: Farmers Home Administration
                 City Center
                 Third Floor
                 89 Main Street
                 Montpelier, VT 05602
                 (802) 828-6001

ECONOMIC INJURY DISASTER LOANS

Office of Disaster Assistance
Small Business Administration (SBA)
409 Third Street, SW
Washington, DC 20416
(202) 205-6734

Description: Provides direct loans to small businesses suffering economic damage under Small Business Administration, Department of Agriculture, and/or presidentially declared disaster. Must be a small business or agricultural concern, located within declared disaster area and unable to obtain credit elsewhere.
$ Given: $78,209,000 est. FY 95; range: up to $1,500,000; average assistance: $50,725
Application Information: Applications are filed with nearest available SBA disaster area or special disaster office.
Deadline: Established for each declaration of disaster.
Contact: Small Business Administration, Region I
                155 Federal Street
                Ninth Floor
                Boston, MA 02110
                (617) 451-2023

NEW JERSEY

EMPLOYMENT SERVICE

United States Employment Service
Employment and Training Administration, Department of Labor
Washington, DC 20210
(202) 219-5257

Description: Provides placement services for job seekers and employers. These include services to special applicant groups, such as veterans, the handicapped, youth, minorities, and older workers; a computerized interstate job listing; and other labor market information.
$ Given: $847,220,000 est. FY 95
Application Information: Contact your state office.
Deadline: Established each year (contact federal agency for deadline for application submission).

Contact: Peter J. Colderme, Commissioner
Department of Labor
John Fitch Plaza
Trenton, NJ 08625
(609) 771-1090
Fax: (609) 633-2884

UNEMPLOYMENT INSURANCE

Unemployment Insurance Service
Employment and Training Administration, Department of Labor
Washington, DC 20210
(202) 219-7831

Description: Provides unemployment insurance for workers whose employers have contributed to state unemployment funds, federal civilian employees, ex–service persons, those who have become unemployed as a result of product imports, and those whose unemployment comes under the purview of a presidentially declared disaster.
$ Given: $23.7 billion est. FY 95
Application Information: Contact the Employment Security Department for your state.
Deadline: Not available
Contact: Peter J. Colderme, Commissioner
Department of Labor
John Fitch Plaza
Trenton, NJ 08625
(609) 771-1090
Fax: (609) 633-2884

EMPLOYMENT AND TRAINING ASSISTANCE— DISLOCATED WORKERS

Employment and Training Administration, Department of Labor
200 Constitution Avenue, NW
Washington, DC 20210
(202) 219-5577

Description: Federal grants given to state and local programs to assist workers through training and employment services. These are workers who have been terminated or laid off or received notice of such and are not likely to return to their previous occupation or industry or who are long-term unemployed. Targeted individuals

include those affected by mass layoffs and natural disasters.
$ Given: $571.1 million total nationwide for FY 93
Application Information: Inquire at Employment Security office listed below.
Deadline: Not available
Contact: Peter J. Colderme, Commissioner
              Department of Labor
              John Fitch Plaza
              Trenton, NJ 08625
              (609) 771-1090
              Fax: (609) 633-2884

WOMEN'S SPECIAL EMPLOYMENT ASSISTANCE

Office of Administrative Management
Women's Bureau
Office of the Secretary
Department of Labor
Washington, DC 20210
(202) 219-6611

Description: Makes referrals as to sources for counseling and disseminates technical information to aid in the employment of women—especially in the realm of nontraditional women's jobs and jobs in new technologies.
$ Given: $8,054,000 est. FY 95
Application Information: Write to Women's Bureau in your region.
Deadline: None
Contact: Mary C. Murphee, Regional Administrator
              Region II, Women's Bureau
              Department of Labor
              201 Varick Street
              Room 601
              New York, NY 10014
              (212) 337-2389

EMERGENCY LOANS

Farmers Home Administration
Department of Agriculture
14th Street and Independence Avenue, SW
Washington, DC 20250
(202) 720-1632

Description: Provides loans to family farmers (either owner or tenant), ranchers, and aquaculture operators to cover losses resulting from natural or other major disasters. Recipients must be unable to obtain credit from other sources.
$ Given: $180 million est. FY 95; average range: $500–$500,000; average assistance: $66,200
Application Information: Consult local telephone directory under United States Government, Department of Agriculture, for Farmers Home Administration office.
Deadline: Not available
Contact: Farmers Home Administration
                Tarnsfield and Woodlane Roads
                Tarnsfield Plaza
                Suite 22
                Mt. Holly, NJ 08060
                (609) 265-3600

ECONOMIC INJURY DISASTER LOANS

Office of Disaster Assistance
Small Business Administration (SBA)
409 Third Street, SW
Washington, DC 20416
(202) 205-6734

Description: Provides direct loans to small businesses suffering economic damage under Small Business Administration, Department of Agriculture, and/or presidentially declared disaster. Must be a small business or agricultural concern, located within declared disaster area and unable to obtain credit elsewhere.
$ Given: $78,209,000 est. FY 95; range: up to $1,500,000; average assistance: $50,725
Application Information: Applications are filed with nearest available SBA disaster area or special disaster office.
Deadline: Established for each declaration of disaster.
Contact: Small Business Administration, Region II
                26 Federal Plaza
                Room 31-08
                New York, NY 10278
                (212) 264-1450

NEW MEXICO

EMPLOYMENT SERVICE

United States Employment Service
Employment and Training Administration, Department of Labor
Washington, DC 20210
(202) 219-5257

Description: Provides placement services for job seekers and employers. These include services to special applicant groups, such as veterans, the handicapped, youth, minorities, and older workers; a computerized interstate job listing; and other labor market information.
$ Given: $847,220,000 est. FY 95
Application Information: Contact your state office.
Deadline: Established each year (contact federal agency for deadline for application submission).
Contact: Patrick G. Baca, Secretary of Labor
              Employment Security Department
              P.O. Box 1928
              Albuquerque, NM 87103
              (505) 841-8409
              Fax: (505) 841-8491

UNEMPLOYMENT INSURANCE

Unemployment Insurance Service
Employment and Training Administration, Department of Labor
Washington, DC 20210
(202) 219-7831

Description: Provides unemployment insurance for workers whose employers have contributed to state unemployment funds, federal civilian employees, ex–service persons, those who have become unemployed as a result of product imports, and those whose unemployment comes under the purview of a presidentially declared disaster.
$ Given: $23.7 billion est. FY 95
Application Information: Contact the Employment Security Department for your state.
Deadline: Not available

Contact: Patrick G. Baca, Secretary of Labor
          Employment Security Department
          P.O. Box 1928
          Albuquerque, NM 87103
          (505) 841-8409
          Fax: (505) 841-8491

EMPLOYMENT AND TRAINING ASSISTANCE— DISLOCATED WORKERS

Employment and Training Administration, Department of Labor
200 Constitution Avenue, NW
Washington, DC 20210
(202) 219-5577

Description: Federal grants given to state and local programs to assist workers through training and employment services. These are workers who have been terminated or laid off or received notice of such and are not likely to return to their previous occupation or industry or who are long-term unemployed. Targeted individuals include those affected by mass layoffs and natural disasters.
$ Given: $571.1 million total nationwide for FY 93
Application Information: Inquire at Employment Security office listed below.
Deadline: Not available
Contact: Patrick G. Baca, Secretary of Labor
          Employment Security Department
          P.O. Box 1928
          Albuquerque, NM 87103
          (505) 841-8409
          Fax: (505) 841-8491

WOMEN'S SPECIAL EMPLOYMENT ASSISTANCE

Office of Administrative Management
Women's Bureau
Office of the Secretary
Department of Labor
Washington, DC 20210
(202) 219-6611

Description: Makes referrals as to sources for counseling and disseminates technical information to aid in the employment of women—especially in the realm of nontraditional women's jobs and jobs in new technologies.

$ Given: $8,054,000 est. FY 95
Application Information: Write to Women's Bureau in your region.
Deadline: None
Contact: Evelyn Smith, Regional Administrator
          Region VI, Women's Bureau
          Department of Labor
          Federal Building
          Suite 731
          525 Griffin Street
          Dallas, TX 75202
          (214) 767-6985

EMERGENCY LOANS

Farmers Home Administration
Department of Agriculture
14th Street and Independence Avenue, SW
Washington, DC 20250
(202) 720-1632

Description: Provides loans to family farmers (either owner or
tenant), ranchers, and aquaculture operators to cover losses resulting from natural or other major disasters. Recipients must be
unable to obtain credit from other sources.
$ Given: $180 million est. FY 95; average range: $500–$500,000;
average assistance: $66,200
Application Information: Consult local telephone directory under
United States Government, Department of Agriculture, for Farmers
Home Administration office.
Deadline: Not available
Contact: Farmers Home Administration
          Federal Building
          Room 3414
          517 Gold Avenue, SW
          Albuquerque, NM 87102
          (505) 766-2462

ECONOMIC INJURY DISASTER LOANS

Office of Disaster Assistance
Small Business Administration (SBA)
409 Third Street, SW
Washington, DC 20416
(202) 205-6734

Description: Provides direct loans to small businesses suffering economic damage under Small Business Administration, Department of Agriculture, and/or presidentially declared disaster. Must be a small business or agricultural concern, located within declared disaster area and unable to obtain credit elsewhere.
$ Given: $78,209,000 est. FY 95; range: up to $1,500,000; average assistance: $50,725
Application Information: Applications are filed with nearest available SBA disaster area or special disaster office.
Deadline: Established for each declaration of disaster.
Contact: Small Business Administration, Region VI
           8625 King George Drive
           Building C
           Dallas, TX 75235-3391
           (214) 767-7643

NEW YORK

EMPLOYMENT SERVICE

United States Employment Service
Employment and Training Administration, Department of Labor
Washington, DC 20210
(202) 219-5257

Description: Provides placement services for job seekers and employers. These include services to special applicant groups, such as veterans, the handicapped, youth, minorities, and older workers; a computerized interstate job listing; and other labor market information.
$ Given: $847,220,000 est. FY 95
Application Information: Contact your state office.
Deadline: Established each year (contact federal agency for deadline for application submission).
Contact: John F. Hudacs, Deputy Commissioner
           Department of Labor
           State Office Campus
           Building 12
           Room 500
           Albany, NY 12240-0002
           (518) 457-2741
           Fax: (518) 457-6908

UNEMPLOYMENT INSURANCE

Unemployment Insurance Service
Employment and Training Administration, Department of Labor
Washington, DC 20210
(202) 219-7831

Description: Provides unemployment insurance for workers whose employers have contributed to state unemployment funds, federal civilian employees, ex–service persons, those who have become unemployed as a result of product imports, and those whose unemployment comes under the purview of a presidentially declared disaster.
$ Given: $23.7 billion est. FY 95
Application Information: Contact the Employment Security Department for your state.
Deadline: Not available
Contact: John F. Hudacs, Deputy Commissioner
            Department of Labor
            State Office Campus
            Building 12
            Room 500
            Albany, NY 12240-0002
            (518) 457-2741
            Fax: (518) 457-6908

EMPLOYMENT AND TRAINING ASSISTANCE— DISLOCATED WORKERS

Employment and Training Administration, Department of Labor
200 Constitution Avenue, NW
Washington, DC 20210
(202) 219-5577

Description: Federal grants given to state and local programs to assist workers through training and employment services. These are workers who have been terminated or laid off or received notice of such and are not likely to return to their previous occupation or industry or who are long-term unemployed. Targeted individuals include those affected by mass layoffs and natural disasters.
$ Given: $571.1 million total nationwide for FY 93
Application Information: Inquire at Employment Security office listed below.
Deadline: Not available

Contact: John F. Hudacs, Deputy Commissioner
          Department of Labor
          State Office Campus
          Building 12
          Room 500
          Albany, NY 12240-0002
          (518) 457-2741
          Fax: (518) 457-6908

WOMEN'S SPECIAL EMPLOYMENT ASSISTANCE

Office of Administrative Management
Women's Bureau
Office of the Secretary
Department of Labor
Washington, DC 20210
(202) 219-6611

Description: Makes referrals as to sources for counseling and disseminates technical information to aid in the employment of women—especially in the realm of nontraditional women's jobs and jobs in new technologies.
$ Given: $8,054,000 est. FY 95
Application Information: Write to Women's Bureau in your region.
Deadline: None
Contact: Mary C. Murphee, Regional Administrator
          Region II, Women's Bureau
          Department of Labor
          201 Varick Street
          Room 601
          New York NY 10014
          (212) 337-2389

EMERGENCY LOANS

Farmers Home Administration
Department of Agriculture
14th Street and Independence Avenue, SW
Washington, DC 20250
(202) 720-1632

Description: Provides loans to family farmers (either owner or tenant), ranchers, and aquaculture operators to cover losses resulting from natural or other major disasters. Recipients must be unable to obtain credit from other sources.

$ Given: $180 million est. FY 95; average range: $500–$500,000; average assistance: $66,200
Application Information: Consult local telephone directory under United States Government, Department of Agriculture, for Farmers Home Administration office.
Deadline: Not available
Contact: Farmers Home Administration
              Federal Building
              100 South Clinton Street
              Room 871
              Syracuse, NY 13261-7318
              (315) 423-5290

ECONOMIC INJURY DISASTER LOANS

Office of Disaster Assistance
Small Business Administration (SBA)
409 Third Street, SW
Washington, DC 20416
(202) 205-6734

Description: Provides direct loans to small businesses suffering economic damage under Small Business Administration, Department of Agriculture, and/or presidentially declared disaster. Must be a small business or agricultural concern, located within declared disaster area and unable to obtain credit elsewhere.
$ Given: $78,209,000 est. FY 95; range: up to $1,500,000; average assistance: $50,725
Application Information: Applications are filed with nearest available SBA disaster area or special disaster office.
Deadline: Established for each declaration of disaster.
Contact: Small Business Administration, Region II
              26 Federal Plaza
              Room 31-08
              New York, NY 10278
              (212) 264-1450

NORTH CAROLINA

EMPLOYMENT SERVICE

United States Employment Service
Employment and Training Administration, Department of Labor
Washington, DC 20210
(202) 219-5257

Description: Provides placement services for job seekers and
employers. These include services to special applicant groups, such
as veterans, the handicapped, youth, minorities, and older workers;
a computerized interstate job listing; and other labor market
information.
$ Given: $847,220,000 est. FY 95
Application Information: Contact your state office.
Deadline: Established each year (contact federal agency for deadline
for application submission).
Contact: Ann Q. Duncan, Chair
            Employment Security Division
            P.O. Box 25903
            700 Wade Avenue
            Raleigh, NC 27611
            (919) 733-7546
            Fax: (919) 733-1129

UNEMPLOYMENT INSURANCE

Unemployment Insurance Service
Employment and Training Administration, Department of Labor
Washington, DC 20210
(202) 219-7831

Description: Provides unemployment insurance for workers whose
employers have contributed to state unemployment funds, federal
civilian employees, ex–service persons, those who have become
unemployed as a result of product imports, and those whose
unemployment comes under the purview of a presidentially declared
disaster.
$ Given: $23.7 billion est. FY 95
Application Information: Contact the Employment Security Department for your state.
Deadline: Not available

Contact: Ann Q. Duncan, Chair
           Employment Security Division
           P.O. Box 25903
           700 Wade Avenue
           Raleigh, NC 27611
           (919) 733-7546
           Fax: (919) 733-1129

EMPLOYMENT AND TRAINING ASSISTANCE— DISLOCATED WORKERS

Employment and Training Administration, Department of Labor
200 Constitution Avenue, NW
Washington, DC 20210
(202) 219-5577

Description: Federal grants given to state and local programs to
assist workers through training and employment services. These are
workers who have been terminated or laid off or received notice of
such and are not likely to return to their previous occupation or
industry or who are long-term unemployed. Targeted individuals
include those affected by mass layoffs and natural disasters.
$ Given: $571.1 million total nationwide for FY 93
Application Information: Inquire at Employment Security office
listed below.
Deadline: Not available
Contact: Ann Q. Duncan, Chair
           Employment Security Division
           P.O. Box 25903
           700 Wade Avenue
           Raleigh, NC 27611
           (919) 733-7546
           Fax: (919) 733-1129

WOMEN'S SPECIAL EMPLOYMENT ASSISTANCE

Office of Administrative Management
Women's Bureau
Office of the Secretary
Department of Labor
Washington, DC 20210
(202) 219-6611

Description: Makes referrals as to sources for counseling and
disseminates technical information to aid in the employment of

women—especially in the realm of nontraditional women's jobs and jobs in new technologies.
$ Given: $8,054,000 est. FY 95
Application Information: Write to Women's Bureau in your region.
Deadline: None
Contact: Delores L. Crockett, Regional Administrator
Region IV, Women's Bureau
Department of Labor
1371 Peachtree Street, NE
Room 323
Atlanta, GA 30367
(404) 347-4461

EMERGENCY LOANS

Farmers Home Administration
Department of Agriculture
14th Street and Independence Avenue, SW
Washington, DC 20250
(202) 720-1632

Description: Provides loans to family farmers (either owner or tenant), ranchers, and aquaculture operators to cover losses resulting from natural or other major disasters. Recipients must be unable to obtain credit from other sources.
$ Given: $180 million est. FY 95; average range: $500–$500,000; average assistance: $66,200
Application Information: Consult local telephone directory under United States Government, Department of Agriculture, for Farmers Home Administration Office.
Deadline: Not available
Contact: Farmers Home Administration
4405 South Band Road
Suite 260
Raleigh, NC 27609
(919) 790-2731

ECONOMIC INJURY DISASTER LOANS

Office of Disaster Assistance
Small Business Administration (SBA)
409 Third Street, SW
Washington, DC 20416
(202) 205-6734

Description: Provides direct loans to small businesses suffering economic damage under Small Business Administration, Department of Agriculture, and/or presidentially declared disaster. Must be a small business or agricultural concern, located within declared disaster area and unable to obtain credit elsewhere.
$ Given: $78,209,000 est. FY 95; range: up to $1,500,000; average assistance: $50,725
Application Information: Applications are filed with nearest available SBA disaster area or special disaster office.
Deadline: Established for each declaration of disaster.
Contact: Small Business Administration, Region IV
                1375 Peachtree Street, NE
                Fifth Floor
                Atlanta, GA 30367-8102
                (404) 347-2797

NORTH DAKOTA

EMPLOYMENT SERVICE

United States Employment Service
Employment and Training Administration, Department of Labor
Washington, DC 20210
(202) 219-5257

Description: Provides placement services for job seekers and employers. These include services to special applicant groups, such as veterans, the handicapped, youth, minorities, and older workers; a computerized interstate job listing; and other labor market information.
$ Given: $847,220,000 est. FY 95
Application Information: Contact your state office.
Deadline: Established each year (contact federal agency for deadline for application submission).
Contact: Gerald P. Balzer, Executive Director
                Job Service North Dakota
                P.O. Box 1537
                1000 East Divide Avenue
                Bismarck, ND 58502-5507
                (701) 224-2836

UNEMPLOYMENT INSURANCE

Unemployment Insurance Service
Employment and Training Administration, Department of Labor
Washington, DC 20210
(202) 219-7831

Description: Provides unemployment insurance for workers whose employers have contributed to state unemployment funds, federal civilian employees, ex–service persons, those who have become unemployed as a result of product imports, and those whose unemployment comes under the purview of a presidentially declared disaster.
$ Given: $23.7 billion est. FY 95
Application Information: Contact the Employment Security Department for your state.
Deadline: Not available
Contact: Gerald P. Balzer, Executive Director
Job Service North Dakota
P.O. Box 1537
1000 East Divide Avenue
Bismarck, ND 58502-5507
(701) 224-2836

EMPLOYMENT AND TRAINING ASSISTANCE— DISLOCATED WORKERS

Employment and Training Administration, Department of Labor
200 Constitution Avenue, NW
Washington, DC 20210
(202) 219-5577

Description: Federal grants given to state and local programs to assist workers through training and employment services. These are workers who have been terminated or laid off or received notice of such and are not likely to return to their previous occupation or industry or who are long-term unemployed. Targeted individuals include those affected by mass layoffs and natural disasters.
$ Given: $571.1 million total nationwide for FY 93
Application Information: Inquire at Employment Security office listed below.
Deadline: Not available

Contact: Gerald P. Balzer, Executive Director
           Job Service North Dakota
           P.O. Box 1537
           1000 East Divide Avenue
           Bismarck, ND 58502-5507
           (701) 224-2836

WOMEN'S SPECIAL EMPLOYMENT ASSISTANCE

Office of Administrative Management
Women's Bureau
Office of the Secretary
Department of Labor
Washington, DC 20210
(202) 219-6611

Description: Makes referrals as to sources for counseling and
disseminates technical information to aid in the employment of
women—especially in the realm of nontraditional women's jobs and
jobs in new technologies.
$ Given: $8,054,000 est. FY 95
Application Information: Write to Women's Bureau in your region.
Deadline: None
Contact: Oleta Crain, Regional Administrator
           Region VIII, Women's Bureau
           Department of Labor
           Federal Office Building
           Room 1452
           1801 California Street
           Suite 905
           Denver, CO 80202-2614
           (303) 391-6755

EMERGENCY LOANS

Farmers Home Administration
Department of Agriculture
14th Street and Independence Avenue, SW
Washington, DC 20250
(202) 720-1632

Description: Provides loans to family farmers (either owner or
tenant), ranchers, and aquaculture operators to cover losses result-

ing from natural or other major disasters. Recipients must be unable to obtain credit from other sources.

$ Given: $180 million est. FY 95; average range: $500–$500,000; average assistance: $66,200

Application Information: Consult local telephone directory under United States Government, Department of Agriculture, for Farmers Home Administration office.

Deadline: Not available

Contact: Farmers Home Administration
Federal Building
Room 208
Third and Roose
P.O. Box 1737
Bismarck, ND 58502
(701) 250-4781

ECONOMIC INJURY DISASTER LOANS

Office of Disaster Assistance
Small Business Administration (SBA)
409 Third Street, SW
Washington, DC 20416
(202) 205-6734

Description: Provides direct loans to small businesses suffering economic damage under Small Business Administration, Department of Agriculture, and/or presidentially declared disaster. Must be a small business or agricultural concern, located within declared disaster area and unable to obtain credit elsewhere.

$ Given: $78,209,000 est. FY 95; range: up to $1,500,000; average assistance: $50,725

Application Information: Applications are filed with nearest available SBA disaster area or special disaster office.

Deadline: Established for each declaration of disaster.

Contact: Small Business Administration, Region VIII
633 17th Street
Seventh Floor
Denver, CO 80202
(303) 294-7186

OHIO

EMPLOYMENT SERVICE

United States Employment Service
Employment and Training Administration, Department of Labor
Washington, DC 20210
(202) 219-5257

Description: Provides placement services for job seekers and
employers. These include services to special applicant groups, such
as veterans, the handicapped, youth, minorities, and older workers;
a computerized interstate job listing; and other labor market
information.
$ Given: $847,220,000 est. FY 95
Application Information: Contact your state office.
Deadline: Established each year (contact federal agency for deadline
for application submission).
Contact: Debra Bowland, Administrator
          Bureau of Employment Services
          145 South Front Street
          P.O. Box 1618
          Columbus, OH 43216
          (614) 466-2100
          Fax: (614) 466-5025

UNEMPLOYMENT INSURANCE

Unemployment Insurance Service
Employment and Training Administration, Department of Labor
Washington, DC 20210
(202) 219-7831

Description: Provides unemployment insurance for workers whose
employers have contributed to state unemployment funds, federal
civilian employees, ex–service persons, those who have become
unemployed as a result of product imports, and those whose
unemployment comes under the purview of a presidentially declared
disaster.
$ Given: $23.7 billion est. FY 95
Application Information: Contact the Employment Security Department for your state.
Deadline: Not available

Contact: Debra Bowland, Administrator
           Bureau of Employment Services
           145 South Front Street
           P.O. Box 1618
           Columbus, OH 43216
           (614) 466-2100
           Fax: (614) 466-5025

EMPLOYMENT AND TRAINING ASSISTANCE— DISLOCATED WORKERS

Employment and Training Administration, Department of Labor
200 Constitution Avenue, NW
Washington, DC 20210
(202) 219-5577

Description: Federal grants given to state and local programs to assist workers through training and employment services. These are workers who have been terminated or laid off or received notice of such and are not likely to return to their previous occupation or industry or who are long-term unemployed. Targeted individuals include those affected by mass layoffs and natural disasters.
$ Given: $571.1 million total nationwide for FY 93
Application Information: Inquire at Employment Security office listed below.
Deadline: Not available
Contact: Debra Bowland, Administrator
           Bureau of Employment Services
           145 South Front Street
           P.O. Box 1618
           Columbus, OH 43216
           (614) 466-2100
           Fax: (614) 466-5025

WOMEN'S SPECIAL EMPLOYMENT ASSISTANCE

Office of Administrative Management
Women's Bureau
Office of the Secretary
Department of Labor
Washington, DC 20210
(202) 219-6611

Description: Makes referrals as to sources for counseling and disseminates technical information to aid in the employment of women—especially in the realm of nontraditional women's jobs and jobs in new technologies.
$ Given: $8,054,000 est. FY 95
Application Information: Write to Women's Bureau in your region.
Deadline: None
Contact: Sandra K. Frank, Regional Administrator
           Region V, Women's Bureau
           Department of Labor
           230 South Dearborn Street
           Room 1022
           Chicago, IL 60604
           (312) 353-6985

EMERGENCY LOANS

Farmers Home Administration
Department of Agriculture
14th Street and Independence Avenue, SW
Washington, DC 20250
(202) 720-1632

Description: Provides loans to family farmers (either owner or tenant), ranchers, and aquaculture operators to cover losses resulting from natural or other major disasters. Recipients must be unable to obtain credit from other sources.
$ Given: $180 million est. FY 95; average range: $500–$500,000; average assistance: $66,200
Application Information: Consult local telephone directory under United States Government, Department of Agriculture, for Farmers Home Administration office.
Deadline: Not available
Contact: Farmers Home Administration
           Federal Building
           Room 507
           200 North High Street
           Columbus, OH 43215
           (614) 469-5606

ECONOMIC INJURY DISASTER LOANS

Office of Disaster Assistance
Small Business Administration (SBA)
409 Third Street, SW
Washington, DC 20416
(202) 205-6734

Description: Provides direct loans to small businesses suffering
economic damage under Small Business Administration, Department of Agriculture, and/or presidentially declared disaster. Must be
a small business or agricultural concern, located within declared
disaster area and unable to obtain credit elsewhere.
$ Given: $78,209,000 est. FY 95; range: up to $1,500,000; average
assistance: $50,725
Application Information: Applications are filed with nearest
available SBA disaster area or special disaster office.
Deadline: Established for each declaration of disaster.
Contact: Small Business Administration, Region V
            Federal Building
            300 South Riverside Plaza
            Room 1975
            Chicago, IL 60606-6611
            (312) 353-5000

OKLAHOMA

EMPLOYMENT SERVICE

United States Employment Service
Employment and Training Administration, Department of Labor
Washington, DC 20210
(202) 219-5257

Description: Provides placement services for job seekers and
employers. These include services to special applicant groups, such
as veterans, the handicapped, youth, minorities, and older workers;
a computerized interstate job listing; and other labor market
information.
$ Given: $847,220,000 est. FY 95
Application Information: Contact your state office.
Deadline: Established each year (contact federal agency for deadline
for application submission).

Contact: Wayne Winn, Executive Director
          Employment Security Commission
          Will Rogers Memorial Office Building
          Oklahoma City, OK 73105
          (405) 557-7200
          Fax: (405) 557-7256

UNEMPLOYMENT INSURANCE

Unemployment Insurance Service
Employment and Training Administration, Department of Labor
Washington, DC 20210
(202) 219-7831

Description: Provides unemployment insurance for workers whose
employers have contributed to state unemployment funds, federal
civilian employees, ex–service persons, those who have become
unemployed as a result of product imports, and those whose
unemployment comes under the purview of a presidentially declared
disaster.
$ Given: $23.7 billion est. FY 95
Application Information: Contact the Employment Security Department for your state.
Deadline: Not available
Contact: Wayne Winn, Executive Director
          Employment Security Commission
          Will Rogers Memorial Office Building
          Oklahoma City, OK 73105
          (405) 557-7200
          Fax: (405) 557-7256

EMPLOYMENT AND TRAINING ASSISTANCE— DISLOCATED WORKERS

Employment and Training Administration, Department of Labor
200 Constitution Avenue, NW
Washington, DC 20210
(202) 219-5577

Description: Federal grants given to state and local programs to
assist workers through training and employment services. These are
workers who have been terminated or laid off or received notice of
such and are not likely to return to their previous occupation or
industry or who are long-term unemployed. Targeted individuals

include those affected by mass layoffs and natural disasters.
$ Given: $571.1 million total nationwide for FY 93
Application Information: Inquire at Employment Security office listed below.
Deadline: Not available
Contact: Wayne Winn, Executive Director
Employment Security Commission
Will Rogers Memorial Office Building
Oklahoma City, OK 73105
(405) 557-7200
Fax: (405) 557-7256

WOMEN'S SPECIAL EMPLOYMENT ASSISTANCE

Office of Administrative Management
Women's Bureau
Office of the Secretary
Department of Labor
Washington, DC 20210
(202) 219-6611

Description: Makes referrals as to sources for counseling and disseminates technical information to aid in the employment of women—especially in the realm of nontraditional women's jobs and jobs in new technologies.
$ Given: $8,054,000 est. FY 95
Application Information: Write to Women's Bureau in your region.
Deadline: None
Contact: Evelyn Smith, Regional Administrator
Region VI, Women's Bureau
Department of Labor
Federal Building
Suite 731
525 Griffin Street
Dallas, TX 75202
(214) 767-6985

EMERGENCY LOANS

Farmers Home Administration
Department of Agriculture
14th Street and Independence Avenue, SW
Washington, DC 20250
(202) 720-1632

Description: Provides loans to family farmers (either owner or tenant), ranchers, and aquaculture operators to cover losses resulting from natural or other major disasters. Recipients must be unable to obtain credit from other sources.
$ Given: $180 million est. FY 95; average range: $500–$500,000; average assistance: $66,200
Application Information: Consult local telephone directory under United States Government, Department of Agriculture, for Farmers Home Administration office.
Deadline: Not available
Contact: Farmers Home Administration
            USDA Agricultural Center Office Building
            Stillwater, OK 74074
            (405) 624-4250

ECONOMIC INJURY DISASTER LOANS

Office of Disaster Assistance
Small Business Administration (SBA)
409 Third Street, SW
Washington, DC 20416
(202) 205-6734

Description: Provides direct loans to small businesses suffering economic damage under Small Business Administration, Department of Agriculture, and/or presidentially declared disaster. Must be a small business or agricultural concern, located within declared disaster area and unable to obtain credit elsewhere.
$ Given: $78,209,000 est. FY 95; range: up to $1,500,000; average assistance: $50,725
Application Information: Applications are filed with nearest available SBA disaster area or special disaster office.
Deadline: Established for each declaration of disaster.
Contact: Small Business Administration, Region VI
            8625 King George Drive
            Building C
            Dallas, TX 75235-3391
            (214) 767-7643

OREGON

EMPLOYMENT SERVICE

United States Employment Service
Employment and Training Administration, Department of Labor
Washington, DC 20210
(202) 219-5257

Description: Provides placement services for job seekers and
employers. These include services to special applicant groups, such
as veterans, the handicapped, youth, minorities, and older workers;
a computerized interstate job listing; and other labor market
information.
$ Given: $847,220,000 est. FY 95
Application Information: Contact your state office.
Deadline: Established each year (contact federal agency for deadline
for application submission).
Contact: Pamela A. Mattson, Administrator
          Employment Division
          Department of Human Resources
          875 Union Street, NE
          Salem, OR 97311
          (503) 378-3210
          Fax: (503) 373-7298

UNEMPLOYMENT INSURANCE

Unemployment Insurance Service
Employment and Training Administration, Department of Labor
Washington, DC 20210
(202) 219-7831

Description: Provides unemployment insurance for workers whose
employers have contributed to state unemployment funds, federal
civilian employees, ex–service persons, those who have become
unemployed as a result of product imports, and those whose
unemployment comes under the purview of a presidentially declared
disaster.
$ Given: $23.7 billion est. FY 95
Application Information: Contact the Employment Security Department for your state.
Deadline: Not available

Contact: Pamela A. Mattson, Administrator
           Employment Division
           Department of Human Resources
           875 Union Street, NE
           Salem, OR 97311
           (503) 378-3210
           Fax: (503) 373-7298

EMPLOYMENT AND TRAINING ASSISTANCE— DISLOCATED WORKERS

Employment and Training Administration, Department of Labor
200 Constitution Avenue, NW
Washington, DC 20210
(202) 219-5577

Description: Federal grants given to state and local programs to assist workers through training and employment services. These are workers who have been terminated or laid off or received notice of such and are not likely to return to their previous occupation or industry or who are long-term unemployed. Targeted individuals include those affected by mass layoffs and natural disasters.
$ Given: $571.1 million total nationwide for FY 93
Application Information: Inquire at Employment Security office listed below.
Deadline: Not available
Contact: Pamela A. Mattson, Administrator
           Employment Division
           Department of Human Resources
           875 Union Street, NE
           Salem, OR 97311
           (503) 378-3210
           Fax: (503) 373-7298

WOMEN'S SPECIAL EMPLOYMENT ASSISTANCE

Office of Administrative Management
Women's Bureau
Office of the Secretary
Department of Labor
Washington, DC 20210
(202) 219-6611

Description: Makes referrals as to sources for counseling and disseminates technical information to aid in the employment of women—especially in the realm of nontraditional women's jobs and jobs in new technologies.

$ Given: $8,054,000 est. FY 95

Application Information: Write to Women's Bureau in your region.

Deadline: None

Contact: Regional Administrator
Region X, Women's Bureau
Department of Labor
111 Third Avenue
Room 885
Seattle, WA 98101-3211
(206) 553-1534

EMERGENCY LOANS

Farmers Home Administration
Department of Agriculture
14th Street and Independence Avenue, SW
Washington, DC 20250
(202) 720-1632

Description: Provides loans to family farmers (either owner or tenant), ranchers, and aquaculture operators to cover losses resulting from natural or other major disasters. Recipients must be unable to obtain credit from other sources.

$ Given: $180 million est. FY 95; average range: $500–$500,000; average assistance: $66,200

Application Information: Consult local telephone directory under United States Government, Department of Agriculture, for Farmers Home Administration office.

Deadline: Not available

Contact: Farmers Home Administration
Federal Building
Room 1590
1220 SW Third Avenue
Portland, OR 97204
(503) 326-2731

ECONOMIC INJURY DISASTER LOANS

Office of Disaster Assistance
Small Business Administration (SBA)
409 Third Street, SW
Washington, DC 20416
(202) 205-6734

Description: Provides direct loans to small businesses suffering
economic damage under Small Business Administration, Department of Agriculture, and/or presidentially declared disaster. Must be
a small business or agricultural concern, located within declared
disaster area and unable to obtain credit elsewhere.
$ Given: $78,209,000 est. FY 95; range: up to $1,500,000; average
assistance: $50,725
Application Information: Applications are filed with nearest
available SBA disaster area or special disaster office.
Deadline: Established for each declaration of disaster.
Contact: Small Business Administration, Region X
           2615 Fourth Avenue
           Room 440
           Seattle, WA 98121
           (206) 442-5676

PENNSYLVANIA

EMPLOYMENT SERVICE

United States Employment Service
Employment and Training Administration, Department of Labor
Washington, DC 20210
(202) 219-5257

Description: Provides placement services for job seekers and
employers. These include services to special applicant groups, such
as veterans, the handicapped, youth, minorities, and older workers;
a computerized interstate job listing; and other labor market
information.
$ Given: $847,220,000 est. FY 95
Application Information: Contact your state office.
Deadline: Established each year (contact federal agency for deadline
for application submission).

Contact: Frank Lynch, Executive Deputy Director
Department of Labor and Industry
1700 Labor and Industry Building
Seventh and Forster Streets
Harrisburg, PA 17120
(717) 787-1745

UNEMPLOYMENT INSURANCE

Unemployment Insurance Service
Employment and Training Administration, Department of Labor
Washington, DC 20210
(202) 219-7831

Description: Provides unemployment insurance for workers whose
employers have contributed to state unemployment funds, federal
civilian employees, ex–service persons, those who have become
unemployed as a result of product imports, and those whose
unemployment comes under the purview of a presidentially declared
disaster.
$ Given: $23.7 billion est. FY 95
Application Information: Contact the Employment Security Department for your state.
Deadline: Not available
Contact: Frank Lynch, Executive Deputy Director
Department of Labor and Industry
1700 Labor and Industry Building
Seventh and Forster Streets
Harrisburg, PA 17120
(717) 787-1745

EMPLOYMENT AND TRAINING ASSISTANCE—DISLOCATED WORKERS

Employment and Training Administration, Department of Labor
200 Constitution Avenue, NW
Washington, DC 20210
(202) 219-5577

Description: Federal grants given to state and local programs to
assist workers through training and employment services. These are
workers who have been terminated or laid off or received notice of
such and are not likely to return to their previous occupation or
industry or who are long-term unemployed. Targeted individuals

include those affected by mass layoffs and natural disasters.
$ Given: $571.1 million total nationwide for FY 93
Application Information: Inquire at Employment Security office
listed below.
Deadline: Not available
Contact: Frank Lynch, Executive Deputy Director
                Department of Labor and Industry
                1700 Labor and Industry Building
                Seventh and Forster Streets
                Harrisburg, PA 17120
                (717) 787-1745

WOMEN'S SPECIAL EMPLOYMENT ASSISTANCE

Office of Administrative Management
Women's Bureau
Office of the Secretary
Department of Labor
Washington, DC 20210
(202) 219-6611

Description: Makes referrals as to sources for counseling and
disseminates technical information to aid in the employment of
women—especially in the realm of nontraditional women's jobs and
jobs in new technologies.
$ Given: $8,054,000 est. FY 95
Application Information: Write to Women's Bureau in your region.
Deadline: None
Contact: Regional Administrator
                Region III, Women's Bureau
                Department of Labor
                Gateway Building
                Room 13280
                3535 Market Street
                Philadelphia, PA 19104
                (206) 553-1534

EMERGENCY LOANS

Farmers Home Administration
Department of Agriculture
14th Street and Independence Avenue, SW
Washington, DC 20250
(202) 720-1632

Description: Provides loans to family farmers (either owner or tenant), ranchers, and aquaculture operators to cover losses resulting from natural or other major disasters. Recipients must be unable to obtain credit from other sources.
$ Given: $180 million est. FY 95; average range: $500–$500,000; average assistance: $66,200
Application Information: Consult local telephone directory under United States Government, Department of Agriculture, for Farmers Home Administration office.
Deadline: Not available
Contact: Farmers Home Administration
One Credit Union Place
Suite 330
Harrisburg, PA 17110-2996
(717) 782-4476

ECONOMIC INJURY DISASTER LOANS

Office of Disaster Assistance
Small Business Administration (SBA)
409 Third Street, SW
Washington, DC 20416
(202) 205-6734

Description: Provides direct loans to small businesses suffering economic damage under Small Business Administration, Department of Agriculture, and/or presidentially declared disaster. Must be a small business or agricultural concern, located within declared disaster area and unable to obtain credit elsewhere.
$ Given: $78,209,000 est. FY 95; range: up to $1,500,000; average assistance: $50,725
Application Information: Applications are filed with nearest available SBA disaster area or special disaster office.
Deadline: Established for each declaration of disaster.
Contact: Small Business Administration, Region III
475 Allendale Road
Suite 201
King of Prussia, PA 19406
(215) 962-3700

PUERTO RICO

EMPLOYMENT SERVICE

United States Employment Service
Employment and Training Administration, Department of Labor
Washington, DC 20210
(202) 219-5257

Description: Provides placement services for job seekers and employers. These include services to special applicant groups, such as veterans, the handicapped, youth, minorities, and older workers; a computerized interstate job listing; and other labor market information.
$ Given: $847,220,000 est. FY 95
Application Information: Contact your state office.
Deadline: Established each year (contact federal agency for deadline for application submission).
Contact: Cesar Juan Almodovar Marchany
              Bureau of Employment Security
              505 Munoz Rivera Avenue
              Hato Rey, PR 00918
              (809) 754-2119
              Fax: (809) 753-9550

UNEMPLOYMENT INSURANCE

Unemployment Insurance Service
Employment and Training Administration, Department of Labor
Washington, DC 20210
(202) 219-7831

Description: Provides unemployment insurance for workers whose employers have contributed to state unemployment funds, federal civilian employees, ex–service persons, those who have become unemployed as a result of product imports, and those whose unemployment comes under the purview of a presidentially declared disaster.
$ Given: $23.7 billion est. FY 95
Application Information: Contact the Employment Security Department for your state.
Deadline: Not available

Contact: Cesar Juan Almodovar Marchany
          Bureau of Employment Security
          505 Munoz Rivera Avenue
          Hato Rey, PR 00918
          (809) 754-2119
          Fax: (809) 753-9550

EMPLOYMENT AND TRAINING ASSISTANCE— DISLOCATED WORKERS

Employment and Training Administration, Department of Labor
200 Constitution Avenue, NW
Washington, DC 20210
(202) 219-5577

Description: Federal grants given to state and local programs to assist workers through training and employment services. These are workers who have been terminated or laid off or received notice of such and are not likely to return to their previous occupation or industry or who are long-term unemployed. Targeted individuals include those affected by mass layoffs and natural disasters.
$ Given: $571.1 million total nationwide for FY 93
Application Information: Inquire at Employment Security office listed below.
Deadline: Not available
Contact: Cesar Juan Almodovar Marchany
          Bureau of Employment Security
          505 Munoz Rivera Avenue
          Hato Rey, PR 00918
          (809) 754-2119
          Fax: (809) 753-9550

WOMEN'S SPECIAL EMPLOYMENT ASSISTANCE

Office of Administrative Management
Women's Bureau
Office of the Secretary
Department of Labor
Washington, DC 20210
(202) 219-6611

Description: Makes referrals as to sources for counseling and disseminates technical information to aid in the employment of women—especially in the realm of nontraditional women's jobs and jobs in new technologies.

$ Given: $8,054,000 est. FY 95
Application Information: Write to Women's Bureau in your region.
Deadline: None
Contact: Mary C. Murphee, Regional Administrator
            Region II, Women's Bureau
            Department of Labor
            201 Varick Street
            Room 601
            New York, NY 10014
            (212) 337-2389

EMERGENCY LOANS

Farmers Home Administration
Department of Agriculture
14th Street and Independence Avenue, SW
Washington, DC 20250
(202) 720-1632

Description: Provides loans to family farmers (either owner or tenant), ranchers, and aquaculture operators to cover losses resulting from natural or other major disasters. Recipients must be unable to obtain credit from other sources.
$ Given: $180 million est. FY 95; average range: $500–$500,000; average assistance: $66,200
Application Information: Consult local telephone directory under United States Government, Department of Agriculture, for Farmers Home Administration office.
Deadline: Not available
Contact: Farmers Home Administration
            New San Juan Center Building
            Room 501
            159 Carlos E. Chardon Street
            G.P.O. Box 6106G
            Hato Rey, PR 00918-5481
            (809) 766-5095

ECONOMIC INJURY DISASTER LOANS

Office of Disaster Assistance
Small Business Administration (SBA)
409 Third Street, SW
Washington, DC 20416
(202) 205-6734

Description: Provides direct loans to small businesses suffering economic damage under Small Business Administration, Department of Agriculture, and/or presidentially declared disaster. Must be a small business or agricultural concern, located within declared disaster area and unable to obtain credit elsewhere.

$ Given: $78,209,000 est. FY 95; range: up to $1,500,000; average assistance: $50,725

Application Information: Applications are filed with nearest available SBA disaster area or special disaster office.

Deadline: Established for each declaration of disaster.

Contact: Small Business Administration, Region II
            26 Federal Plaza
            Room 31-08
            New York, NY 10278
            (212) 264-7772

RHODE ISLAND

EMPLOYMENT SERVICE

United States Employment Service
Employment and Training Administration, Department of Labor
Washington, DC 20210
(202) 219-5257

Description: Provides placement services for job seekers and employers. These include services to special applicant groups, such as veterans, the handicapped, youth, minorities, and older workers; a computerized interstate job listing; and other labor market information.

$ Given: $847,220,000 est. FY 95

Application Information: Contact your state office.

Deadline: Established each year (contact federal agency for deadline for application submission).

Contact: Marvin Perry, Director
            Department of Employment Security and Training
            101 Friendship Street
            Providence, RI 02903-3740
            (401) 277-3732
            Fax: (401) 277-1473

UNEMPLOYMENT INSURANCE

Unemployment Insurance Service
Employment and Training Administration, Department of Labor
Washington, DC 20210
(202) 219-7831

Description: Provides unemployment insurance for workers whose employers have contributed to state unemployment funds, federal civilian employees, ex–service persons, those who have become unemployed as a result of product imports, and those whose unemployment comes under the purview of a presidentially declared disaster.
$ Given: $23.7 billion est. FY 95
Application Information: Contact the Employment Security Department for your state.
Deadline: Not available
Contact: Marvin Perry, Director
           Department of Employment Security and Training
           101 Friendship Street
           Providence, RI 02903-3740
           (401) 277-3732
           Fax: (401) 277-1473

EMPLOYMENT AND TRAINING ASSISTANCE— DISLOCATED WORKERS

Employment and Training Administration, Department of Labor
200 Constitution Avenue, NW
Washington, DC 20210
(202) 219-5577

Description: Federal grants given to state and local programs to assist workers through training and employment services. These are workers who have been terminated or laid off or received notice of such and are not likely to return to their previous occupation or industry or who are long-term unemployed. Targeted individuals include those affected by mass layoffs and natural disasters.
$ Given: $571.1 million total nationwide for FY 93
Application Information: Inquire at Employment Security office listed below.
Deadline: Not available

Contact: Marvin Perry, Director
Department of Employment Security and Training
101 Friendship Street
Providence, RI 02903-3740
(401) 277-3732
Fax: (401) 277-1473

WOMEN'S SPECIAL EMPLOYMENT ASSISTANCE

Office of Administrative Management
Women's Bureau
Office of the Secretary
Department of Labor
Washington, DC 20210
(202) 219-6611

Description: Makes referrals as to sources for counseling and disseminates technical information to aid in the employment of women—especially in the realm of nontraditional women's jobs and jobs in new technologies.
$ Given: $8,054,000 est. FY 95
Application Information: Write to Women's Bureau in your region.
Deadline: None
Contact: Martha Izzi, Regional Administrator
Region I, Women's Bureau
Department of Labor
One Congress Street
Boston, MA 02214
(617) 565-1988

EMERGENCY LOANS

Farmers Home Administration
Department of Agriculture
14th Street and Independence Avenue, SW
Washington, DC 20250
(202) 720-1632

Description: Provides loans to family farmers (either owner or tenant), ranchers, and aquaculture operators to cover losses resulting from natural or other major disasters. Recipients must be unable to obtain credit from other sources.
$ Given: $180 million est. FY 95; average range: $500–$500,000; average assistance: $66,200

Application Information: Consult local telephone directory under
United States Government, Department of Agriculture, for Farmers
Home Administration office.
Deadline: Not available
Contact: Farmers Home Administration
              451 West Street
              Amherst, MA 01002
              (413) 253-4300

ECONOMIC INJURY DISASTER LOANS

Office of Disaster Assistance
Small Business Administration (SBA)
409 Third Street, SW
Washington, DC 20416
(202) 205-6734

Description: Provides direct loans to small businesses suffering
economic damage under Small Business Administration, Department of Agriculture, and/or presidentially declared disaster. Must be
a small business or agricultural concern, located within declared
disaster area and unable to obtain credit elsewhere.
$ Given: $78,209,000 est. FY 95; range: up to $1,500,000; average
assistance: $50,725
Application Information: Applications are filed with nearest
available SBA disaster area or special disaster office.
Deadline: Established for each declaration of disaster.
Contact: Small Business Administration, Region I
              155 Federal Street
              Ninth Floor
              Boston, MA 02110
              (617) 451-2023

SOUTH CAROLINA

EMPLOYMENT SERVICE

United States Employment Service
Employment and Training Administration, Department of Labor
Washington, DC 20210
(202) 219-5257

Description: Provides placement services for job seekers and employers. These include services to special applicant groups, such as veterans, the handicapped, youth, minorities, and older workers; a computerized interstate job listing; and other labor market information.
$ Given: $847,220,000 est. FY 95
Application Information: Contact your state office.
Deadline: Established each year (contact federal agency for deadline for application submission).
Contact: Robert E. David, Executive Director
Employment Security Commission
P.O. Box 995
1550 Gadsden Street
Columbia, SC 29202
(803) 737-2617
Fax: (803) 737-2617

UNEMPLOYMENT INSURANCE

Unemployment Insurance Service
Employment and Training Administration, Department of Labor
Washington, DC 20210
(202) 219-7831

Description: Provides unemployment insurance for workers whose employers have contributed to state unemployment funds, federal civilian employees, ex–service persons, those who have become unemployed as a result of product imports, and those whose unemployment comes under the purview of a presidentially declared disaster.
$ Given: $23.7 billion est. FY 95
Application Information: Contact the Employment Security Department for your state.
Deadline: Not available
Contact: Robert E. David, Executive Director
Employment Security Commission
P.O. Box 995
1550 Gadsden Street
Columbia, SC 29202
(803) 737-2617
Fax: (803) 737-2617

EMPLOYMENT AND TRAINING ASSISTANCE— DISLOCATED WORKERS

Employment and Training Administration, Department of Labor
200 Constitution Avenue, NW
Washington, DC 20210
(202) 219-5577

Description: Federal grants given to state and local programs to assist workers through training and employment services. These are workers who have been terminated or laid off or received notice of such and are not likely to return to their previous occupation or industry or who are long-term unemployed. Targeted individuals include those affected by mass layoffs and natural disasters.
$ Given: $571.1 million total nationwide for FY 93
Application Information: Inquire at Employment Security office listed below.
Deadline: Not available
Contact: Robert E. David, Executive Director
              Employment Security Commission
              P.O. Box 995
              1550 Gadsden Street
              Columbia, SC 29202
              (803) 737-2617
              Fax: (803) 737-2617

WOMEN'S SPECIAL EMPLOYMENT ASSISTANCE

Office of Administrative Management
Women's Bureau
Office of the Secretary
Department of Labor
Washington, DC 20210
(202) 219-6611

Description: Makes referrals as to sources for counseling and disseminates technical information to aid in the employment of women—especially in the realm of nontraditional women's jobs and jobs in new technologies.
$ Given: $8,054,000 est. FY 95
Application Information: Write to Women's Bureau in your region.
Deadline: None

Contact: Delores L. Crockett, Regional Administrator
Region IV, Women's Bureau
Department of Labor
1371 Peachtree Street, NE
Room 323
Atlanta, GA 30367
(404) 347-4461

EMERGENCY LOANS

Farmers Home Administration
Department of Agriculture
14th Street and Independence Avenue, SW
Washington, DC 20250
(202) 720-1632

Description: Provides loans to family farmers (either owner or tenant), ranchers, and aquaculture operators to cover losses resulting from natural or other major disasters. Recipients must be unable to obtain credit from other sources.
$ Given: $180 million est. FY 95; average range: $500–$500,000; average assistance: $66,200
Application Information: Consult local telephone directory under United States Government, Department of Agriculture, for Farmers Home Administration office.
Deadline: Not available
Contact: Farmers Home Administration
Strom Thurmond Federal Building
1835 Assembly Street
Room 1007
Columbia, SC 29201
(803) 765-5163

ECONOMIC INJURY DISASTER LOANS

Office of Disaster Assistance
Small Business Administration (SBA)
409 Third Street, SW
Washington, DC 20416
(202) 205-6734

Description: Provides direct loans to small businesses suffering economic damage under Small Business Administration, Department of Agriculture, and/or presidentially declared disaster. Must be

a small business or agricultural concern, located within declared
disaster area and unable to obtain credit elsewhere.
$ Given: $78,209,000 est. FY 95; range: up to $1,500,000; average
assistance: $50,725
Application Information: Applications are filed with nearest
available SBA disaster area or special disaster office.
Deadline: Established for each declaration of disaster.
Contact: Small Business Administration, Region IV
               1375 Peachtree Street, NE
               Fifth Floor
               Atlanta, GA 30367-8102
               (404) 347-2797

SOUTH DAKOTA

EMPLOYMENT SERVICE

United States Employment Service
Employment and Training Administration, Department of Labor
Washington, DC 20210
(202) 219-5257

Description: Provides placement services for job seekers and
employers. These include services to special applicant groups, such
as veterans, the handicapped, youth, minorities, and older workers;
a computerized interstate job listing; and other labor market
information.
$ Given: $847,220,000 est. FY 95
Application Information: Contact your state office.
Deadline: Established each year (contact federal agency for deadline
for application submission).
Contact: Grant Gormley
               Department of Labor
               Kneip Building
               700 Governors Drive
               Pierre, SD 57501-2277
               (605) 773-3101

UNEMPLOYMENT INSURANCE

Unemployment Insurance Service
Employment and Training Administration, Department of Labor
Washington, DC 20210
(202) 219-7831

Description: Provides unemployment insurance for workers whose
employers have contributed to state unemployment funds, federal
civilian employees, ex–service persons, those who have become
unemployed as a result of product imports, and those whose
unemployment comes under the purview of a presidentially declared
disaster.
$ Given: $23.7 billion est. FY 95
Application Information: Contact the Employment Security Department for your state.
Deadline: Not available
Contact: Grant Gormley
           Department of Labor
           Kneip Building
           700 Governors Drive
           Pierre, SD 57501-2277
           (605) 773-3101

EMPLOYMENT AND TRAINING ASSISTANCE—
DISLOCATED WORKERS

Employment and Training Administration, Department of Labor
200 Constitution Avenue, NW
Washington, DC 20210
(202) 219-5577

Description: Federal grants given to state and local programs to
assist workers through training and employment services. These are
workers who have been terminated or laid off or received notice of
such and are not likely to return to their previous occupation or
industry or who are long-term unemployed. Targeted individuals
include those affected by mass layoffs and natural disasters.
$ Given: $571.1 million total nationwide for FY 93
Application Information: Inquire at Employment Security office
listed below.
Deadline: Not available

Contact: Grant Gormley
          Department of Labor
          Kneip Building
          700 Governors Drive
          Pierre, SD 57501-2277
          (605) 773-3101

WOMEN'S SPECIAL EMPLOYMENT ASSISTANCE

Office of Administrative Management
Women's Bureau
Office of the Secretary
Department of Labor
Washington, DC 20210
(202) 219-6611

Description: Makes referrals as to sources for counseling and
disseminates technical information to aid in the employment of
women—especially in the realm of nontraditional women's jobs and
jobs in new technologies.
$ Given: $8,054,000 est. FY 95
Application Information: Write to Women's Bureau in your region.
Deadline: None
Contact: Oleta Crain, Regional Administrator
          Region VIII, Women's Bureau
          Department of Labor
          Federal Office Building
          Room 1452
          1801 California Street
          Suite 905
          Denver, CO 80202-2614
          (303) 391-6755

EMERGENCY LOANS

Farmers Home Administration
Department of Agriculture
14th Street and Independence Avenue, SW
Washington, DC 20250
(202) 720-1632

Description: Provides loans to family farmers (either owner or
tenant), ranchers, and aquaculture operators to cover losses result-

ing from natural or other major disasters. Recipients must be unable to obtain credit from other sources.
$ Given: $180 million est. FY 95; average range: $500–$500,000; average assistance: $66,200
Application Information: Consult local telephone directory under United States Government, Department of Agriculture, for Farmers Home Administration office.
Deadline: Not available
Contact: Farmers Home Administration
Huron Federal Building
Room 308
200 Fourth Street, SW
Huron, SD 57350
(605) 353-1430

ECONOMIC INJURY DISASTER LOANS

Office of Disaster Assistance
Small Business Administration (SBA)
409 Third Street, SW
Washington, DC 20416
(202) 205-6734

Description: Provides direct loans to small businesses suffering economic damage under Small Business Administration, Department of Agriculture, and/or presidentially declared disaster. Must be a small business or agricultural concern, located within declared disaster area and unable to obtain credit elsewhere.
$ Given: $78,209,000 est. FY 95; range: up to $1,500,000; average assistance: $50,725
Application Information: Applications are filed with nearest available SBA disaster area or special disaster office.
Deadline: Established for each declaration of disaster.
Contact: Small Business Administration, Region VIII
633 17th Street
Seventh Floor
Denver, CO 80202
(303) 294-7186

TENNESSEE

EMPLOYMENT SERVICE

United States Employment Service
Employment and Training Administration, Department of Labor
Washington, DC 20210
(202) 219-5257

Description: Provides placement services for job seekers and employers. These include services to special applicant groups, such as veterans, the handicapped, youth, minorities, and older workers; a computerized interstate job listing; and other labor market information.
$ Given: $847,220,000 est. FY 95
Application Information: Contact your state office.
Deadline: Established each year (contact federal agency for deadline for application submission).
Contact: James A. Davenport, Commissioner
            Department of Employment Security
            Volunteer Plaza Building
            12th Floor
            500 James Robertson Parkway
            Nashville, TN 37245-0001
            (615) 741-2131
            Fax: (615) 741-3203

UNEMPLOYMENT INSURANCE

Unemployment Insurance Service
Employment and Training Administration, Department of Labor
Washington, DC 20210
(202) 219-7831

Description: Provides unemployment insurance for workers whose employers have contributed to state unemployment funds, federal civilian employees, ex–service persons, those who have become unemployed as a result of product imports, and those whose unemployment comes under the purview of a presidentially declared disaster.
$ Given: $23.7 billion est. FY 95
Application Information: Contact the Employment Security Department for your state.
Deadline: Not available

Contact: James A. Davenport, Commissioner
Department of Employment Security
Volunteer Plaza Building
12th Floor
500 James Robertson Parkway
Nashville, TN 37245-0001
(615) 741-2131
Fax: (615) 741-3203

EMPLOYMENT AND TRAINING ASSISTANCE—DISLOCATED WORKERS

Employment and Training Administration, Department of Labor
200 Constitution Avenue, NW
Washington, DC 20210
(202) 219-5577

Description: Federal grants given to state and local programs to assist workers through training and employment services. These are workers who have been terminated or laid off or received notice of such and are not likely to return to their previous occupation or industry or who are long-term unemployed. Targeted individuals include those affected by mass layoffs and natural disasters.
$ Given: $571.1 million total nationwide for FY 93
Application Information: Inquire at Employment Security office listed below.
Deadline: Not available
Contact: James A. Davenport, Commissioner
Department of Employment Security
Volunteer Plaza Building
12th Floor
500 James Robertson Parkway
Nashville, TN 37245-0001
(615) 741-2131
Fax: (615) 741-3203

WOMEN'S SPECIAL EMPLOYMENT ASSISTANCE

Office of Administrative Management
Women's Bureau
Office of the Secretary
Department of Labor
Washington, DC 20210
(202) 219-6611

Description: Makes referrals as to sources for counseling and
disseminates technical information to aid in the employment of
women—especially in the realm of nontraditional women's jobs and
jobs in new technologies.
$ Given: $8,054,000 est. FY 95
Application Information: Write to Women's Bureau in your region.
Deadline: None
Contact: Delores L. Crockett, Regional Administrator
           Region IV, Women's Bureau
           Department of Labor
           1371 Peachtree Street, NE
           Room 323
           Atlanta, GA 30367
           (404) 347-4461

EMERGENCY LOANS

Farmers Home Administration
Department of Agriculture
14th Street and Independence Avenue, SW
Washington, DC 20250
(202) 720-1632

Description: Provides loans to family farmers (either owner or
tenant), ranchers, and aquaculture operators to cover losses resulting from natural or other major disasters. Recipients must be
unable to obtain credit from other sources.
$ Given: $180 million est. FY 95; average range: $500–$500,000;
average assistance: $66,200
Application Information: Consult local telephone directory under
United States Government, Department of Agriculture, for Farmers
Home Administration office.
Deadline: Not available
Contact: Farmers Home Administration
           3322 West End Avenue
           Suite 300
           Nashville, TN 37203-1071
           (615) 736-7341

ECONOMIC INJURY DISASTER LOANS

Office of Disaster Assistance
Small Business Administration (SBA)
409 Third Street, SW
Washington, DC 20416
(202) 205-6734

Description: Provides direct loans to small businesses suffering economic damage under Small Business Administration, Department of Agriculture, and/or presidentially declared disaster. Must be a small business or agricultural concern, located within declared disaster area and unable to obtain credit elsewhere.
$ Given: $78,209,000 est. FY 95; range: up to $1,500,000; average assistance: $50,725
Application Information: Applications are filed with nearest available SBA disaster area or special disaster office.
Deadline: Established for each declaration of disaster.
Contact: Small Business Administration, Region IV
           1375 Peachtree Street, NE
           Fifth Floor
           Atlanta, GA 30367-8102
           (404) 347-2797

TEXAS

EMPLOYMENT SERVICE

United States Employment Service
Employment and Training Administration, Department of Labor
Washington, DC 20210
(202) 219-5257

Description: Provides placement services for job seekers and employers. These include services to special applicant groups, such as veterans, the handicapped, youth, minorities, and older workers; a computerized interstate job listing; and other labor market information.
$ Given: $847,220,000 est. FY 95
Application Information: Contact your state office.
Deadline: Established each year (contact federal agency for deadline for application submission).

Contact: William Grossenbacher, Administrator
          Texas Employment Commission
          638 TEC Building
          15th and Congress Avenue
          Austin, TX 78778
          (512) 463-2652
          Fax: (512) 475-1133

UNEMPLOYMENT INSURANCE

Unemployment Insurance Service
Employment and Training Administration, Department of Labor
Washington, DC 20210
(202) 219-7831

Description: Provides unemployment insurance for workers whose
employers have contributed to state unemployment funds, federal
civilian employees, ex–service persons, those who have become
unemployed as a result of product imports, and those whose
unemployment comes under the purview of a presidentially declared
disaster.
$ Given: $23.7 billion est. FY 95
Application Information: Contact the Employment Security Department for your state.
Deadline: Not available
Contact: William Grossenbacher, Administrator
          Texas Employment Commission
          638 TEC Building
          15th and Congress Avenue
          Austin, TX 78778
          (512) 463-2652
          Fax: (512) 475-1133

EMPLOYMENT AND TRAINING ASSISTANCE—
DISLOCATED WORKERS

Employment and Training Administration, Department of Labor
200 Constitution Avenue, NW
Washington, DC 20210
(202) 219-5577

Description: Federal grants given to state and local programs to
assist workers through training and employment services. These are

workers who have been terminated or laid off or received notice of such and are not likely to return to their previous occupation or industry or who are long-term unemployed. Targeted individuals include those affected by mass layoffs and natural disasters.
$ Given: $571.1 million total nationwide for FY 93
Application Information: Inquire at Employment Security office listed below.
Deadline: Not available
Contact: William Grossenbacher, Administrator
Texas Employment Commission
638 TEC Building
15th and Congress Avenue
Austin, TX 78778
(512) 463-2652
Fax: (512) 475-1133

WOMEN'S SPECIAL EMPLOYMENT ASSISTANCE

Office of Administrative Management
Women's Bureau
Office of the Secretary
Department of Labor
Washington, DC 20210
(202) 219-6611

Description: Makes referrals as to sources for counseling and disseminates technical information to aid in the employment of women—especially in the realm of nontraditional women's jobs and jobs in new technologies.
$ Given: $8,054,000 est. FY 95
Application Information: Write to Women's Bureau in your region.
Deadline: None
Contact: Evelyn Smith, Regional Administrator
Region VI, Women's Bureau
Department of Labor
Federal Building
Suite 731
Dallas, TX 75202
(214) 767-6985

EMERGENCY LOANS

Farmers Home Administration
Department of Agriculture
14th Street and Independence Avenue, SW
Washington, DC 20250
(202) 720-1632

Description: Provides loans to family farmers (either owner or tenant), ranchers, and aquaculture operators to cover losses resulting from natural or other major disasters. Recipients must be unable to obtain credit from other sources.
$ Given: $180 million est. FY 95; average range: $500–$500,000; average assistance: $66,200
Application Information: Consult local telephone directory under United States Government, Department of Agriculture, for Farmers Home Administration office.
Deadline: Not available
Contact: Farmers Home Administration
         Federal Building
         Suite 102
         101 South Main Street
         Temple, TX 76501
         (817) 774-1301

ECONOMIC INJURY DISASTER LOANS

Office of Disaster Assistance
Small Business Administration (SBA)
409 Third Street, SW
Washington, DC 20416
(202) 205-6734

Description: Provides direct loans to small businesses suffering economic damage under Small Business Administration, Department of Agriculture, and/or presidentially declared disaster. Must be a small business or agricultural concern, located within declared disaster area and unable to obtain credit elsewhere.
$ Given: $78,209,000 est. FY 95; range: up to $1,500,000; average assistance: $50,725
Application Information: Applications are filed with nearest available SBA disaster area or special disaster office.
Deadline: Established for each declaration of disaster.

Contact: Small Business Administration, Region VI
          8625 King George Drive
          Building C
          Dallas, TX 75235-3391
          (214) 767-7633

UTAH

EMPLOYMENT SERVICE

United States Employment Service
Employment and Training Administration, Department of Labor
Washington, DC 20210
(202) 219-5257

Description: Provides placement services for job seekers and
employers. These include services to special applicant groups, such
as veterans, the handicapped, youth, minorities, and older workers;
a computerized interstate job listing; and other labor market
information.
$ Given: $847,220,000 est. FY 95
Application Information: Contact your state office.
Deadline: Established each year (contact federal agency for deadline
for application submission).
Contact: Floyd G. Astin, Administrator
          Department of Employment Security
          P.O. Box 11249
          140 East 300 South
          Salt Lake City, UT 84147-0249
          (801) 536-7401

UNEMPLOYMENT INSURANCE

Unemployment Insurance Service
Employment and Training Administration, Department of Labor
Washington, DC 20210
(202) 219-7831

Description: Provides unemployment insurance for workers whose
employers have contributed to state unemployment funds, federal
civilian employees, ex–service persons, those who have become
unemployed as a result of product imports, and those whose

unemployment comes under the purview of a presidentially declared disaster.

$ Given: $23.7 billion est. FY 95

Application Information: Contact the Employment Security Department for your state.

Deadline: Not available

Contact: Floyd G. Astin, Administrator
Department of Employment Security
P.O. Box 11249
140 East 300 South
Salt Lake City, UT 84147-0249
(801) 536-7401

EMPLOYMENT AND TRAINING ASSISTANCE— DISLOCATED WORKERS

Employment and Training Administration, Department of Labor
200 Constitution Avenue, NW
Washington, DC 20210
(202) 219-5577

Description: Federal grants given to state and local programs to assist workers through training and employment services. These are workers who have been terminated or laid off or received notice of such and are not likely to return to their previous occupation or industry or who are long-term unemployed. Targeted individuals include those affected by mass layoffs and natural disasters.

$ Given: $571.1 million total nationwide for FY 93

Application Information: Inquire at Employment Security office listed below.

Deadline: Not available

Contact: Floyd G. Astin, Administrator
Department of Employment Security
P.O. Box 11249
140 East 300 South
Salt Lake City, UT 84147-0249
(801) 536-7401

WOMEN'S SPECIAL EMPLOYMENT ASSISTANCE

Office of Administrative Management
Women's Bureau
Office of the Secretary
Department of Labor
Washington, DC 20210
(202) 219-6611

Description: Makes referrals as to sources for counseling and disseminates technical information to aid in the employment of women—especially in the realm of nontraditional women's jobs and jobs in new technologies.
$ Given: $8,054,000 est. FY 95
Application Information: Write to Women's Bureau in your region.
Deadline: None
Contact: Oleta Crain, Regional Administrator
        Region VIII, Women's Bureau
        Department of Labor
        Federal Office Building
        Suite 1452
        1801 California Street
        Suite 905
        Denver, CO 80202-2614
        (303) 391-6755

EMERGENCY LOANS

Farmers Home Administration
Department of Agriculture
14th Street and Independence Avenue, SW
Washington, DC 20250
(202) 720-1632

Description: Provides loans to family farmers (either owner or tenant), ranchers, and aquaculture operators to cover losses resulting from natural or other major disasters. Recipients must be unable to obtain credit from other sources.
$ Given: $180 million est. FY 95; average range: $500–$500,000; average assistance: $66,200
Application Information: Consult local telephone directory under United States Government, Department of Agriculture, for Farmers Home Administration office.
Deadline: Not available

Contact: Farmers Home Administration
           Federal Building
           Room 5438
           125 South State Street
           Salt Lake City, UT 84138
           (801) 524-4063

ECONOMIC INJURY DISASTER LOANS

Office of Disaster Assistance
Small Business Administration (SBA)
409 Third Street, SW
Washington, DC 20416
(202) 205-6734

Description: Provides direct loans to small businesses suffering
economic damage under Small Business Administration, Department of Agriculture, and/or presidentially declared disaster. Must be
a small business or agricultural concern, located within declared
disaster area and unable to obtain credit elsewhere.
$ Given: $78,209,000 est. FY 95; range: up to $1,500,000; average
assistance: $50,725
Application Information: Applications are filed with nearest
available SBA disaster area or special disaster office.
Deadline: Established for each declaration of disaster.
Contact: Small Business Administration, Region VIII
           633 17th Street
           Seventh Floor
           Denver, CO 80202
           (303) 294-7186

VERMONT

EMPLOYMENT SERVICE

United States Employment Service
Employment and Training Administration, Department of Labor
Washington, DC 20210
(202) 219-5257

Description: Provides placement services for job seekers and
employers. These include services to special applicant groups, such
as veterans, the handicapped, youth, minorities, and older workers;

a computerized interstate job listing; and other labor market information.

$ Given: $847,220,000 est. FY 95

Application Information: Contact your state office.

Deadline: Established each year (contact federal agency for deadline for application submission).

Contact: Susan Auld, Commissioner
Department of Employment Security and Training
P.O. Box 488
5 Green Mountain Drive
Montpelier, VT 05602
(802) 828-4151
Fax: (802) 828-4022

UNEMPLOYMENT INSURANCE

Unemployment Insurance Service
Employment and Training Administration, Department of Labor
Washington, DC 20210
(202) 219-7831

Description: Provides unemployment insurance for workers whose employers have contributed to state unemployment funds, federal civilian employees, ex–service persons, those who have become unemployed as a result of product imports, and those whose unemployment comes under the purview of a presidentially declared disaster.

$ Given: $23.7 billion est. FY 95

Application Information: Contact the Employment Security Department for your state.

Deadline: Not available

Contact: Susan Auld, Commissioner
Department of Employment Security and Training
P.O. Box 488
5 Green Mountain Drive
Montpelier, VT 05602
(802) 828-4151
Fax: (802) 828-4022

EMPLOYMENT AND TRAINING ASSISTANCE— DISLOCATED WORKERS

Employment and Training Administration, Department of Labor
200 Constitution Avenue, NW
Washington, DC 20210
(202) 219-5577

Description: Federal grants given to state and local programs to assist workers through training and employment services. These are workers who have been terminated or laid off or received notice of such and are not likely to return to their previous occupation or industry or who are long-term unemployed. Targeted individuals include those affected by mass layoffs and natural disasters.
$ Given: $571.1 million total nationwide for FY 93
Application Information: Inquire at Employment Security office listed below.
Deadline: Not available
Contact: Susan Auld, Commissioner
             Department of Employment Security and Training
             P.O. Box 488
             5 Green Mountain Drive
             Montpelier, VT 05602
             (802) 828-4151
             Fax: (802) 828-4022

WOMEN'S SPECIAL EMPLOYMENT ASSISTANCE

Office of Administrative Management
Women's Bureau
Office of the Secretary
Department of Labor
Washington, DC 20210
(202) 219-6611

Description: Makes referrals as to sources for counseling and disseminates technical information to aid in the employment of women—especially in the realm of nontraditional women's jobs and jobs in new technologies.
$ Given: $8,054,000 est. FY 95
Application Information: Write to Women's Bureau in your region.
Deadline: None

Contact: Martha Izzi, Regional Administrator
           Region I, Women's Bureau
           Department of Labor
           One Congress Street
           Boston, MA 02214
           (617) 565-1988

EMERGENCY LOANS

Farmers Home Administration
Department of Agriculture
14th Street and Independence Avenue, SW
Washington, DC 20250
(202) 720-1632

Description: Provides loans to family farmers (either owner or
tenant), ranchers, and aquaculture operators to cover losses resulting from natural or other major disasters. Recipients must be
unable to obtain credit from other sources.
$ Given: $180 million est. FY 95; average range: $500–$500,000;
average assistance: $66,200
Application Information: Consult local telephone directory under
United States Government, Department of Agriculture, for Farmers
Home Administration office.
Deadline: Not available
Contact: Farmers Home Administration
           City Center
           Third Floor
           89 Main Street
           Montpelier, VT 05602
           (802) 828-6001

ECONOMIC INJURY DISASTER LOANS

Office of Disaster Assistance
Small Business Administration (SBA)
409 Third Street, SW
Washington, DC 20416
(202) 205-6734

Description: Provides direct loans to small businesses suffering
economic damage under Small Business Administration, Department of Agriculture, and/or presidentially declared disaster. Must be
a small business or agricultural concern, located within declared
disaster area and unable to obtain credit elsewhere.

$ Given: $78,209,000 est. FY 95; range: up to $1,500,000; average assistance: $50,725
Application Information: Applications are filed with nearest available SBA disaster area or special disaster office.
Deadline: Established for each declaration of disaster.
Contact: Small Business Administration, Region I
155 Federal Street
Ninth Floor
Boston, MA 02110
(617) 451-2023

VIRGINIA

EMPLOYMENT SERVICE

United States Employment Service
Employment and Training Administration, Department of Labor
Washington, DC 20210
(202) 219-5257

Description: Provides placement services for job seekers and employers. These include services to special applicant groups, such as veterans, the handicapped, youth, minorities, and older workers; a computerized interstate job listing; and other labor market information.
$ Given: $847,220,000 est. FY 95
Application Information: Contact your state office.
Deadline: Established each year (contact federal agency for deadline for application submission).
Contact: Kenneth A. Bolles, Commissioner
Virginia Employment Commission
P.O. Box 1358
Richmond, VA 23211
(804) 786-3001
Fax: (804) 225-3923

UNEMPLOYMENT INSURANCE

Unemployment Insurance Service
Employment and Training Administration, Department of Labor
Washington, DC 20210
(202) 219-7831

Description: Provides unemployment insurance for workers whose employers have contributed to state unemployment funds, federal civilian employees, ex–service persons, those who have become unemployed as a result of product imports, and those whose unemployment comes under the purview of a presidentially declared disaster.

$ Given: $23.7 billion est. FY 95

Application Information: Contact the Employment Security Department for your state.

Deadline: Not available

Contact: Kenneth A. Bolles, Commissioner
            Virginia Employment Commission
            P.O. Box 1358
            Richmond, VA 23211
            (804) 786-3001
            Fax: (804) 225-3923

EMPLOYMENT AND TRAINING ASSISTANCE— DISLOCATED WORKERS

Employment and Training Administration, Department of Labor
200 Constitution Avenue, NW
Washington, DC 20210
(202) 219-5577

Description: Federal grants given to state and local programs to assist workers through training and employment services. These are workers who have been terminated or laid off or received notice of such and are not likely to return to their previous occupation or industry or who are long-term unemployed. Targeted individuals include those affected by mass layoffs and natural disasters.

$ Given: $571.1 million total nationwide for FY 93

Application Information: Inquire at Employment Security office listed below.

Deadline: Not available

Contact: Kenneth A. Bolles, Commissioner
            Virginia Employment Commission
            P.O. Box 1358
            Richmond, VA 23211
            (804) 786-3001
            Fax: (804) 225-3923

WOMEN'S SPECIAL EMPLOYMENT ASSISTANCE

Office of Administrative Management
Women's Bureau
Office of the Secretary
Department of Labor
Washington, DC 20210
(202) 219-6611

Description: Makes referrals as to sources for counseling and disseminates technical information to aid in the employment of women—especially in the realm of nontraditional women's jobs and jobs in new technologies.
$ Given: $8,054,000 est. FY 95
Application Information: Write to Women's Bureau in your region.
Deadline: None
Contact: Regional Administrator
          Region III, Women's Bureau
          Department of Labor
          Gateway Building
          Room 13280
          3535 Market Street
          Philadelphia, PA 19104
          (215) 596-1184

EMERGENCY LOANS

Farmers Home Administration
Department of Agriculture
14th Street and Independence Avenue, SW
Washington, DC 20250
(202) 720-1632

Description: Provides loans to family farmers (either owner or tenant), ranchers, and aquaculture operators to cover losses resulting from natural or other major disasters. Recipients must be unable to obtain credit from other sources.
$ Given: $180 million est. FY 95; average range: $500–$500,000; average assistance: $66,200
Application Information: Consult local telephone directory under United States Government, Department of Agriculture, for Farmers Home Administration office.
Deadline: Not available

Contact: Farmers Home Administration
          Culpeper Building
          Suite 238
          1606 Santa Rosa Road
          Richmond, VA 23229
          (804) 828-1550

ECONOMIC INJURY DISASTER LOANS

Office of Disaster Assistance
Small Business Administration (SBA)
409 Third Street, SW
Washington, DC 20416
(202) 205-6734

Description: Provides direct loans to small businesses suffering
economic damage under Small Business Administration, Department of Agriculture, and/or presidentially declared disaster. Must be
a small business or agricultural concern, located within declared
disaster area and unable to obtain credit elsewhere.
$ Given: $78,209,000 est. FY 95; range: up to $1,500,000; average
assistance: $50,725
Application Information: Applications are filed with nearest
available SBA disaster area or special disaster office.
Deadline: Established for each declaration of disaster.
Contact: Small Business Administration, Region III
          475 Allendale Road
          Suite 201
          King of Prussia, PA 19406
          (215) 962-3700

VIRGIN ISLANDS

EMPLOYMENT SERVICE

United States Employment Service
Employment and Training Administration, Department of Labor
Washington, DC 20210
(202) 219-5257

Description: Provides placement services for job seekers and
employers. These include services to special applicant groups, such
as veterans, the handicapped, youth, minorities, and older workers;

a computerized interstate job listing; and other labor market information.
$ Given: $847,220,000 est. FY 95
Application Information: Contact your state office.
Deadline: Established each year (contact federal agency for deadline for application submission).
Contact: Luis Llanos, Commissioner
             Employment Security Agency
             Virgin Islands Department of Labor
             2131 Hospital Street
             Christiansted, St. Croix, VI 00820
             (809) 773-1994
             Fax: (809) 774-5908

UNEMPLOYMENT INSURANCE

Unemployment Insurance Service
Employment and Training Administration, Department of Labor
Washington, DC 20210
(202) 219-7831

Description: Provides unemployment insurance for workers whose employers have contributed to state unemployment funds, federal civilian employees, ex–service persons, those who have become unemployed as a result of product imports, and those whose unemployment comes under the purview of a presidentially declared disaster.
$ Given: $23.7 billion est. FY 95
Application Information: Contact the Employment Security Department for your state.
Deadline: Not available
Contact: Luis Llanos, Commissioner
             Employment Security Agency
             Virgin Islands Department of Labor
             2131 Hospital Street
             Christiansted, St. Croix, VI 00820
             (809) 773-1994
             Fax: (809) 774-5908

EMPLOYMENT AND TRAINING ASSISTANCE— DISLOCATED WORKERS

Employment and Training Administration, Department of Labor
200 Constitution Avenue, NW
Washington, DC 20210
(202) 219-5577

Description: Federal grants given to state and local programs to assist workers through training and employment services. These are workers who have been terminated or laid off or received notice of such and are not likely to return to their previous occupation or industry or who are long-term unemployed. Targeted individuals include those affected by mass layoffs and natural disasters.
$ Given: $571.1 million total nationwide for FY 93
Application Information: Inquire at Employment Security office listed below.
Deadline: Not available
Contact: Luis Llanos, Commissioner
             Employment Security Agency
             Virgin Islands Department of Labor
             2131 Hospital Street
             Christiansted, St. Croix, VI 00820
             (809) 773-1994
             Fax: (809) 774-5908

WOMEN'S SPECIAL EMPLOYMENT ASSISTANCE

Office of Administrative Management
Women's Bureau
Office of the Secretary
Department of Labor
Washington, DC 20210
(202) 219-6611

Description: Makes referrals as to sources for counseling and disseminates technical information to aid in the employment of women—especially in the realm of nontraditional women's jobs and jobs in new technologies.
$ Given: $8,054,000 est. FY 95
Application Information: Write to Women's Bureau in your region.
Deadline: None

Contact: Mary C. Murphree, Regional Administrator
          Region II, Women's Bureau
          Department of Labor
          201 Varick Street
          Room 601
          New York, NY 10014
          (212) 337-2389

EMERGENCY LOANS

Farmers Home Administration
Department of Agriculture
14th Street and Independence Avenue, SW
Washington, DC 20250
(202) 720-1632

Description: Provides loans to family farmers (either owner or
tenant), ranchers, and aquaculture operators to cover losses resulting from natural or other major disasters. Recipients must be
unable to obtain credit from other sources.
$ Given: $180 million est. FY 95; average range: $500–$500,000;
average assistance: $66,200
Application Information: Consult local telephone directory under
United States Government, Department of Agriculture, for Farmers
Home Administration office.
Deadline: Not available
Contact: Farmers Home Administration
          City Center
          Third Floor
          89 Main Street
          Montpelier, VT 05602
          (802) 828-6001

ECONOMIC INJURY DISASTER LOANS

Office of Disaster Assistance
Small Business Administration (SBA)
409 Third Street, SW
Washington, DC 20416
(202) 205-6734

Description: Provides direct loans to small businesses suffering
economic damage under Small Business Administration, Depart-

ment of Agriculture, and/or presidentially declared disaster. Must be a small business or agricultural concern, located within declared disaster area and unable to obtain credit elsewhere.
$ Given: $78,209,000 est. FY 95; range: up to $1,500,000; average assistance: $50,725
Application Information: Applications are filed with nearest available SBA disaster area or special disaster office.
Deadline: Established for each declaration of disaster.
Contact: Small Business Administration, Region II
         26 Federal Plaza
         Room 31-08
         New York, NY 10278
         (212) 264-1450

WASHINGTON

EMPLOYMENT SERVICE

United States Employment Service
Employment and Training Administration, Department of Labor
Washington, DC 20210
(202) 219-5257

Description: Provides placement services for job seekers and employers. These include services to special applicant groups, such as veterans, the handicapped, youth, minorities, and older workers; a computerized interstate job listing; and other labor market information.
$ Given: $847,220,000 est. FY 95
Application Information: Contact your state office.
Deadline: Established each year (contact federal agency for deadline for application submission).
Contact: Vernon E. Stoner, Commissioner
         Employment Security Department
         212 Maple Park
         P.O. Box 9046
         Olympia, WA 98507-9046
         (206) 753-5114
         Fax: (206) 753-4851

UNEMPLOYMENT INSURANCE

Unemployment Insurance Service
Employment and Training Administration, Department of Labor
Washington, DC 20210
(202) 219-7831

Description: Provides unemployment insurance for workers whose employers have contributed to state unemployment funds, federal civilian employees, ex–service persons, those who have become unemployed as a result of product imports, and those whose unemployment comes under the purview of a presidentially declared disaster.
$ Given: $23.7 billion est. FY 95
Application Information: Contact the Employment Security Department for your state.
Deadline: Not available
Contact: Vernon E. Stoner, Commissioner
      Employment Security Department
      212 Maple Park
      P.O. Box 9046
      Olympia, WA 98507-9046
      (206) 753-5114
      Fax: (206) 753-4851

EMPLOYMENT AND TRAINING ASSISTANCE— DISLOCATED WORKERS

Employment and Training Administration, Department of Labor
200 Constitution Avenue, NW
Washington, DC 20210
(202) 219-5577

Description: Federal grants given to state and local programs to assist workers through training and employment services. These are workers who have been terminated or laid off or received notice of such and are not likely to return to their previous occupation or industry or who are long-term unemployed. Targeted individuals include those affected by mass layoffs and natural disasters.
$ Given: $571.1 million total nationwide for FY 93
Application Information: Inquire at Employment Security office listed below.
Deadline: Not available

Contact: Vernon E. Stoner, Commissioner
           Employment Security Department
           212 Maple Park
           P.O. Box 9046
           Olympia, WA 98507-9046
           (206) 753-5114
           Fax: (206) 753-4851

WOMEN'S SPECIAL EMPLOYMENT ASSISTANCE

Office of Administrative Management
Women's Bureau
Office of the Secretary
Department of Labor
Washington, DC 20210
(202) 219-6611

Description: Makes referrals as to sources for counseling and
disseminates technical information to aid in the employment of
women—especially in the realm of nontraditional women's jobs and
jobs in new technologies.
$ Given: $8,054,000 est. FY 95
Application Information: Write to Women's Bureau in your region.
Deadline: None
Contact: Regional Administrator
             Region X, Women's Bureau
             Department of Labor
             1111 Third Avenue
             Room 885
             Seattle, WA 98101-3211
             (206) 553-1534

EMERGENCY LOANS

Farmers Home Administration
Department of Agriculture
14th Street and Independence Avenue, SW
Washington, DC 20250
(202) 720-1632

Description: Provides loans to family farmers (either owner or
tenant), ranchers, and aquaculture operators to cover losses resulting from natural or other major disasters. Recipients must be
unable to obtain credit from other sources.

$ Given: $180 million est. FY 95; average range: $500–$500,000; average assistance: $66,200
Application Information: Consult local telephone directory under United States Government, Department of Agriculture, for Farmers Home Administration office.
Deadline: Not available
Contact: Farmers Home Administration
             Federal Building
             Room 319
             P.O. 2427
             Wenatchee, WA 98807
             (509) 664-0240

ECONOMIC INJURY DISASTER LOANS

Office of Disaster Assistance
Small Business Administration (SBA)
409 Third Street, SW
Washington, DC 20416
(202) 205-6734

Description: Provides direct loans to small businesses suffering economic damage under Small Business Administration, Department of Agriculture, and/or presidentially declared disaster. Must be a small business or agricultural concern, located within declared disaster area and unable to obtain credit elsewhere.
$ Given: $78,209,000 est. FY 95; range: up to $1,500,000; average assistance: $50,725
Application Information: Applications are filed with nearest available SBA disaster area or special disaster office.
Deadline: Established for each declaration of disaster.
Contact: Small Business Administration, Region X
             2615 Fourth Avenue
             Room 440
             Seattle, WA 98121
             (206) 442-5676

WEST VIRGINIA

EMPLOYMENT SERVICE

United States Employment Service
Employment and Training Administration, Department of Labor
Washington, DC 20210
(202) 219-5257

Description: Provides placement services for job seekers and employers. These include services to special applicant groups, such as veterans, the handicapped, youth, minorities, and older workers; a computerized interstate job listing; and other labor market information.
$ Given: $847,220,000 est. FY 95
Application Information: Contact your state office.
Deadline: Established each year (contact federal agency for deadline for application submission).
Contact: Andrew N. Richardson, Commissioner
Bureau of Employment Programs
State Office Building
112 California Avenue
Charleston, WV 25302
(304) 558-2630
Fax: (304) 558-2992

UNEMPLOYMENT INSURANCE

Unemployment Insurance Service
Employment and Training Administration, Department of Labor
Washington, DC 20210
(202) 219-7831

Description: Provides unemployment insurance for workers whose employers have contributed to state unemployment funds, federal civilian employees, ex–service persons, those who have become unemployed as a result of product imports, and those whose unemployment comes under the purview of a presidentially declared disaster.
$ Given: $23.7 billion est. FY 95
Application Information: Contact the Employment Security Department for your state.
Deadline: Not available

Contact: Andrew N. Richardson, Commissioner
           Bureau of Employment Programs
           State Office Building
           112 California Avenue
           Charleston, WV 25302
           (304) 558-2630
           Fax: (304) 558-2992

EMPLOYMENT AND TRAINING ASSISTANCE— DISLOCATED WORKERS

Employment and Training Administration, Department of Labor
200 Constitution Avenue, NW
Washington, DC 20210
(202) 219-5577

Description: Federal grants given to state and local programs to assist workers through training and employment services. These are workers who have been terminated or laid off or received notice of such and are not likely to return to their previous occupation or industry or who are long-term unemployed. Targeted individuals include those affected by mass layoffs and natural disasters.
$ Given: $571.1 million total nationwide for FY 93
Application Information: Inquire at Employment Security office listed below.
Deadline: Not available
Contact: Andrew N. Richardson, Commissioner
           Bureau of Employment Programs
           State Office Building
           112 California Avenue
           Charleston, WV 25302
           (304) 558-2630
           Fax: (304) 558-2992

WOMEN'S SPECIAL EMPLOYMENT ASSISTANCE

Office of Administrative Management
Women's Bureau
Office of the Secretary
Department of Labor
Washington, DC 20210
(202) 219-6611

Description: Makes referrals as to sources for counseling and disseminates technical information to aid in the employment of women—especially in the realm of nontraditional women's jobs and jobs in new technologies.
$ Given: $8,054,000 est. FY 95
Application Information: Write to Women's Bureau in your region.
Deadline: None
Contact: Regional Administrator
          Region III, Women's Bureau
          Department of Labor
          Gateway Building
          Room 13280
          3535 Market Street
          Philadelphia, PA 19104
          (206) 553-1534

EMERGENCY LOANS

Farmers Home Administration
Department of Agriculture
14th Street and Independence Avenue, SW
Washington, DC 20250
(202) 720-1632

Description: Provides loans to family farmers (either owner or tenant), ranchers, and aquaculture operators to cover losses resulting from natural or other major disasters. Recipients must be unable to obtain credit from other sources.
$ Given: $180 million est. FY 95; average range: $500–$500,000; average assistance: $66,200
Application Information: Consult local telephone directory under United States Government, Department of Agriculture, for Farmers Home Administration office.
Deadline: Not available
Contact: Farmers Home Administration
          75 High Street
          P.O. Box 678
          Morgantown, WV 26505
          (304) 291-4791

ECONOMIC INJURY DISASTER LOANS

Office of Disaster Assistance
Small Business Administration (SBA)
409 Third Street, SW
Washington, DC 20416
(202) 205-6734

Description: Provides direct loans to small businesses suffering
economic damage under Small Business Administration, Department of Agriculture, and/or presidentially declared disaster. Must be
a small business or agricultural concern, located within declared
disaster area and unable to obtain credit elsewhere.
$ Given: $78,209,000 est. FY 95; range: up to $1,500,000; average
assistance: $50,725
Application Information: Applications are filed with nearest
available SBA disaster area or special disaster office.
Deadline: Established for each declaration of disaster.
Contact: Small Business Administration, Region III
           475 Allendale Road
           Suite 201
           King of Prussia, PA 19406
           (215) 962-3700

WISCONSIN

EMPLOYMENT SERVICE

United States Employment Service
Employment and Training Administration, Department of Labor
Washington, DC 20210
(202) 219-5257

Description: Provides placement services for job seekers and
employers. These include services to special applicant groups, such
as veterans, the handicapped, youth, minorities, and older workers;
a computerized interstate job listing; and other labor market
information.
$ Given: $847,220,000 est. FY 95
Application Information: Contact your state office.
Deadline: Established each year (contact federal agency for deadline
for application submission).

Contact: Carol Skornicka, Secretary
           Department of Industry, Labor, and Human Relations
           P.O. Box 7946
           201 East Washington Avenue
           Madison, WI 53707
           (608) 266-7552
           Fax: (608) 266-1784

UNEMPLOYMENT INSURANCE

Unemployment Insurance Service
Employment and Training Administration, Department of Labor
Washington, DC 20210
(202) 219-7831

Description: Provides unemployment insurance for workers whose
employers have contributed to state unemployment funds, federal
civilian employees, ex–service persons, those who have become
unemployed as a result of product imports, and those whose
unemployment comes under the purview of a presidentially declared
disaster.
$ Given: $23.7 billion est. FY 95
Application Information: Contact the Employment Security Department for your state.
Deadline: Not available
Contact: Carol Skornicka, Secretary
           Department of Industry, Labor, and Human Relations
           P.O. Box 7946
           201 East Washington Avenue
           Madison, WI 53707
           (608) 266-7552
           Fax: (608) 266-1784

EMPLOYMENT AND TRAINING ASSISTANCE—
DISLOCATED WORKERS

Employment and Training Administration, Department of Labor
200 Constitution Avenue, NW
Washington, DC 20210
(202) 219-5577

Description: Federal grants given to state and local programs to
assist workers through training and employment services. These are
workers who have been terminated or laid off or received notice of

such and are not likely to return to their previous occupation or industry or who are long-term unemployed. Targeted individuals include those affected by mass layoffs and natural disasters.
$ Given: $571.1 million total nationwide for FY 93
Application Information: Inquire at Employment Security office listed below.
Deadline: Not available
Contact: Carol Skornicka, Secretary
Department of Industry, Labor, and Human Relations
P.O. Box 7946
201 East Washington Avenue
Madison, WI 53707
(608) 266-7552
Fax: (608) 266-1784

WOMEN'S SPECIAL EMPLOYMENT ASSISTANCE

Office of Administrative Management
Women's Bureau
Office of the Secretary
Department of Labor
Washington, DC 20210
(202) 219-6611

Description: Makes referrals as to sources for counseling and disseminates technical information to aid in the employment of women—especially in the realm of nontraditional women's jobs and jobs in new technologies.
$ Given: $8,054,000 est. FY 95
Application Information: Write to Women's Bureau in your region.
Deadline: None
Contact: Sandra K. Frank, Regional Administrator
Region V, Women's Bureau
Department of Labor
230 South Dearborn Street
Room 1022
Chicago, IL 60604
(312) 353-6985

EMERGENCY LOANS

Farmers Home Administration
Department of Agriculture
14th Street and Independence Avenue, SW
Washington, DC 20250
(202) 720-1632

Description: Provides loans to family farmers (either owner or
tenant), ranchers, and aquaculture operators to cover losses resulting from natural or other major disasters. Recipients must be
unable to obtain credit from other sources.
$ Given: $180 million est. FY 95; average range: $500–$500,000;
average assistance: $66,200
Application Information: Consult local telephone directory under
United States Government, Department of Agriculture, for Farmers
Home Administration office.
Deadline: Not available
Contact: Farmers Home Administration
         4949 Kirschling Court
         Stevens Point, WI 54481
         (715) 345-7625

ECONOMIC INJURY DISASTER LOANS

Office of Disaster Assistance
Small Business Administration (SBA)
409 Third Street, SW
Washington, DC 20416
(202) 205-6734

Description: Provides direct loans to small businesses suffering
economic damage under Small Business Administration, Department of Agriculture, and/or presidentially declared disaster. Must be
a small business or agricultural concern, located within declared
disaster area and unable to obtain credit elsewhere.
$ Given: $78,209,000 est. FY 95; range: up to $1,500,000; average
assistance: $50,725
Application Information: Applications are filed with nearest
available SBA disaster area or special disaster office.
Deadline: Established for each declaration of disaster.

Contact: Small Business Administration, Region V
          Federal Building
          300 South Riverside Plaza
          Room 1975
          Chicago, IL 60606-6611
          (312) 353-0359

WYOMING

EMPLOYMENT SERVICE

United States Employment Service
Employment and Training Administration, Department of Labor
Washington, DC 20210
(202) 219-5257

Description: Provides placement services for job seekers and
employers. These include services to special applicant groups, such
as veterans, the handicapped, youth, minorities, and older workers;
a computerized interstate job listing; and other labor market
information.
$ Given: $847,220,000 est. FY 95
Application Information: Contact your state office.
Deadline: Established each year (contact federal agency for deadline
for application submission).
Contact: Beth Nelson, Deputy Director
          Department of Employment
          Division of Employment Security
          P.O. Box 2760
          Center and Midwest Streets
          Casper, WY 82602
          (307) 235-3254

UNEMPLOYMENT INSURANCE

Unemployment Insurance Service
Employment and Training Administration, Department of Labor
Washington, DC 20210
(202) 219-7831

Description: Provides unemployment insurance for workers whose
employers have contributed to state unemployment funds, federal

civilian employees, ex–service persons, those who have become unemployed as a result of product imports, and those whose unemployment comes under the purview of a presidentially declared disaster.

$ Given: $23.7 billion est. FY 95

Application Information: Contact the Employment Security Department for your state.

Deadline: Not available

Contact: Beth Nelson, Deputy Director
                Department of Employment
                Division of Employment Security
                P.O. Box 2760
                Center and Midwest Streets
                Casper, WY 82602
                (307) 235-3254

EMPLOYMENT AND TRAINING ASSISTANCE— DISLOCATED WORKERS

Employment and Training Administration, Department of Labor
200 Constitution Avenue, NW
Washington, DC 20210
(202) 219-5577

Description: Federal grants given to state and local programs to assist workers through training and employment services. These are workers who have been terminated or laid off or received notice of such and are not likely to return to their previous occupation or industry or who are long-term unemployed. Targeted individuals include those affected by mass layoffs and natural disasters.

$ Given: $571.1 million total nationwide for FY 93

Application Information: Inquire at Employment Security office listed below.

Deadline: Not available

Contact: Beth Nelson, Deputy Director
                Department of Employment
                Division of Employment Security
                P.O. Box 2760
                Center and Midwest Streets
                Casper, WY 82602
                (307) 235-3254

WOMEN'S SPECIAL EMPLOYMENT ASSISTANCE

Office of Administrative Management
Women's Bureau
Office of the Secretary
Department of Labor
Washington, DC 20210
(202) 219-6611

Description: Makes referrals as to sources for counseling and disseminates technical information to aid in the employment of women—especially in the realm of nontraditional women's jobs and jobs in new technologies.
$ Given: $8,054,000 est. FY 95
Application Information: Write to Women's Bureau in your region.
Deadline: None
Contact: Oleta Crain, Regional Administrator
Region VIII, Women's Bureau
Department of Labor
Federal Office Building
Room 1452
1801 California Street
Suite 905
Denver, CO 80202-2614
(303) 391-6755

EMERGENCY LOANS

Farmers Home Administration
Department of Agriculture
14th Street and Independence Avenue, SW
Washington, DC 20250
(202) 720-1632

Description: Provides loans to family farmers (either owner or tenant), ranchers, and aquaculture operators to cover losses resulting from natural or other major disasters. Recipients must be unable to obtain credit from other sources.
$ Given: $180 million est. FY 95; average range: $500–$500,000; average assistance: $66,200
Application Information: Consult local telephone directory under United States Government, Department of Agriculture, for Farmers Home Administration office.
Deadline: Not available

Contact: Farmers Home Administration
           Federal Building
           Room 1005
           100 East B Street
           P.O. Box 820
           Casper, WY 82602
           (307) 261-5271

ECONOMIC INJURY DISASTER LOANS

Office of Disaster Assistance
Small Business Administration (SBA)
409 Third Street, SW
Washington, DC 20416
(202) 205-6734

Description: Provides direct loans to small businesses suffering
economic damage under Small Business Administration, Department of Agriculture, and/or presidentially declared disaster. Must be
a small business or agricultural concern, located within declared
disaster area and unable to obtain credit elsewhere.
$ Given: $78,209,000 est. FY 95; range: up to $1,500,000; average
assistance: $50,725
Application Information: Applications are filed with nearest
available SBA disaster area or special disaster office.
Deadline: Established for each declaration of disaster.
Contact: Small Business Administration, Region VIII
           633 17th Street
           Seventh Floor
           Denver, CO 80202
           (303) 294-7186

Index